WYRD ALLIES

Harnessing the Chaos
in Your Relationships

TOM GRAVES

GOTHIC IMAGE
PUBLICATIONS

Gothic Image Publications
7 High Street, Glastonbury,
Somerset, BA6 9DP

© Tom Graves 1996

Cover illustration by Peter Woodcock
and Frameworks, Bristol

Editorial service by Jim Nagel
Abbey Press Glastonbury
Set in Acorn Monotype Garamond

Printed and bound in Great Britain by
WBC Book Manufacturers Ltd,
Brigend, Mid-Glamorgan

A catalogue record for this book is available
from the British Library

ISBN 0 906362 32 6

CONTENTS

ACKNOWLEDGEMENTS

Every book — especially one of this nature — is the result of interactions and ideas created by and between many different people. What follows is my own interpretation of what I've seen and shared with others, but I do need to acknowledge that others have contributed to this — sometimes consciously, in some cases not.

Writers whose ideas I've used or adapted include Douglas Adams, Eric Berne, John Bradshaw, Bryan Branston, James Burke, Joseph Campbell, Marion Campbell, Lewis Carroll, Carlos Castaneda, Jeremy Cherfas, members of the Conflict Resolution Network, members of the Duluth Domestic Abuse Intervention Project, Paul Feyerabend, Kate Fillion, Ian Fleming, Betty Friedan, Alan Garner, James Gleick, Germaine Greer, Felicitas Goodman, John Gribbin, Douglas Hofstadter, Robert Hughes, Susan Jeffers, Robert Johnson, Sam Keen, Thomas Kuhn, Carol Lee, Ursula Le Guin, Hugh Mackay, George Orwell, Robert Pirsig, Terry Pratchett, Starhawk (Miriam Simos), Gloria Steinem, Ann Summers, Glen Tomasetti, Gerald Weinberg, and Naomi Wolf. In some cases the ideas I've 'borrowed' have been taken into very different contexts from the original, but I believe—or hope!—that in each case I've done so with the respect that their ideas deserve.

Friends, colleagues and others who've provided ideas and

feedback include Roy Bailey; Coral Baragwanath; Stuart Birks; Graeme Burnett; Cass Carter; Ross Daly; Phil Day; Donna; Cheryle Dean; Bob Dingley; Bonnie Gibson; Valerie Graves; Martin Hungerford; Lindsay Jackel; Hanson Jeong; Dess Kammason; Marina Moss; Cindy Pavlinac; the People's Equality Network crew, particularly Don Bruce, Judy Hardman, Ray O'Sullivan, Tanya Trott and Ian Young; the People Knowhow/Zoeros crew, especially Diana Coverdale, Annie Davies-McCubbin, Roger Harman, Robert Meredith, St-John Miall, Robert Prinable and Gai Roper; Susannah Sabine; Soni Stecker; John Venables; Peter Vogel; Brooke Wade; Paul Whyte; and Janne Williams.

Particular thanks are due to Linda Moore and Catherine Caulwell, both of whom spent much time tossing ideas and practical examples back and forth across the world; to Cary Meehan and to Frances Howard-Gordon, who did likewise, and was also my editor and publisher.

Other than these authors and others mentioned above, all personal names in the narrative section of the text—all except the Introduction chapter—refer to fictitious characters, such as the imaginary narrator Chris Kelley. Although most stories and examples are based on real-life incidents, they are in most cases adapted from the experiences of many different people, and are not intended to refer to any actual person, alive or dead.

INTRODUCTION

People are weird. It doesn't take much of an understanding of reality to know that. Sometimes, without warning, unexpected troubles or unexpected enemies appear, to turn our life into turmoil; and in the midst of hard times, unknown allies arise to help restore some sense of calm and self, of meaning and purpose. The weird part, and the one we'll usually fail to notice, is how often the 'enemies' and the 'allies' turn out to be the same people... and that the only real 'enemy' we have is ourself...

A key part of what's generally called 'personal growth' is learning to come to terms with that fact—coming to terms with our true selves and our true relationships with others. But it's often hard to see—and even harder to accept. And there's a hint of weirdness that can make it even harder: at times it can seem that the whole world is against us, thwarting us at every turn; while at others everything can seem impossibly smooth and easy —for a while at least... Just when we're certain we really know someone, they change—or perhaps *we* change—and we're faced with new challenges and new choices in relationship with them. The same issues, the same problems, the same fears, the same joys, all keep weaving through our relationships with others, always wearing similar yet strangely different faces. And as we work on our path of personal growth—expanding our awareness of ourselves and our hidden choices—everyone we meet, it seems, acts as a weird kind of mirror, showing us not only themselves, but the results of our own choices too.

There's always a choice in any interaction with others; but there's also always a twist, an uncertainty, a subtle chaos that underlies even the most ordered of relationships. That uncertainty is what keeps relationships interesting, but it does also add to the difficulties! In our less happy moments, relationships might seem like nothing but a series of tests and trials: yet if we've had more than a passing involvement with personal growth, we'll know that most of life is like that anyway — and relationships are no different... The only difference is that the issues are *inter*personal rather than personal — and even in that there's a weird sense in which they're the same anyway.

So it's to this weirdness in the process of interpersonal growth — accepting the weirdness in our relationships, and working *with* them rather than trying to fight against them—that this book is addressed. It extends into the interpersonal realm the exploration of personal work and personal awareness described in *Positively Wyrd*, the previous book in this series. Like its predecessor, this book is also addressed to the realities of the process and its often uncomfortable twists and turns: as such, it develops a rather different sequence of approach to issues. In particular, there's an emphasis on some issues which are often missed out in other books in this field — such as a detailed exploration of personal power and personal responsibility, and of the subtle and self-destructive traps of the 'blame-game'. And there are also some guidelines on how to work with the bad times—and how not to get lost in some illusory 'good' ones.

As with the previous book, all the text after this introductory chapter is framed as if spoken by an imaginary narrator, named Chris Kelley. Throughout this book, from the next chapter onwards, 'I' is Chris Kelley, not me. 'Chris' is in fact a composite, whose life is drawn from the real-life experiences of many different people — both men and women. One reader commented, about an incident of Chris's in *Positively Wyrd*, "Your narrator, I *really* identified with her there—it's something which *only* happens to women": but in fact the real-life story behind the incident was actually a man's... So I'd argue that despite the strong emphasis on gender in so many current books on interpersonal issues, we do all have the same human needs and, for the most part, the same human problems: which is why you'll find that although Chris should be readily identifiable as a person, Chris's sex (and for that matter sexual preference) is intentionally uncertain — and likewise that of many of the people with whom Chris interacts. Make your own choices on this, if you wish—but remember there's always a twist...!

So although this introduction is somewhat formal, the rest of the book is not. The stories that Chris tells are highly personal, and illustrate clearly the intensity of *feeling* of many of these states — so if you find yourself in the same kind of emotional spaces or practical predicaments that this imaginary 'I' describes, you'll know you're not alone in that experience. We've all been there too: sometimes that fact alone can be a great deal of help in some of the darker times...

The aim of personal growth is to create constructive changes within ourselves and the ways in which we relate with others and to the world at large. But since nothing changes without our choosing to be involved in the change, there's also a strong emphasis in this book on the practical: examples to put the concepts into practice will be found on almost every page. As with *Positively Wyrd*, these typically consist of a personal experience from Chris that illustrates the point being made, followed by some suggestions about how to put this into practice, and questions about the resultant experience — questions to which only *you* have the answers—to help you explore the issues in your own personal context. All of these examples have been tested in practice, by myself, friends and colleagues as well as many others, and often over long periods of time: they work. Whether they work for you in the same way is up to you to decide, based on your own experience: but unless you *do* try them for yourself, you'll never know!

This book develops a sequence of observations and

changes, starting with relationship to self, moving onward to close and intimate relationships, and outward to relationships with the world in general. Be warned, though, that the sequence may not always be what you expect: some themes are threaded throughout the book, twisting and looping back in ever-changing forms, so the apparent repetition that occurs in many places is intentional, and is not simply due to poor editing! One of these themes is the problem of blame, which weaves through most relationships in its own weird way: an example 'sets the stage' in the first chapter, which opens the way toward the subtle freedom that can be found from a better understanding of the original meaning of 'weird' — another central theme of the book, explored in depth in the chapter which follows.

The next section, consisting of roughly a third of the book, looks at the kind of pressures and issues which apply in all kinds of relationships. We learn to watch how our own fears and confusions, and the habits we've been taught from childhood onwards, can dominate our relationships with others, and even with ourselves—and how we can begin to reclaim real choices in this. We explore the weird boundary between 'I' and 'not-I'; and we begin to discover that while there *is* such a thing as 'fate', we do have choices even in this—although there's always a twist in what happens next...

The third section is concerned mainly with practical tools: it consists of five chapters, each of which focusses on a specific problem-issue in all kinds of relationship. We observe the strange confusions that arise from some common ways of relating which view others as 'object' or 'subject'; we explore ways to break free from the destructive pervasiveness of blame; we look more closely at what exactly we mean by 'I', and its weird relationship with others. And we learn to become aware of the subtle boundary between use and abuse of both self and others; and also the subtle distinction between sympathy and empathy, without which no true relationship is possible.

In the final section we start to put into practice this new experience of ourselves and the true 'weirdness' of relationships. We find a new understanding of sex—in all its senses—and strange meetings with 'soul-mates'; we explore a new world of trust and joy, in commitment to ourselves, to others and to the wider world. We learn to recognise the allies that we already have in this; and discover that we *can* create, in any relationship, the allies we truly need. There's always a twist, perhaps, but in every relationship we *always* have choice, and the power to choose. And that choice, and the responsibility for that choice, are always ours: it's up to us to build the relationships we need.

Using this book

In keeping with the nature of 'weirdness', this book can be read in a number of different ways, depending on what *you* need from it. At one level, this is, of course, a perfectly ordinary book, developing a sequence of ideas with a beginning, a middle and an end. So if you want, you can read it in the usual way, from cover to cover: but you don't *have* to do this in order to make use of it.

For example, if all you're interested in is ideas, you might choose to skip over all the 'boxes' of practical material. In theory it might seem to make little difference, because the ideas and concepts are mostly explored in the main text. But the boxes provide the *context* in which those ideas make practical sense: and since that's the main point of the book, I wouldn't recommend ignoring them.

At the other extreme, you could skip over all the main text, and read only the 'boxes': that'll work too, but you're likely to miss out on understanding *why* the practical material works in the way that it does. Without that understanding, you may well be able to create *some* useful changes in your relationships, for a while: but in time you'll find yourself reverting back to the same old loops and patterns in which you were caught before. So I wouldn't recommend doing that either.

What I'd recommend instead, from many people's experience with the previous book in this series, is to use a combination of all these methods. Read the first two chapters carefully, to give you a general idea of what the book is about; then skim through the whole of the remainder once, fairly quickly, stopping only to read in detail a few passages that particularly catch your eye. That'll give you enough background information such that the practical material will then make practical sense, whatever you do next. Once you've done this, go back to the beginning again, and as you read each section of the main text, try out the practical examples described in the respective boxes. You don't even have to do this in sequence: for example, as the whim takes you, dip in at random anywhere in the book, to find an idea or a practical piece—you'll usually find it has some apposite comment on your current situation. Use this book to work *with* the weirdness of change, the weirdness of relationships: that's how it works best.

A word of warning, though: once you start to put the material into practice, take it *slowly* — don't rush. Experience suggests that, beyond that first couple of introductory chapters, it's best not to try to work with more than a single section—two or three pages — a day. Change, while valuable, can also be uncomfortable and even frightening, to yourself and to others: and the practical material in this book, if it's used properly, *does* trigger real changes in the way we view and work with ourselves and each other. If you try to rush it, or force the pace of change, you'll either miss some key points and find yourself back in the same old loops, or else you'll give yourself — and others — an unnecessarily rough time. So don't do it. Just take it slow: "Beyond a wholesome discipline, be gentle on yourself" — and on others too!

Whichever way you choose to use this book, welcome to a different world: at times a weird way of relating with others, perhaps, though one that turns out to be far more practical — and more empowering for everyone. It's a world in which we *do* have choices in our relationships — and yet, somehow, there's always a weird twist of fate in everything that happens...

1

WEIRD IS A NOUN

Weird is a noun. I'm surprised to find that it *is* what the dictionary shows, too: it's from the Old English word *wyrd*, "the principle, power or agency by which events are predetermined; fate, destiny", and also "a happening, event, occurrence; predetermined events collectively". The dictionary also says that the use of 'weird' as an adjective, to mean 'strange', is quite recent—it started only a couple of hundred years ago, picked up by Victorian scholars from Shakespeare's description of the "three Weird Sisters" in *Macbeth*. But 'weird' the noun, 'weird' the event, is an idea which goes back many centuries, even thousands of years. Those three weird sisters weren't only strange: they *were* the wyrd, "the power by which events are predetermined"—though it's obvious they're also weird in that sense of strange.

Fascinating. But so what? How is that supposed to help me sort out my hassles with everyone else? Judging by the chaos in *my* life, most events certainly aren't 'predetermined' by me... are they? And if my problems really *are* predetermined, really *are* prescribed by fate or destiny, where does choice come into it? If there *is* a choice, where does fate—or wyrd—come into it? And what's that about "there's always a choice, there's always a twist"?

Stop for a moment, and think about some of your own relationships with others. Some are probably all too predictable — predetermined indeed! — with the same comments and same responses coming up in the same context, time after time after time. By contrast, other relationships might seem chaotic, completely unpredictable, uncertain, even unsafe. And some may seem to be stuck in repeating loops or patterns of frustration, with blame and bickering endlessly echoing back and forth. In each case, where are the choices? For that matter, *who* seems to have the choices there? You? Or only others? Or what?

It would probably be worthwhile to write some notes to yourself on this, to come back to later in the book.

But from that description, whatever wyrd is, it obviously affects everyone. It's also about feelings — that feeling of 'weirdness' that comes up so often in so many of these situations. If there *are* choices involved — those "choices hidden in the weavings of the wyrd" — then it's also about awareness: awareness of what really *is* 'predetermined' and what isn't. And there's evidently a story behind it: so that's probably the best place to start.

Wyrd is a story

Imagine the weird scene as Shakespeare describes it in *Macbeth*: on a dark, bare heathland stands a single huge tree, the wind twisting and turning in its leaves and branches. Beneath the tree stand three 'secret, black and midnight hags' — or as Holinshed, Shakespeare's source for the story, put it, 'weirdly sisters in straunge and wild apparell, resembling creatures of elder world' — stirring a cauldron, casting men's lives into the roiling waters above the fire. As Banquo and Macbeth enter the scene, the women each greet Macbeth in turn: "All haile, Makbeth, thane of Glammis!" "Haile, Makbeth, thane of Cawder!" "All haile, Makbeth, that hereafter shall be king of Scotland!" And as

Shakespeare's play shows, all these greetings come true: but there is also a certain amount of twist in that story...

Just a story... or a bit more than a story? Holinshed's *Chronicles*, first published in Shakespeare's time, purports to be a genuine history of Scotland: Macbeth, Banquo and the others were real people, and Shakespeare's play is based — with a fair amount of poetic licence — on what seem, from historical evidence, to be real facts. That much is known. But who were these 'weird sisters'? And how come they're supposed to be able to control, or direct, people's lives in this strange, twisted way?

To answer that, we need to go a little deeper into the myth behind the story. It's actually a variant of the common myth of the three sisters of fate — called the Moirai by the Greeks, the Parcae by the Romans, or the Nornir in Old Norse. The Greeks named the three sisters Clotho (from whom we get the word 'cloth'), Lachesis and Atropos (whose name literally means 'one who will not be turned'). Individually, they are blind — hence 'blind fate' — though they share one eye, passing it endlessly between them; yet it's doubtful if they really need it, because they seem to see the weavings of the world with weirder 'eyes'. And they're the weavers of the fabric of human lives: one spins, one weaves, one cuts. In the Greek story, though, there's no choice: although the cross-warp of 'blind chance' holds the fabric together, each thread of life within it is predestined, 'meted out' — and the fates will not be turned. Life *is*: and the only choices are held in the mysterious hands of fate.

> Would you say that's true for you — that for much of the time you seem to have no choice, that "the only choices are held in the mysterious hands of fate"? How do you *feel* about that?
>
> And what happens if you try to "wrest control of your life from the fates"? Does it work — in other words do you gain absolute certainty, absolute predictability in your life? If not, what *does* happen then?

The Greek story has a certain amount of truth, but it's not

really enough. We do always have *some* choice in what happens to us — even if the choices we make usually turn out to be the wrong ones! The Nordic version of the same story gives it a slightly different twist—which is where 'wyrd' comes in.

Wyrd—or rather *Urðr*, in the original—is actually the name of the first of the three sisters; the others are Verðandi and Skuld, and their names roughly translate as Past, Present and Future. So these three 'maidens from Giantland'—as the Nordic myth describes them—are not only the weavers of the fabric of life, they're also the sisters of *time*. The crucial difference in the Nordic story is that, unlike the Moirai, the 'sisters of wyrd' weave a fabric of *life*, not lives. Each life is not a single, isolated thread on a flat cloth, but a pathway of *choices* in something more like a Celtic knotwork — infinitely interwoven within itself, yet with a pattern and a structure all its own. Where the Greek story of the Fates has rigid rules and harsh retributions, the story of the Weird Sisters is more like modern chaos theory and fractal topology: everywhere there is 'self-similarity', with patterns of "sudden leaps and jagged edges" which never quite repeat, but appear on many different levels and areas at once. Douglas Hofstadter described chaos theory succinctly: "It turns out that behind apparent order lies an eerie kind of chaos; but behind that chaos lies an even eerier kind of order"—and he could just as well have been describing the concept of wyrd. The wyrd— the world of those Weird Sisters—may look chaotic at first: but behind the surface chaos it does indeed have its own "even eerier kind of order"...

"Behind apparent order lies an eerie kind of chaos; but behind that chaos lies an even eerier kind of order". At the time things happen — all those strange twists and turns in our lives — we're probably only aware of the chaos! But looking back, can you perhaps see in the pattern of your life "an even eerier kind of order"—or at least a thread or two of continuity, seeming to push you along a particular path? What's happened in your life — particularly those "sudden leaps and jagged edges"

> where, in a brief space of time, your life has changed its whole direction? That's wyrd—that's what wyrd *is*...
>
> Who else was with you at those times? Who else was involved in these sudden twists of fate? What part did you think then that they played in this? Looking back, with the benefit of hindsight, what part do you now think they played?
>
> And what part did fate, coincidence, providence — call it what you will — play in those changes? Because that's wyrd too—that's what wyrd *is*...

Each thread within the fabric of wyrd is not a single person's life, as with the Fates, but more a stereotype or arche-type: what a life would be like if *one* choice was followed from its beginning all the way through to its logical conclusion. Every thread, every choice, has its dénouément, its often ignominious ending: even the 'good' and 'moral' choices, as the Greeks used to warn, often fade away into hubris, the pride that goes before a fall. So unlike the story of the Fates, our life-path within the wyrd is not a single, fixed, predetermined thread, but instead consists of an endless series of choices, moving our life-path from thread to thread—and trying not to be misled into poor choices or trapped in 'self-similar' loops by the twisted confu-sions of the wyrd. No one can ever truly control what happens, to themselves or to anyone; but with awareness we can each *direct* our path through the wyrd—that distinction is subtle, but vitally important! At every moment, there's a choice: to stay on the current thread, the logical extension of the current choice; or to move off onto any one of a myriad of other threads, other paths, that intersect with this one, here, now. So what choice should I make? What do I do now? Which way do I turn? There's always a choice, there's always a twist: yet it's the interweavings of those twists of 'weirdness' that make the choices possible—if we can allow ourselves to see them.

And there's a further twist, because each thread not only passes through everyone — or everyone through each thread — but also through everywhere, and every*when*: every choice has its echoes in every place, and every time. In the Greek story this aspect of the weaving is maintained not by the Fates, but by Pan, whose name literally means 'everywhere'. Yet there is no such separation in the Nordic story: the wyrd is all of these. The Sisters of Weird are the spinners and weavers of the wyrd's fabric; as the 'sisters of time', they control — or choose — the everchanging nature of Now; and they also keep watch over the world itself—the tree they stand beside is Yggdrasil, the World-Tree, which they tend constantly with water from the world's well. Even the name of the first — and originally the only — sister, Urðr, echoes this interweaving of everywhere: in Scottish the 'ð' or 'eth' in her name is hardened to a 'd'-sound, giving us the word 'weird'; but in Old German it was originally softened to a 'th'-sound, becoming the name of an important deity, Erthe or Eartha—the goddess of the earth, the goddess of everywhere. The wyrd is everything, everyone, everywhere, everywhen.

The other crucial difference between these two stories is in the way they view relationship. As far as Fate is concerned, relationship might as well not exist: each life is a distinct, separate, isolated thread, and such connection as it might happen to have with any other is fixed by the weavings of 'blind chance'—there's certainly no choice about it. But the wyrd is a fabric of *life*: an infinity of lives, each choosing their own path within a roiling, seething, effervescent interweaving of choices and chances. So every life, every choice, affects everyone and everything within the wyrd, everywhere and everywhen: everyone is on, or in, the *same* interweaving. Two people, following the same path—the same choice—compare notes on their experiences: for each of them this new information leads to further choices—and, of course, to further twists. So every moment is the interweaving of every choice, everywhere, everywhen; the wyrd, quite simply, *is* relationship, with everyone.

Wyrd is everyone

The threads of wyrd are archetypes, human characteristics: every one of them passes through everyone, everywhere, creating a web of connections which Carl Jung described as 'the collective unconscious'. More accurately, it's a kind of collective *sub*conscious: most of the time we're aware only of the handful of threads that form what we each tend to think of as 'I'—or at least the 'I' that we present to others—yet within each one of us is *every* thread, *every* characteristic, *every* human possibility. And we share all of these with everyone else: the wyrd *is* everyone.

I'm walking down the street, in the centre of the city, not particularly thinking of anything. Quite without warning, quite unbidden, a sense of *knowing* arises: I *know* that I *am* everyone — share humanity with everyone — and everyone *is* me. There is no separation between us, no distinction between us, no boundary between us — and yet I'm still 'I'. And the moment fades, and there's the street around me, and there are all the other people in the street, entirely separate, living their — our — own separate yet interweaving lives. A brief moment of weirdness, illustrating once more for me the nature of the wyrd.

When do you find yourself *knowing* that sense of connection with everyone? What *feelings* arise when it happens? If you think that you've never known this — that you feel only your isolation, your separateness from others — how do you think it *would* feel if you became aware of this sense of connection?

Each 'I', in this sense, is no more than that set of threads which we choose to present as 'I': our character, so to speak, or, in Jung's terms, our 'persona'—literally, a mask, 'that through which I sound'. *Every* thread passes through us, but usually we're only aware of a few—and are either unaware of the rest, or like to pretend that they *don't* pass through us!

I'm not keen on the idea that *every* thread, every human characteristic passes through me: "*I'm* not bitchy and vindictive — am I?" But then if every thread *does* pass through me, that includes all the 'good' characteristics

---

that I think only other people have: "I'll never be as confident as she is — will I?" The wyrd weaves in both directions: ultimately, we each *choose* our own 'I'.

If every thread, every human characteristic passes through you, which ones would you prefer to say *aren't* part of you? Bitchiness? Vindictiveness? Cruelty? Callousness? What else?

And which threads do you think aren't 'you' which you'd like to be so? Beauty? Charm? Confidence? Certainty? Strength? What else?

What if all of these were part of your 'I' — right now? In what ways would you feel different? And if you're not aware of these characteristics in you now, what would happen to your sense of self, of 'I', if you *did* accept them as part of 'I'?

In the short term, our 'character'—made up of the threads that are visible on the surface — is fairly stable. Over time, though, it does change—sometimes a lot—because our *choices* change: and yet it's always the same 'I'. So 'I' is not that which changes: 'I' is that which *chooses*.

Yet as we choose, so does everyone else; and every choice changes the choices for everyone else. Every choice we make echoes up and down the threads, affecting everyone: although in itself each thread may be fixed, and the path it defines predetermined, the wyrd itself—the interweaving of choice and chance —is anything *but* fixed. "No man is an island, entire of itself": whether we 'choose' so or not, we're *always* in relationship—with everyone.

Within the context of the wyrd, each 'I' is like a nexus or clustering of the threads—the *same* threads. Every thread passes through everyone: which means that we always have access to *every* possible human characteristic, human feeling. And it also means that we can always reach inside *ourselves* to understand others—which sounds weird, perhaps, but it works!

We can see *why* it works by using a slightly different analogy for 'I'. From a basic perspective, there's a clear boundary between 'I', and 'not-I' — in other words everyone else, everything else. It's like a wall around our sense of self: a wall or 'boundary' which sometimes—often, perhaps—we feel we have to defend.

> Are you aware of a kind of wall or boundary which you maintain around you, protecting your sense of 'I'? How does it *feel* when someone or something comes too close? How do you respond when someone intentionally, or even accidentally, breaches that boundary?

But for an analogy, cut off a strip about an inch wide from the long side of a piece of standard letter-paper, and join the ends flat together to turn it into a loop, a circle. Imagine that this forms the boundary between 'I' and 'not-I', with a definite inside — 'I' — and an equally definite outside — 'not-I'. Now take the loop apart, and give the strip of paper a *half*-twist before joining the ends together again, into what's called a Möbius loop. It's twisted, like the threads of wyrd, but it's still a loop, a circle, forming a definite boundary. Or not so definite a boundary: there's still an inside—an 'I'—and there's still an outside—'not-I' —but there is also *no* boundary, because somehow the inside of the strip becomes the outside becomes the inside. (Follow the side of the strip with your finger if this isn't obvious.) There is a boundary, but the boundary blurs — and there's no break, no specific point, at which it does so. Weird.

We can take this analogy a couple of steps further. Take a pair of scissors, and cut *along* the middle of the strip of paper. You'll notice that if you start cutting on the outside of the circle, at some point you'll find yourself cutting from what seems to be the inside, but just keep going till you come back to where you started. As you complete the cut, the circle falls apart—not into two circles, but into a single larger one with *two* twists. So once more cut along the middle of this longer strip of paper: and as the cut completes this time, it *does* fall into two circles — but interwoven with each other, and each with a single twist. We're back where we started: except now we have two interlocking circles where before we had one. So the more we divide this strip

—this thread of wyrd—the more we create a web of interlocking, interweaving threads, creating a more and more tightly defined boundary that is also, at the same time, no boundary.

So imagine, then, that this boundary between 'I' and 'not-I' is made up, not of a single strip of paper, but of an infinite number of threads of wyrd, all with the same twisted property, where somehow the inside becomes the outside becomes the inside, where 'I' *interweaves* with 'not-I'. *That's* wyrd: that's what wyrd *is*.

We interweave with everyone through the wyrd: its twisted threads create choices that allow us to relate to others in many different ways. However strange or difficult a relationship may seem, there's always a choice *we* can take which can make it work for everyone—if we so choose. But to find this we first need to understand the twisted nature of the wyrd: and perhaps the best way to start is to remember that 'weird' is also, and always, a *feeling*.

Wyrd is a feeling

Strange. Peculiar. Odd. Uncertain. *Weird*. They're all words to describe a particular, almost indescribable feeling. There's often a hint of fear, of panic almost, in that feeling, but there's also exhilaration, excitement, even elation. A very strange feeling...

> Something's weird, you say. Where do you *feel* it?
>
> Go back through some memories of events or situations — or even people — that you'd describe as weird. Explore the *feelings* you associate with each—"it sent shivers up my spine", perhaps.
>
> Having done that, notice the circumstances where that same feeling comes up in your everyday life. What does that tell you about 'weirdness' itself?

That feeling is also one of the hallmarks of wyrd in action: a signal that we can *know* we have new choices, that we're being presented, in the moment, with the possibility of looking at ourselves, or our relationship with the wider world, in a different and more empowering way.

Perhaps the greatest problem here, though, is fear. There's always *some* fear that comes up whenever we meet the wyrd — mainly because, being wyrd, it weaves its way past that carefully-constructed boundary around our sense of 'I'. In that moment of weirdness, we're being shown something that we don't usually see, and often don't *want* to see — especially about ourselves. The feelings that come with that are not exactly pleasant... And yet if we don't accept what's being shown to us by the twists of wyrd — if we hide from it in embarrassed, angry fear — we won't be able to see that we're also being shown *choices*: new ways to understand and express our own power. Power — 'the ability to act within the world, as an expression of our own choice' — is inextricably interwoven with fear: "Where there is fear, there is power; where there is power, there is fear," as the old witchcraft saying puts it. But if we hide in fear from what the wyrd shows us about our own power — our own choices — we can hardly complain if we end up feeling powerless...

> What are you afraid of? What do you fear? Why?
> In what weird ways do the weavings of the world remind you of that fear? When that fear returns — if only for a brief moment — what do you *feel*?

Our fears reduce only when we face them, and usually grow when we refuse to face them: that's one of the standard lessons in all forms of what's called personal growth. And a certain kind of wry humour can play an important part in this: by its nature, humour is weird, yet it's also one of the ways in which we come to allow ourselves to face our own fears. The weirdness of humour is that it juxtaposes different ways of looking at a particular issue — particularly, ways which we wouldn't usually allow ourselves to see. In the midst of the laughter, it's often easy to miss that the twists of humour conceal choices: what it's really showing us is that the way we see the world is the way we *choose* to see it — and that other ways of seeing it can allow us to reduce the fears we all have about it.

> Another chaotic mess of confusion and blame: no choice... I can't face it... it's so bad this time I just don't know whether to laugh or cry...
>
> Yet even here I *do* still have a choice — namely to laugh, or to cry. Which would be more useful? Which would be more empowering? An interesting question...
>
> When you're as overloaded emotionally as that, which do you choose? What happens with each of those choices — what do you *feel* in each case? And notice, no matter how powerless you feel, that you still have the power to make that choice...

That's what personal growth is about. But when we're working on our relationships with others, it's not just personal growth we're concerned with: it's also *inter*personal growth, the development of shared feeling and shared awareness. One of the aims of interpersonal growth is to become personally familiar with another feeling: "Je ne regrette rien" — no regrets, no anguishing about what 'could' or 'should' or 'might' have happened, but simply an acceptance of what *did* happen, and an acknowledgement of what we and others learned from it. A quiet state of active acceptance, yet active involvement, that's described as both non-attachment *and* non-detachment. Yet we won't be able to reach that state without awareness: awareness of ourselves, awareness of others, and awareness of the twisted nature of the wyrd and its choices. With awareness, the wyrd provides us with awareness of *itself* — and of the empowering choices that lie within its twists.

Wyrd is an awareness

"Evolution is chaos with feedback," wrote one of the early researchers on the mathematics of chaos. *Life* is chaos with feedback: but if we're not aware of the feedback, all we'll see is the chaos...

The usual approach to chaos is to try to take control, to

reduce it to some kind of order, a predictable pattern. Then, we hope, it will all make sense—somehow. Many personal development programmes aim, or at least claim, to show how to "take control of your life!" — which is unfortunate, because Reality Department is, by its nature, inherently chaotic, and hence true control is impossible, a myth. Any semblance of order we try to place on reality — such as the simple concept of cause-and-effect, or a more sophisticated concept such as the Indian notion of 'karma' — is exactly that: a semblance, an illusion, not the thing itself.

One of the common misunderstandings about modern chaos theory is the assumption that it makes the unpredictable predictable at last. It doesn't: all it does is make predictable the *degree* of unpredictability—within those bounds, chaos remains as unpredictable as ever. Even a simple coin-toss is completely unpredictable: no matter how many times it's come up heads or tails before, there's always an exactly even chance as to which way it will land—a mistake that has cost many gamblers dearly... And no matter how much we may talk about the 'laws' of science, or psychology, or economics, or whatever, in reality there is only one true law: the weirdness of Murphy's Law—"If something can go wrong, it probably will." Ultimately, all the other so-called 'laws' are only guidelines, patterns of high or even very high probability: but Murphy's Law really *is* a law—the only law in town.

> "If something can go wrong, it probably will." What's your experience of Murphy's Law: the car refusing to start on the one morning you're in a hurry, for example?
> Remind yourself of some other examples of your own. What do you *feel* when this happens?

The twist is that Murphy's Law is so much of a law that it normally applies to itself—"If Murphy's Law can go wrong, it probably will"—which gives us the illusion that the other 'laws' are real. The apparent predictability of scientific law and social custom occurs because the unpredictabilities tend to cancel

13

themselves out — but it's essential never to forget that the uncertainty is *always* there, and can never be 'legislated' away. We may think things 'ought to' or 'should' work in the way that we want them to: but sometimes this just doesn't happen — at all. We may think people 'ought to' or 'should' always do exactly what we want them to: but sometimes this just doesn't happen — at all. It's then interesting to note how we respond to the 'failure' of the world in general to conform to *our* expectations...

> "Damn! Kaye promised she'd update the report for me while I was stuck with that client. But Mary says she's gone home, says she's feeling ill — blast her, I *need* that report, right now! Why does she always let me down just when I really need her help?"
>
> What's your experience of Murphy's Law with *people*: particularly where you've depended on someone, and they've unintentionally let you down. What do you *feel* when this happens?

Anger. Irritation. Blame — "It's *their* fault it isn't working!" Common though these are, none of them help to resolve anything — in fact, they almost always make it worse. And they also conveniently block the awareness that the world *has* worked perfectly well, in its own way: it's *our* expectation of it that hasn't...

Being more realistic about what we expect from the world will help. Being more aware of our own involvement in the weavings of the world will help. And so too, especially, will an awareness and an acceptance of the ways that the world *does* work. For example, there's another twist that we might call 'inverse Murphy': "Things *can* go right — if you let them." The uncertainties of Murphy's Law can work both ways, to our advantage as well as to our detriment: and if we only allow things to work in the ways we expect, can we honestly complain when things don't seem to be working out for us?

> "Things *can* go right — if you let them": what's your experience of 'inverse Murphy'?
>
> What do you *feel* when something works in a way that you didn't expect? Are you pleased that it's working? Or annoyed, angry, even frightened, perhaps, that it didn't work in the way that you expected? What else?

So it's useful to develop a shift in awareness: when things don't work out in the ways that we expect, it's not so much the world 'going wrong', but a warning that our expectation of the world is wrong — or at least too fixed, too rigid. Life is 'chaos with feedback': so what we get back from the weird chaos of the world is its feedback, its response to us. And it's up to us to notice it, accept that that's what it is, and work *with* it — not complain about it! With that awareness, every 'failure' instead becomes a *lesson*, reminding us that the world, and our relationships within it, *can* work for us—but only if we let them.

It may seem weird... wyrd... but it *does* work. It's often difficult, though, to see that most of what happens 'to' us *is* feedback from the wyrd. We choose, and something happens; but the 'feedback' often isn't as simple as cause-and-effect, because every choice echoes up and down the wyrd, often coming back to us from the most unexpected directions. At times, the ways in which the wyrd 'responds' can be very weird indeed... and it's up to us to recognise them, and make use of them as best we can.

That's what we'll explore here. And the first stage is to look at one of the most common experiences of 'wyrdness': the repeating patterns and loops into which our lives — and especially our relationships — tend to get stuck. Round and round the garden, getting nowhere slowly... that's the feeling. So when that feeling comes again—as it so often does, for all of us — it's time to look more closely at what's going on, in our interaction with others, and with the wyrd.

2

ROUND AND ROUND
THE GARDEN

Every now and then, that strange yet familiar feeling returns: *déjà vu*, it's called... Been here, done that, I'd thought—but now I'm back here again. Again. And again. "Round and round the garden, *like* a teddy bear...".: those weird loops keep happening in my life. The same issues come up again and again with different people, in different places, in different contexts; exactly the same words, even. I do understand that there's no way those people could have known that those words have specific—and painful —meanings for me, that just that gesture brings back memories that I really don't want to recall; and yet... *how*? How does it happen? More to the point, *why* does it happen?

> I've been on a long trip with a colleague, and she's been asking me detailed questions every inch of the way: every time I stop for breath, for a pause, she sends another question hurtling at me. We reach our destination; are greeted by my colleague's partner. "I'm exhausted," she says to him, mockingly, "Chris was talking at me *all the way*, and I couldn't get a word in edgeways!" Suddenly I'm furious: *she'd* been pestering *me* all the way, and now she's mocking me for answering her questions! And yes, I do have some reason to be

> upset—but not *that* much. By the time I cool down a bit, I realise it isn't much to do with her at all: what really hurts so much is that it's an exact repeat, even to the same words, of what happened so often back in school and at home — answers being demanded, and then being mocked for answering as demanded. That all happened many years ago, in another place, and with other people: yet here it is again, now, in this moment. Weird...
>
> What issues keep returning for you — wearing different faces, different places, but still the same thread? What do you *feel* when they return? And how do you feel towards the people who—usually unwittingly— bring these threads back into your life?

About all I can answer is that it *does* happen—a lot. And a lot more than I'm willing to admit: allow myself to notice, and it becomes clear that life is full of these weird loops. If all these things which happen to me are supposed to be the results of my own choices, then what on earth did I choose? It's crazy, frightening: better be careful not to notice it too much, or ask too many questions about it, because that way madness lies — that's what it feels like, anyway. Almost like something out of one of Lewis Carroll's stories: a weird garden full of strange characters and even stranger experiences, all woven together with a thread of logic so twisted that it *almost* seems to make sense... in *a* sense, at least.

Round and round the garden... a garden full of Carroll's weird characters... that's another analogy that's worth exploring for a while. So imagine walking in a quiet park-like garden: you hear voices in the middle distance, and you begin to move towards them...

Running nowhere

Turning a corner past a clump of bushes, you walk almost straight into a bevy of some of the strangest-looking people you've ever seen. They look like animals, or birds, and sound just like them too—but they're all human-sized, and they're all fully dressed in normal, if outdated, human clothes.

> Slightly off the thread, perhaps, but do some people remind you of particular animals or birds? A fox, perhaps, or a rabbit; a mouse or a rat, a pig, a hawk, a swan, a startled deer? What are the characteristics — appearance, mannerisms, habits — which these people seem to you to share with the respective animal or bird?
>
> Given that you *choose* to perceive those people that way, *why* do you do so? What difference does it make? How does it change the way you relate with them?
>
> The same threads, or characteristics, are present in everyone: all that changes is the degree to which they're visible — or that we choose to see them. If so, what makes it easier for you to see them in some people, and not in others—especially yourself?

It's a caucus-race, they say—whatever that is—and they want you to join in. They're so enthusiastic about it all that it's obvious they wouldn't be able to notice even if you said "No"; and suddenly they, and you, are all off in this race. Or dance. Or something. It seems to consist of running madly round in circles, bumping into each other, making lots of loud noises, jumping up and down in wild excitement—a kind of cross between a stock-car race and the mad circus of the Stock Exchange. Just as suddenly, it all stops: everyone flops onto the ground in whatever way they can. Everyone has won, apparently; but now they're all looking at *you*, because they seem to think that *you're* the one who's going to give everybody prizes...

> The caucus-race sounds crazy, but there's no shortage of everyday examples: is your workplace one, perhaps? Do you feel you have to join in with everyone else's mad dance, even when you don't want to? Why? And what happens when they make it clear that they're all expecting some kind of prize or 'gift' from you?

A few mumbled apologies, and you're on your way again:

they're so engrossed in their game that they've forgotten you already. You've barely made your escape, though, when it becomes clear that you're not going to get away *that* easily... Striding towards you, from the other direction, is a tall, spiky woman, dressed all in dark red—*everything* about her is the same dark red, from her shoes and her long dress to her face, her hair, her hands, and the pointed crown she wears on her head. "If you're going to get anywhere," she snaps at you, "you've got to *run!*" She grabs hold of your arm, and starts running, dragging you with her—without asking where *you* want to go, of course. "Faster!" she yells, "Faster! Faster!" You're both running so fast that everything's a blur—but she still wants you to run faster than ever. Exhausted, you stop—and realise that you haven't moved an inch. You're in exactly the same place where you started: all that running, just to stay still! "Of course!" snaps the Red Queen. "What did you expect? If you actually want to move somewhere else, you have to run *much* faster than that!" And with that comment, she vanishes: presumably she *can* run fast enough to get away from here...

> Having to run ever faster and faster, just to stay still: how often has that happened in your life? What was the context? Who are the people with whom you find yourself doing this?
>
> When you *know* you've run—or worked, or whatever —as hard as you can, and somebody tells you "That's not good enough—you'll have to do better than *that!*" what do you *feel*—towards yourself, and towards them?

Over to the left you can hear the clinking of china and cutlery—it's obvious that that's going to be the Mad Hatter's tea-party, and it'd be best to watch from a distance! There are quite a few people there, and they seem to be playing a strange variant of 'musical chairs': running round and round the long table, chanting something, then all suddenly sitting down and shouting and pointing at the one who hasn't found a chair. You get a little closer to hear what's going on—taking care to keep out of sight!

—and hear them chant, over and over, as they run: "Round and round in the usual old game—I take the credit and you take the blame." Then when they stop, they shout *"It's all your fault!"* — and the hapless victim runs off into the bushes, head hanging in shame and despair. Not exactly a pleasant game—but a disturbingly familiar one...

> "Round and round in the usual old game — I take the credit and you take the blame": that ever-popular pastime called 'passing the buck'! How often have you found yourself caught in one of these 'blame-games', where everyone is trying to grab the credit if it works, but set someone else up as the scapegoat in case it doesn't? What were the circumstances? In what ways — and why —were you involved?
>
> If you found yourself being set up as the scapegoat, how did it *feel* when all the blame was dumped on you? Were you able to see it coming? And if you did, why weren't you able to pull out of the game in time?
>
> On the times when you managed to avoid being the scapegoat, what did you *feel* when someone else was landed with everyone's blame? How did you feel towards the scapegoat—and towards yourself?

Time to get away from here. But you find that you can't: there's something weird going on—the path seems straightforward enough, but somehow it must have a hidden wriggle or twist, because whatever you do, you keep coming back to the same place. Who can you turn to for help? Not the Mad Hatter —that's for sure! Perhaps the gardener you can see over to the right, crooning his little rhyme: "He thought he saw a banker's clerk descending from a bus; he looked again and found it was a hippopotamus... if that should stay to dine, he said, there won't be much for us..." Oh. Perhaps not the gardener, then... But there must be *someone* in this mad garden you can turn to for advice—musn't there?

A garden-full of advice

"Depends what you mean by *someone*," says a quiet voice just beside you. But there's no one there, in among the mass of flowers: no one you can see, anyway. "I don't think it knows we can talk," says another voice. *Who?* The flowers, of course... this is getting crazier every minute... "If you want to get out of the garden," says another of the flowers, "It's no use going the way you expect—life's never as simple as that! When you're stuck, and can't get to where you want, you have to walk *away* from it instead—keep your goal in mind, but walk the other way!"

The flowers' advice—"Keep your goal in mind, but walk the other way"—may seem a little crazy, but it's another variant on Inverse Murphy: if things aren't working in expected ways, allow them to work in *un*expected ways! Sometimes — often — this weird approach to problems *does* work out: when has it happened in your life?

What do you *feel* when you're stuck, and someone gives you apparently nonsensical advice? *Where* do you feel this feeling? And what do you feel—about them, and about yourself—when their advice turns out to be right?

You're thinking about whether to put this crazy advice into practice, when you're startled by a loud yell from behind. "Ahoy! Check!" comes the yell again, as a man on horseback canters up to you, and promptly falls off. As he picks himself up off the ground and dusts himself down—white armour clanking as he does so—you notice that his horse is festooned with an incredible amount of junk and jetsam: tattered bags and bits of old rope, a piece of fence, a wooden sword, a tin dustbin-lid, even the wreckage of what appears to have once been a beehive. "Ah, I'm glad you noticed that," he says, pointing at a small object you hadn't yet noticed. "It's my own invention." You look at the tangled mass of wire, in the midst of which is a tiny piece of cheese: is this some kind of mousetrap? "It's to prevent mice from climbing on the back of the horse when I'm sitting on it," he says with pride. But mice wouldn't do that anyway, would they? "Ah, but they *might*, you know. So I invented this, just in case!" Oh, no, not another one...

> Who do you know that's an inveterate collector of 'unconsidered trifles', their pockets and bags kept full of all sorts of unlikely items 'just in case'? Do you, perhaps? If so, what are all these items? How often—if ever —have you used them for the purpose you expected? How often have you used them for a purpose you *didn't* expect?
>
> The White Knight was in some ways Lewis Carroll's self-portrait: a shy, timid man, he too used to travel around with all sorts of toys and trinkets in his pockets, with which to start up a conversation with a child and her parents. You've probably shared with others quite a few of your own collection of items: a pin or a pen, perhaps; a tissue or a packet of mints. What conversations or other weird twists have ensued from that simple choice to share something with strangers?

It's clear that you're about to receive a lengthy lecture on the climbing habits of mice and the finer points of mousetrap design, but instead you both see a glint of red armour in the wood beyond. The White Knight leaps into action... sort of... it takes him some time to struggle into the saddle, and he falls off three times even before he gets to the trees... As he vanishes erratically into the shadows, you can still hear his thin voice calling out the challenge, "Ahoy! Ahoy! Check!"

Shaking your head in disbelief, you wander off to the side, and hear two more voices in earnest discussion. One seems a little upset: in fact, it's the Mock Turtle, sobbing sonorously at the Gryphon, who in turn is paying little attention to anyone but itself.

> The Gryphon and the Mock Turtle: two more archetypes —two more threads of the wyrd!
>
> Who do you know who, like the Mock Turtle, is

constantly crying and complaining, trying to claim what John Bradshaw described as "that special attention which is the prerogative of the miserable"? Does this habit of theirs make it easier, or harder, to relate with them?

And who do you know who, like the Gryphon, are so full of themselves that they're interested only in reflections of their own ideas? How do you relate *with* them — rather than being talked *at* by them?

How often do you find yourself meeting up with people like these — people who demand your attention, but rarely if ever reciprocate? When you find yourself sucked into their space, how do you *feel*, towards them, and towards yourself? How did you come to be trapped there? And how, at last, did you break free?

While you're there, how easy is it to notice that, in the midst of the constant stream of "Me! me! me!" there *is* useful information for *you*? If you *did* notice it, what did you learn?

Self-centred though they may be, they don't seem *quite* as mad as the others, so you walk up to meet them. Their conversation—if that's what one would call it—seems at first to be about school, because they keep on talking about lessons. But it turns out that the conversation's more about the lessons of life itself—which is why the Mock Turtle's tears are flowing. "I'd... be happier... if... the same old hurts didn't... keep... coming back," it sobs, sadly. "Ah," says the Gryphon, "that's the point about the lessons, you see. Everything that happens is a lesson: we're supposed to learn from them. Don't know *why*, but we are—call it fate, if you like. If you don't understand what the lesson *is*, old thing, you get to do it again. And again. And again. The lessons tend to come back anyway, but each time you grasp a bit more of it, it doesn't come back so hard. The whole idea, y'see, is to get the lessons to lessen. Hah! Rather proud of that," it says, turning to you. "Clever pun, don't you think: 'get the lessons to lessen'?"

Whatever you may think of the Gryphon's attempts at humour, it may have a point. If, as it suggests, most

> things which happen to us are more like 'lessons' from the weavings of the wyrd — happening not so much 'to' us as *with* us — then it's up to us to understand what that lesson is: or it'll simply come back again. More to the point, *we* bring it back again, in order to find out what it is we have to learn. In my own case, one of the 'lessons' was about having consciously played the scapegoat role, in order to keep others 'happy': it's taken many repetitions of that particular 'lesson' before I finally understood that my playing that role wasn't helping anyone — least of all me...
>
> Are you aware of some of your own 'lessons'? For examples, look at some of the repeating patterns and loops that have happened in your own life. How many not-quite-repeats of the loop did it take before you began to understand the lesson? And what did it take for you to 'get the lessons to lessen'?

Enough 'advice' for the moment, perhaps? It's obvious that the Gryphon and the Mock Turtle will continue talking at each other all day, and they'll do it whether you're there or not. So you wander away, back towards the trees, and see another figure in white, lying on the ground, apparently sleeping — and wearing, like the Red Queen, a crown.

A royal muddle

Whoever it is, it's snoring loudly; or rather *he's* snoring, because his small, straggly beard and moustache are just visible. Twitching slightly: presumably he's dreaming. "Dreaming about *you*," says a sharp voice in your ear — which turns out to be that of the Red Queen again, irritable as ever. "You're only a figment of his imagination, a character in his dream," she says; "when he wakes up, you'll vanish, as if you'd never been." And she moves as if to wake him...

> "Last night," wrote one of the old Zen poets, "I dreamed I was a butterfly. Or is it that it's *now* that I'm asleep, and that I'm a butterfly dreaming I'm a man?" There's no way

we can tell: dreams have their own weird reality. And yet the existential anxiety this creates is all too real: Who am I? *What* am I? How can I prove that I exist? Perhaps this is one of those 'lessons' that we'd like to lessen...

Is this an experience with which you're familiar? If so, under what kind of context—and with whom—does it tend to arise?

And who do you know that, like the Red Queen here, deliberately plays on your fears? Why do they do it? If you do it to others, why do *you* do it?

Looking pleased at your obvious discomfiture, the Red Queen leaves the White King to his snoring, and returns to talk at you. "You've been talking with the Gryphon and the Mock Turtle, I see—not that those idiots know anything, of course." You mention that the Gryphon had some interesting comments to make about the lessons of life. "Lessons? What do they know about *lessons?* Why, in *my* school they taught us *everything* there is to know about arithmetic: I doubt if they taught *you* that." You attempt to murmur that, yes, you did indeed study arithmetic at school, and a great deal more besides, but the Queen quickly cuts you off. "Prove it! Divide a loaf by a knife—what's the answer? Can't say? There, you see, I knew it. Useless! Doesn't know any arithmetic at all! The answer's *sliced bread*, of course!" And with a patronising—matronising?—smile, she vanishes again.

You'll know, in a matter of moments, that *nothing* you say here would be right: nothing is going to shift the Red Queen's smug certainty in herself. It really doesn't matter whether she's right or wrong, because you're the one who'll take the blame in any case: you know she'll always be able find *some* way to twist whatever you said, to make you out to be the fool every time...

Familiar, perhaps? Who do you know that's like this — constantly constructing put-downs so as to prop up their delusions of their own superiority?

Placating someone like the Red Queen doesn't work: they simply take, and never give in return.

> Responding aggressively to their selfish rudeness doesn't work either: you'll get hit with a torrent of right-eous indignation and blame. Since almost everything they do is based on setting up a 'no-win' for others, if you play the game their way, you'll always lose. So how *do* you create a relationship with them in which everyone *does* 'win'?

A sigh of relief: she's gone. But you hear a rustling noise; you look up, and there in the tree above you is an enormous cat. Grinning. At you. Showing all its many sharp teeth, yet with wry amusement, as if it knows something you'd rather it didn't. It makes a most peculiar sound in its throat — a cross between a yowl and a purr, but with a hint of words—and then fades away, leaving behind only its grin. A cat without a grin, yes; but a grin without a cat? What's *that* supposed to mean? Weird indeed...

Confused, you walk round a corner, and there in the distance are a group of very thin people—thin from the side, at least—apparently painting a rose-bush. Not painting a picture of the bush—painting the bush itself... *why?* You walk a little closer.

They're thin, these people, yet wide — almost like playing-cards with head and limbs attached. And they *are* putting paint onto the roses, as quick as they can. They see you; jump up and down in evident panic, trying to hide the paint-brushes; and then realise that you're not who they thought you were, and go back to painting the flowers again, even more hurriedly than before. What are they so frightened about? Intriguing... weird...

You walk right up to them, and ask what they're doing. "Oh, you give us a fright then!" says one—literally One, it has a single bright red heart-shape on its flat back, while others have more. "Thought you was the Queen, like. What're we doin'? Correctin' a little error like wot Three 'ere bin and done. Queen wanted red roses, din't she? Three thought 'e'd planted a red one, but when it growed, the flowers come up white. She won't like that, will the Queen: have our heads off if we ain't careful... Oh no! 'Ere she comes!"

And here she comes indeed: not the Red Queen, but the

Queen of Hearts, with her full entourage — including the Executioner, his axe at the ready. "*What* is the meaning of this! There shall be *no* mistakes in my realm! Off with their heads!"

I can remember, all too vividly, a real-life example of the Queen of Hearts: a senior sales manager from the head office of a large supermarket chain, visiting a local branch. "We have a national special on strawberry gateau!" he yelled—he never merely *spoke* to anyone if he could help it; "*why is it not on display?*" "We don't *have* any," said the branch manager; "we ordered it, but Distribution hasn't sent us any yet." "That's *your* problem!" shouted the head-office man; "I want it on display, and I want it there *now!*" Terrified, the branch manager turned to the warehouse supervisor: "Ah... ah... get the strawberry gateau on display—quickly!" The supervisor in turn started to say, "but we haven't got any in stock"; then realised that her manager knew that too, so turned to the nearest junior staff member and said loudly, "Get the strawberry gateau from stock—now!" The junior took only a moment to realise what was going on, and then took the only sensible action under those circumstances —he ran to the warehouse, and hid, until the visitor had gone!

Who do you know that, like the Queen of Hearts or the head-office man, tries to rule by fear and intimidation? How do you work with—or in any way relate to— such people? What effect does their bullying have on other people's relationships with each other? And what effect does it have on everyone's ability to get the job done well? In that sense, does the bullying 'work'? If not, what *does* the bullying do?

The painters try to hide behind you, but they're quickly caught, and dragged away. There is the terrifying 'crunch' of an axe hitting something that isn't wood... And now, for the first time, the Queen turns to notice you. "What is this... this..."—she looks you up and down, in evident disgust — "this *thing?*" She looks round angrily at her terrified entourage, then back at you. "*What* is it doing in my realm? Take it away—at once! Executioner!" she screams, at the top of her voice, "Executioner! Off with its head!"

This madwoman screaming at you, and people beginning to move towards you: they're so frightened of her that it's clear they'll literally do *anything*—even "Off with its head!"—just to keep her quiet... You're terrified, panicking, you want to run away, anywhere but here... But for some weird reason you remember the flowers' advice—"Go the other way!"—and you go *towards* the Queen instead...

It works!

Either you've vanished, or they've vanished: it's impossible to tell—whichever it is, you're free, and out of the garden at last.

You still feel a few of the effects of the fear the Queen of Hearts set out to create in you: sweating hands, pounding heart, and so on. But they're fading too, like the last vestiges of the Cheshire Cat's grin. Stuck in her bullying, she probably thought that fear *is* power—that others' fear is *her* power; yet by facing that fear, and coming towards it in a different, and perhaps weird way, you found your *own* power to break free from hers. Where there's power, there's fear; but by facing our own fear we can find that where there's fear, there can also be power—our *own* power. So fear and power, and the weird mistakes we all make about them, are what we'd better look at next.

3

POWER AND FEAR

Free of the confusions and craziness of the imaginary garden, and back in the ordinary—sometimes mistakenly called 'real'—world, it's time to stop and think for a while: look a bit more closely at what we saw there.

Imaginary though they all were, each of the characters in the garden would also have been recognisable—perhaps all too recognisable—in examples of people you know in your day-to-day world. In their own different ways, each of those characters —even the Mock Turtle—thought that they were being power-ful: that what they were doing was the right way, or even the only way, in which they could get what they wanted in the world. A few of them—the Queen of Hearts especially—were playing on other people's fears, and probably thought that fear — other people's fear, at least—*was* 'power'. Some of the others—such as the White Knight, and the mad gardener whom we quietly avoided — were away in their own private worlds, with only a tenuous grasp on what was actually happening around them. And some—like those at the caucus-race, or around the Mad Hatter's table — had a kind of shared world, with mutually-agreed rules, but which in practice perhaps had even less of a grasp on reality. The results are chaotic: the same destructive patterns, the same habitual responses, repeated — with minor variations—over and over again. Round and round the garden...

Some people may — and evidently do — choose to be caught in loops like these: and if we're not careful, they'll often try to drag us in to join them. We don't *have* to join them: but sometimes it can seem that there's no choice—and often others will try very hard to make it seem that way. The way out of those loops is to recognise that they *are* loops in the weavings of the wyrd, and then notice the twists — like the flowers' advice — which open up hidden choices that allow us to move to alternative paths. But first we need to see that, no matter what it may look like, we *do* always have a choice: and to find this we need to understand more about power and fear, and the weird interactions between them.

A problem of power

What *is* power? Most people would say that they want it, that someone else has it, but don't ever seem to be able to say what it is. Power is apparently linked in some way with money, or with a supposed 'right' to bully others, or to offload work onto others; but then we come across some chance encounter which triggers what we could only call powerful changes in our lives, but which has little or nothing to do with money, or bullying, or anything other than the weirdness of the moment itself. Power is... something... but it's surprisingly difficult to pin down exactly what that something *is*.

> What, to you, *is* power? Who has it? Where does it come from? Where does it go?
>
> What is *your* power? Where does it come from? Where does it go?
>
> What happens to your power when you're with others? With whom, and under what circumstances, do you seem to gain power? With whom, and in what circumstances, does it seem to fade—or be taken from you?
>
> It might be worthwhile to write some notes on this, and review these questions often as you go through the book.

Whatever definition of power we choose, it *is* still a choice —which means a twist is also attached to that choice. As with all other definitions, how our choice of how we define 'power' also determines how we perceive it—and how we experience it.

For example, there's the so-called 'common-sense' notion that power is a kind of limited and rare commodity: some people have it, and most don't, but everybody wants it. If that's how power is perceived, *all* transactions between people are described in terms of a 'zero-sum' of power—the old Marxist concept that "It is in the nature of power that it is impossible for one to have more without others having less"—and hence *all* relationships are viewed in terms of 'win-lose'. If that's what I believe, then I'll also believe that the only way I can win is to make sure that you lose. So if you hold the same concept of power, we're set for a life-time of struggle... and even if you didn't hold it to start with, you probably would quite soon, because you'd get very annoyed, very quickly, at my constant attempts to prop myself up by putting you down.

> "It is in the nature of power that it is impossible for one to have more without others having less": in what ways is that true in your own life? In what ways is it *not* true?
>
> Is there a difference in the meaning of 'power' in each case? Or is it more a difference in what you—or others—choose to perceive as 'power'?
>
> How do you relate with someone who regards that definition of power as true — someone who constantly attempts to prop themselves up by putting others down? In what ways, and under what circumstances, do *you* attempt to prop yourself up by putting others down? How do others relate with you when *you* do this?

The twist in 'win-lose' is that since everyone's energy is expended on struggling to be 'the winner' — and especially in trying to avoid being 'the loser'—*nobody* ever really 'wins': all that happens is that an increasing number of people spend ever-increasing amounts of energy going nowhere, 'round and round the garden'. Since one of the most popular means of gaining 'power' is to manufacture fear in one sense or another, it's all too true that "where there's fear, there's power; where there's power, there's fear". But the supposed winner's feeling of having gained power over others masks the reality that *everyone* loses — and in practice even the most definite 'final victory' can be short-lived...

Each concept of power is a thread of the wyrd: each has its own path, its own consequences, its own dénouement. So we *can* change our experience of power — and other people's experience of power, when in relationship with us — simply by changing the way *we* choose to perceive it. If we perceive power as a fixed commodity, that's what it'll be; if we treat every relationship as a 'zero-sum', that's what we'll have. And if, as the slogan for one of the *Godfather* films put it, we base our life on the notion that "true power cannot be given — it must be *taken*", we will, in the usual weird way, find plenty of people who are willing to play: a few will accept it as their fate that they have to lose to us, but there'll be many, many more who are also trying to 'win' that much-prized feeling of power — and are all too willing to fight us for it... In a very real sense it *is* true that "life doesn't have to be a struggle" — and that if it is a struggle for us, it's probable that our past and present choices have helped to make it so.

There's always a choice, there's always a twist: we don't have much choice about the twists, but we *do* have choice about the choices. So we can choose, for example, to perceive power not as a finite commodity, but as something variable and volatile, something created — or destroyed — *by* us, or in the space *between* us. Power — or the lack of it — depends on *us*, and how we relate with each other. In this sense, when people relate with each other, there's a whole spectrum of power-transactions from 'win-win' to 'lose-lose'; in this sense, 'win-lose' is just an odd type of 'lose-lose', in which the illusion of gaining at one level masks an overall loss at another. The constant 'win-lose' battles for power-over and power-under — manipulation, deceit and so on — are replaced by stronger need for power *with* others to help us find, and share, a deeper and more personal kind of power-from-within. The struggles still exist, in a sense: but rather than being *against* others, they're more *for* understanding—especially understanding of ourselves, and of what our own power *is*.

> The 'power-games' of power-over and power-under are probably all too familiar: but what is your experience of power-with — a power that exists *because* it's shared with others? In what ways does this kind of power feel different from power-over and power-under? What difference does it make to your *own* sense of power — your own power-from-within? With whom, and in what circumstances, does this sense of power-with arise?
>
> Even if—or perhaps even *because*—this concept of power-with seems alien to you, experiment with it for a while. Assume that in every interaction with others, it's always in part *your* choice as to whether it will be 'win-win', 'lose-lose', or the illusory 'win-lose'—and that you *always* have that choice. What difference does this make to the way you perceive those others? What difference does this make to the way they interact with you? If, in some weird way, you find yourself interacting with different people, in what ways are they different from the type of people you meet when you assume that 'power cannot be given—it can only be taken'?
>
> Despite the damage it causes, 'win-lose' can sometimes seem easier than the constant search for constructive solutions that 'win-win' demands... Why is this? What's the difference in what 'win-win' asks from *you*?

This description also matches more closely with the physics definition of power, where 'power' — or, more accurately, 'potential' — is "the ability to do work". (In 'win-lose', by comparison, power often seems more like "the ability to avoid work"—which is probably why so little actually gets done!) That bald physics definition, though, applies mainly to machines, which work in only one way and have no choice in what they do. By the time we apply it to people, we'd have to expand that physics definition somewhat: we'd have to say that power is "the ability to do work, as an expression of *choice*"; and not only is the definition of 'work' entirely open, but there is also no distinction between 'work' and 'play'. This may take a bit of explaining...

First, power may be the ability to do work, but work itself is not power: without awareness, that mistake leads inevitably to the illusion that 'arbeit macht frei' ('work makes freedom')—the slogan over the gates at Auschwitz... If the work is not done by choice, there is no power: being forced to do someone else's work rarely *feels* like power, at any rate! In practice, that's what 'win-lose' is really about: people not so much searching for any real power, as trying desperately—at any cost, to anyone—to avoid the terrifying feeling of power*less*ness.

> "Power is the ability to do work, as an expression of choice": what's the difference you *feel* between when you're doing something you choose to do, and something that you don't?
>
> There's an odd sense in which power and time interweave: the sisters of wyrd are the sisters of *time*. So does time seem to go by faster when you're doing what you want to do, or when you're doing what you don't want to do?

Next, it's essential to understand that the meaning of 'work' is entirely open: for example, to dig a ditch, to solve a complex equation, to calm a fractious child, and to reclaim hope from despair are all *work*. In physics, 'work' is defined as "the rate at which energy is expended": energy is certainly expended in all those examples of work, so that definition would still apply! But they're different *kinds* of energy: physical effort, mental effort, emotional effort, and what would probably be called a spiritual effort—where 'spiritual', in this sense, has little to do with religion and the like, but is more 'a sense of meaning and purpose, a sense of self and of that which is greater than self'. Even in physics, there are different types of energy — electromagnetic, gravity, weak nuclear, strong nuclear—which interact with each other and in some ways change into each other; in the same way, those different kinds of human energy interact with each other and in some ways change into each other—they change *through* us, as an expression of our choices. Our power exists through the work *we* choose to do, in whatever form we choose.

> We each have our own choices in the wyrd, our own preferred ways of working in the world: so what *form* does your power most easily take? Do you find it easier working with machines than with people, perhaps? Do you prefer the challenge of a technical problem to the challenge of keeping the house tidy and clean? Would you rather face the rigours of a mountain-climb than face the rigours of exploring your own sense of self?
>
> Although you'll find some forms of work easier than others, we all have to do most of them at some time — especially the mundane tasks like tax forms and the weekly washing. Where do you find your own power in these other forms of work?

The last point is perhaps the hardest: the idea that, as far as power is concerned, there's no distinction between work and play. Children don't distinguish between them: a child's 'work' *is* play—and there's usually plenty of energy being expended! It's in children's play that they develop their many skills, and come to understand their own 'ability to do work, as an expression of choice'. But by the time we get to adulthood, somewhere the idea creeps in that work isn't supposed to be enjoyable, isn't supposed to be meaningful to us, whereas what we still call 'play-time' is: hence the common notion, as a friend put it to me the other day, that "work is what I do to pay for my play". If we're doing work that has no meaning to us, no purpose in itself, we're not exactly likely to feel powerful about it...

> What, to you, is 'work'? What, to you, is 'play'? What form — if any — does your own sense of power take in each of these?
>
> Do 'work' and 'play' ever coincide, as far as you're concerned? If so, how, and in what way? And who are you with, when—or if—they coincide?
>
> "Work is what I do to pay for my play"—is that close

to your own attitude to work? If so, how can you *create* a
sense of being powerful at work? And in those times
when work *does* seem also like play — especially with
others—what happens to how you *feel* about your work?

Yet in its own weird way this attitude to work is just as
much of a choice as is the notion of 'win-lose'—and with much
the same results. In terms of the wyrd, if we choose to view
work as boring, disempowering, something we have to do in
order to pay for what we *really* want to do... well, that's what
we're likely to get, because that is what we *choose*. And just as
with 'win-lose', we're likely to meet up with people who'll help to
reinforce that choice. We *can* choose to view work in a different
way: for example, as Joseph Campbell put it, we can choose to
"follow our bliss", or as Castaneda's perhaps imaginary 'teacher'
Don Juan put it, we can "choose a path that has heart"—though
at times it can be far from easy to do. Yet if we do that, we'll find
there are people who'll help to reinforce that choice, too. It's up
to us: we always have that choice.

But the twist is that to make that change happen, we also
have to change our choices about power, and about work. And
to do that, we have to face the real issue behind all of this: an
infamous four-letter word called 'fear'...

A problem of fear

Here we need to return to that idea that 'where there's fear,
there's power'. When we're afraid, we lose our power—we lose
our ability to do work, for the simple reason that we're too busy
being afraid to do much of anything else...

When you were a child, what were you afraid of? *Who*
were you afraid of? Why? What led you to be afraid?
And how much of what you feared did actually come to
pass?

What are you afraid of now? *Who* are you afraid of?
Why? How much—if ever—does what you fear actually
happen to *you*?

> What are you afraid of in yourself? Are you afraid of what you might do with your anger, perhaps? Explore those inner fears a little...

Fear is a useful and natural tool: it always has something to tell us about the way we interact with the world, and we often do need to listen to what it has to say. But it can easily become a hindrance rather than a help, for a number of reasons: when we *don't* listen to it, for example—and hence get damaged; or when we pay too much attention to the feeling of fear itself, rather than listening to what it's trying to tell us; or when others set out to augment our natural fears, in the hope that this will allow them to 'take away' our power. The idea there seems to be that, if we lose our power to fear, then if we can be induced into feeling afraid, that power will be lying around—so to speak—for someone else to claim. Where there's fear, there's power; and I'll have it from you, thanks...

Fear is natural. What *isn't* 'natural' is the way in which so many people—especially those focussed on a 'win-lose' model of power—deliberately set out to make others frightened. In some ways our whole society is based on this: "Do *you* have enough insurance?" asks a television advertisement; "Shouldn't you be afraid of going out at night?" asks an apparently well-meaning relative. Often it's dressed up as 'for your own good'—"Don't go near the dog! All dogs bite!"—but sometimes, as with the sales-manager's shouted demands for the strawberry special, there's not even an attempt at disguise: it's just plain ordinary bullying. "It is in the nature of power that it is impossible for some to have less without one having more, so the more powerless and afraid I can make others feel, the more powerful I'll be": that seems to be the idea, anyway.

> We've already looked at the problems of relating with those who bully others in the belief that 'where's there's fear, there's power': but how much do *you* do this? How much, for example, do you set out to make children frightened of something 'for their own good'? *Why* do you do this? Do you feel more, or less, powerful when

you see that they're now more afraid?

It isn't likely to be comfortable to face this, or to admit to doing it at all, but face it anyway... what do you find out about yourself? If you can acknowledge it as something that you do, what do you *feel* when you face this fact?

Who do you do this to? Children? Adults? Work colleagues? Your partner? How do others relate to *you* when you try to make them fearful?

Fear *always* exists, in all of us; no matter what may be claimed, no one is ever truly without fear. (Even the 'common-sense' idea that men are naturally less fearful than women is wrong: in reality, most men are haunted by the fear of the abuse they'd get if they fail to *simulate* 'fearlessness'...) And there's a simple twist: if we face fear, it shrinks, though never quite disappears; but if we refuse to face it, it grows — and the wyrd, obliging as ever, keeps coming back with 'lessons' to remind us of the fact. So up comes another common notion: the idea that, rather than facing the fear ourselves, we can *export* it to someone else: then it's their problem, not ours. I'll take your power, and you can have my fear: that's a fair exchange, isn't it? That's part of what the desire for 'power' is really about: because if I'm truly 'powerful', I'll always be able to find someone whom I can force to face my fears for me... We've seen this already, for example, with the sales manager and his demands about the strawberry special: he exported the problem — and his unad-mitted fears — by yelling at the supermarket manager, who 'passed the buck' to the supervisor. She in turn passed it on, quickly, to the junior, who 'solved' the problem for everyone by running away in a panic. We could note that nothing was actually *done* — no cake was displayed, because it didn't exist — so if power is 'the ability to do work', *no one* was actually powerful. In this sense, it might be more accurate to say that "where there's fear, there *isn't* power"...

We'll be looking at this in more detail later, but for now, who do you know who routinely tries to use their sup-

posed 'power' to attempt to export their fear to others?
What are they afraid of? In the short term, and
individually, it may *seem* to work: but what effect does it
have on the people around them?

What fears of your own do *you* try to export or
offload onto others? How do you do this? Does it work—
or do the fears quietly come back to haunt you later in
some weird way, 'large as life and twice as natural'?

This idea that fear can be exported is so common, and so
pervasive, that most people think it's natural, normal, just the
way things are. But it's not: it's just another choice — another
thread of the wyrd, with the usual weird twist in its tail. So we
can choose to look at fear in a different way: a way which accepts
that fear *is* normal, and a way which can be more empowering
for *everyone*.

As usual, we can find that choice by watching for a twist of
wyrdness hidden in the usual ways of looking at the world. The
twist here comes from noticing that our fears—whatever those
fears might be—often grow when we refuse to face them, and
certainly *do* shrink when we do turn round to face them. Hence
we arrive at the 'win-win' version of that phrase about "where
there's fear, there's power": we find our power—both our own
power-from-within, and the power-with that we share with
others — by facing our own fears, and helping others to face
theirs. Fear itself has its own weird power: and as we come to
respect it within ourselves, we begin to find out more about
what our own power *is*.

The weird power of fear

Trying to export fear to others often *feels* powerful, but isn't;
facing fear means that we have to face the terrifying feeling of
powerlessness, and yet it's one of the most empowering things
we can do. Weird... wyrd...

In the same way that fear and power are closely interwoven,

39

so too is fear deeply interwoven with the wyrd. Perhaps the most common *feeling* of fear is what we call 'panic'—everything comes together all at once, and there's a desperate need to be anywhere but here! Yet the 'pan-' prefix literally means 'everywhere': so what we're doing in panic is trying to run away from interweaving of everywhere, everyone, everywhen — running from Pan, running from the weavings of the sisters of wyrd. But there's nowhere to run, because everywhere is already *here*, and at the same moment 'here' *is* everything, everywhere. No boundaries, no limits: no 'I', just a swirling, chaotic sea of 'is'-ness, in which we're about to dissolve into nothing — that's what it feels like. No wonder it's frightening...

And yet 'I' is always here: 'I' is not that which changes, 'I' is that which *chooses*. So we *always* have the choice to stand our ground, to accept the fear, acknowledge the fear, but turn round and face it. And in the act of turning round, the act of *choosing*, the fear shrinks—and we find that we *do* have the power to face it. Fear itself *changes* into power, simply by turning round and facing it.

> "Fear itself changes into power, simply by turning round and facing it": what's your experience of this? It may well sound a bit too utopian, too idealistic, at first, but remind yourself of some of your old childhood fears—fear of the dark, perhaps: how did they come to fade? What — if anything—did you do to make them fade?
> How did others help you to face those fears? In what ways have you helped others to face *their* fears? In your experience, what works for this? What doesn't?

Fear isn't rational: it's a response to something—anything—that seems to be a threat to our sense of being. But then power isn't exactly rational either—and neither is the wyrd. Facing facts — acknowledging what's *actually* happening, rather than only what we think is happening—is an important part of facing fear, and of reclaiming our power, but that kind of rationality alone is not enough. We do need to accept that fear *is* weird, and that the wyrd itself brings its own fears—especially in our interweavings with others.

For example, if we involve ourselves in personal growth, exploring our personal power, we're likely to find that some of those around us—perhaps even those closest to us—become noticeably nervous about what we're doing. And they may well indulge in power-over or power-under—usually mild at first, but sometimes definitely not—to try to stop us: because as we make different choices, their world suddenly becomes uncertain, and *feels* unsafe. In other words, they're afraid. Making different choices brings up others' fear—not from something we *do*, but simply from who we *are*. That can make life difficult at times...

> One friend commented that, as a teenager, he found that some people seemed to be unnaturally afraid of him. Often, on a night-time street, women would even cross to the other side of the road, and then re-cross when he'd gone past. It was upsetting, he said: "It felt like I was seen as some kind of monster, a leper, an unwanted outcast. I hadn't done anything, and they were treating me like that! Eventually I realised it was because they were frightened of *me* — solely because I'm tall and male. But I can't help being who I am—and it still hurts when they do the same now..."
>
> Have you had the experience of others being afraid of you, not because of anything you've done, but simply because of who you *are*? If you have, how do you feel about that? How do you cope with the reality that there's little or nothing you can *do* about it—because it's *their* fear, not yours?

Another part of the weirdness is that we can find ourselves in a kind of unconscious connection with others—resonating with their wyrd, if you like. Without knowing it, we'll find ourselves doing exactly what others most fear, or most desire; or without knowing it, they'll be doing exactly what *we* most fear, or most desire. It can feel so uncanny—so weird—that some people even imagine that we must have some kind of strange powers, to make this happen to them. We don't: all we have is an accidental weaving of the wyrd, working in its own weird if entirely normal way. But when people are confused about that kind of power, they either hope that we'll be able magically to take away all their fears — the old 'guru-game', described in Christian terms as 'the one who dies to take away our sins'—or else drift off into the old habitual 'win-lose' thinking. Afraid that because we seem to have some kind of strange power that they don't understand — can't rationalise — we must therefore be aiming to have power *over* them, they start to attack us for what are actually the results of *their* fears. That's not exactly fun either...

> For me, this has been so common that, unpleasant as it is, I've had to accept it as part of my wyrd. I walk into an office, and casually ask a question: it turns out later that it's been the one question everyone's been avoiding — which is why I'd had an entirely unexpected and unwarranted torrent of anger and blame thrown at me. And there've been so many would-be partners with whom, quite unconsciously, I've done just what they've most desired: hence they first assumed that I must be their one and only god-given 'soul-mate'—and then reacted violently when their delusions finally dissolved, and they discovered that I'm no omnipotent 'saviour', but just a perfectly ordinary human being with issues of my own. *No* fun... not fun at all...
>
> What kind of unconscious connections have you had with others? When you became aware of it, what was the *feeling* of the power—the ability to *share* work—that you sensed there? What happened—both to that feeling of power, and to your relationship—when either or both of you became aware that this sense of connection could not last indefinitely?

Power is weird; and one of the key sources of our power is through the wyrd itself, our connection with everyone. Our fears block our access to that power: when we face the fears—and the weirdnesses with which and through which they interweave—we start to discover that we *do* have a very real power, a real 'ability to do work' as an expression of what *we* choose.

But here we run into an even stranger problem: once we begin to grasp the weird nature of power, we discover that most people have an even weirder fear of power itself—even though it's the one thing they keep saying they want. Something doesn't quite make sense here... something else we need to understand before we can move on.

The weird fear of power

Power is the ability to do work, as an expression of choice. So at first it'd seem obvious that when someone says "I want to be powerful", or "I want *you* to be powerful", what they want is to express their choices in action, or for us to do so. But it doesn't quite work that way... what they're more likely to mean is that *they* don't want to *feel* power*less*—which is not the same thing at all. Given the usual fears about 'win-lose'—and the assumption that someone who's finding their power will inevitably strive for power-over others—relationships can become strangely strained whenever one person starts to change: "He always used to be able to talk," said a friend, "but in the past year it's almost as if he's afraid of what I've been learning and trying to express, while because of this fear, or criticism, or whatever, I've become less willing to express it, particularly when I've found understanding elsewhere." End of relationship—very quickly, in some cases — unless *both* parties come to realise that someone's succumbed to the weird fear of power: and need to work to find their power-*with* each other to create their relationship anew.

Who's afraid of *your* power, your expression of choice? In what ways do you change your choices, and hold yourself back, because you know others are afraid of you — or try to pull you down, which comes to much the same thing — when you express *your* choices in the world?

Whose power are *you* afraid of? What are you afraid

> that they would do? In what ways do you try to pull others down, or restrict them, because you're afraid of their power, their ability to express themselves?

We're afraid of other people's power; we're even afraid of our own power. A colleague asked a group of business-people to describe their greatest fears: 'fear of making a mistake' came at or near the top of the list for every one of them. If no one's willing to make a move, for fear of making a mistake, is anyone actually being powerful? No one's 'taken' anyone else's power—but where has it gone? Into thin air, apparently... or back into the wyrd?

> A while back, I taught myself juggling: no particular reason, it was just a fun thing to do. But it was fascinating to see how many people, when I offered to show them how to do it themselves, backed off, almost in panic, saying "No, no, I can't do that, I couldn't do that!" Their fear of making a mistake—or being seen to make a mistake—was so strong that they wouldn't even try.
>
> What do you prevent yourself from learning to do, for fear of failure? What do you *feel* when you see someone else doing what you'd like to do, but are too afraid to face all the mistakes you'd make as you learn to do it yourself?
>
> "If *I* can't do it, nobody can!"—do you find yourself putting others down if they can do things that you as yet can't? If so, how? Why? What are the *feelings* that lead to this?

And, equally common, there's even a weird fear of success: even if we *do* get right, it still feels wrong... Or we're told by others that we ought to feel wrong about it: because *they* don't like anyone else having a 'power' that they won't let themselves have...

> "Huh! Setting yourself up as teacher's pet, are you, Chris? Trying to make out you're better than the rest of us, hey? Well, don't bother trying to follow *us* around, you smart-ass..." I *want* to do the work, and I *want* to get it right; but if I want any friends at all, looks like I'd better

> not be seen to do so... And even when I *do* get it right, I always seem to be lumbered with extra work—more like a punishment than a reward! Just not fair... no point... Getting it right just doesn't seem worth it...
>
> In what ways do you hold yourself back, for fear of success as much as of failure? What are you afraid will happen if you *do* 'get it right'?

It's not just other people's put-downs that are the problem —though it'd always be easy to blame them for everything! What we're more likely to be afraid of is blame itself: and since most people confuse responsibility and blame, most are afraid—if not terrified—of the sense of responsibility that inevitably accompanies 'getting it right'. "Round and round in the usual old game —I take the credit and you take the blame": everyone wants the credit of having done something—whatever it is—but no one wants to face the risk of getting the blame if it doesn't work out as intended. And since the wyrd all but guarantees that *nothing* ever quite works as intended, the possibility for blame is always present—especially if someone else can grab the credit by doing so...

That's the way that those loops of wyrd get formed: by placating others, rebelling against others, avoiding responsibility, or trying to cover up for our own fears or someone else's, *everyone* gets dragged into some kind of 'game', seemingly trapped into going 'round and round the garden'. The way out is to notice those 'lessons' that come weaving back on the wyrd. But first we do have to *notice* them: and that usually needs an almost childlike awareness of the weavings of the world. Yet a child*ish* evasion of responsibility is the source of most of the problems in the first place: 'danger—children at play'! So before we can move on, we need a much better understanding of the difference between childish and childlike—and that's what we'd better look at next.

4

DANGER — CHILDREN AT PLAY

Childhood — in principle, at least — is a time of wonder, of magic, of innocence. Over time, though, we become 'adulterated', tainted with the bleak realities and complex compromises of the everyday world: and slowly — unless we're careful, or lucky, or both — the magic and the laughter begin to fade, and we wake up to find ourselves stranded in an ever-more-chaotic but supposedly adult world, wondering where on earth the magic went.

So we look around, and there *are* people out there having fun, just like we used to. But we look a little more closely, and notice that while, yes, there *are* a few people who've retained that sense of childlike wonder, and can share it with others, much of what passes for 'fun' among adults is something subtly different. Not so much childlike as child*ish*, and often with a solid streak of self-centred nastiness: not the same thing at all. Danger — children at play...

The centre of the universe

Remember, remember... go right back before childhood, before you were born. You rested in your mother's womb, and grew there; everything was provided for you, and you didn't have to do a thing to gain any of it. All you had to do was *be*. Nothing else. Nothing else to do; no challenges, no threats; no problem. Although you might perhaps have sensed vague happenings at its fringes, the space you were in was the sum of your universe— and you were its centre.

Then you were born: for many, a rough awakening to the so-called 'real world'. But even here, at first, there's only you, at the centre of the universe. If you're fortunate, everything is provided, just when you need it. There are more sensations — many more—than before, and you can now do more; but there's only you, and a blur that provides. If there's any discomfort, all you have to do is howl, and something happens: it may take longer than you want, and you may not always get exactly what you want, but something *does* happen. You're in control: you're still the centre of the universe, and you're also comfortably certain that you're at the centre of everyone else's universe too. They exist to serve you: and as far as you're concerned, that's the only reason they exist.

And then, quite suddenly, it stops.

I'm not the centre of the universe; I'm not the reason the world exists; there are many, many others out there, and they're just the same as me. When that realisation finally dawns, it's literally life-shattering. So shattering that many people spend their lives running away from it... and that's what we mean by 'childish'.

Do you have any memory of when you first became aware that you *were not* the centre of everyone's universe? Who do you know who tries to cling to the idea that they *should* be the centre of everyone's universe — and will do *anything* to try to force others to conform to their will? In what ways would it be fair to describe that behaviour as 'childish'? What behaviours of your own would you admit to as being childish? Notice the feeling of embarrassment, but continue looking a little closer... Then notice that, even if you *are* sometimes 'childish', so is everyone else. What difference does that knowledge

> make to you? What difference does that make to your
> relationships with others?

Exactly *how* that realisation dawns doesn't matter that much. For some, it's the arrival of a younger sibling, or that first day at day-care or kindergarten; for others, it's the intransigence of adults during that devastating period known as the 'terrible twos'. Whatever the nominal cause, we discover that we *don't* always get what we want, especially when others are involved; and even worse, we have to accept the idea that we need to *share*—sharing affection, sharing resources, accepting differences—and surrender what has been, until now, our rightful place as the sole centre of the universe. That's hard: to a child, it can be *very* hard...

Yet there's another aspect of childhood that can vanish at the same time—and even if it doesn't, it can be steadily crushed in the pressures of socialisation and the enforced indoctrination that's mistakenly described as 'education'. It's a sense of wonder, of magic, of connection, of possibility: an open, innocent awareness that we call 'child*like*'. It's the state in which we can most easily become aware of the interweavings of the wyrd—not just in children's fantasies, but also in the complex connections of adult life. (All science, for example, arises from people continuing to ask the childlike question 'Why?') Once we lose this sense of 'childlikeness', it can sometimes be hard to reclaim it: but every now and then the wyrd will show itself to us in its own weird way—and return us, for an unknowable instant, back to that state of wonder.

> On a warm summer afternoon, I'm sitting in the back yard, watching a column of ants marching purposefully up and down a tree, while a blackbird whistles and warbles overhead. Everything, everywhere, everywhen quietly coincide: and in this place, at this moment, in this context, I *am* the eyes and ears and senses of the wyrd. I *am* the centre of the universe, and not—at the same time. A strangely childlike state...
> Remind yourself of some times when you've had the

feeling of *knowing*, for a brief moment, that sense of being 'the centre of the universe', the point around which —or *through* which—the world turns. What did you see in that state? What did you learn? Does this kind of experience happen mostly on your own, or with others— and if with others, who?

In this state it *is* true that we're the centre of the universe; but it's true only because *everywhere* is that centre—at the same moment. The threads of wyrd pass through everywhere, everyone, everywhen: it has no centre as such—it simply *is*. But everywhere is its centre, because every choice made anywhere within it echoes throughout the interweavings of the wyrd. And by *knowing* that wherever we are, we are *at* the centre of the universe, we have access to every possibility—which means that we *always* have a choice when we need one.

Ultimately, awareness of this can become a way of life, as was shown by an ancient Celtic chieftain who was captured and dragged off to Rome. History records that the Emperor asked him two questions: the first was "What is your greatest fear?" His reply: "That the sky shall fall on my head." "Where is the centre of the earth?" "Between my feet," came the reply. The Romans laughed at his answers — they thought him strangely childish. But the Roman army lost many battles — even whole legions—before they realised that those answers were far more than they seemed: child*like*, perhaps, but in no way child*ish*. The Celts may have admitted fears about things which rarely, if ever, happened—such as a falling sky; but they had few fears about things which *did*—such as death and dying. And if each warrior knew, for certain, that wherever they stood, that was the centre of the earth, there was nowhere else to go but here—so *here, now* was the time to stand and fight. A different kind of game, played by different rules... a different choice, leading to a different twist.

Playing fair

The first lesson of sharing is 'playing fair': failure to do so can lead to war... if only at a childish level, as any number of playground squabbles would indicate! But what do we mean by 'fair' or 'equal'? The answers depend entirely on the individual: and if someone's still clinging to the childish idea that they are, or should be, the sole centre of the universe, there's going to be trouble...

> When we were growing up, big sister Anne had a very clear concept of 'fair': it was *only* fair when she had what she wanted, otherwise it was definitely, *deliberately* unfair — and all hell would break loose. If we tried to play a board-game, for example, everything would be fine — as long as she seemed to be winning: but the moment it became clear that she was likely to lose, the tantrums would start — we would all be accused of cheating, the board would fly into the air, and she'd hurl game-pieces across the room while everyone else ducked for cover. We gave up playing board-games eventually... no fun for anyone...When you were growing up, was there someone among your family or friends who tended to do this? At what age did they stop? Or did they simply continue the behaviour in a more sophisticated, 'adult' form?You've probably done it too, to some extent — but to what extent? Look closely: to what extent, and in what ways, do you still do the same now?

Equality is an enormously complex concept. At first it seems easy enough—just share everything out, and that'll be fine —but once we start to look closely, we discover just how weird it really is. 'Identical' is easy—or relatively easy—to set up, but is rarely equal in the sense of 'fair': a 'child's portion' in a restaurant wouldn't satisfy a hollow-legged teenager! And at public events, and in public places such as theatres, men and women are usually allocated the same amount of toilet space: but because of the simple facts of anatomy, women need about five times as much space as men, to get the same number through in the same time—hence all those agonising queues... *Not* fair at all...

In many circumstances like these, identical can be far from

equal: everyone is different, and has different needs. In some ways, *what* is done is less important than the *intent* that whatever happens should be fair: it's more about feelings than strictly tangible results. So a fuller understanding of fair would be something like "equally deserving of respect"—or perhaps, as the 'philosophy statement' of an organisation I know puts it, that "the needs, concerns, feelings and fears of men and of women are of exactly equal value and importance". But it's sad to notice how many people have difficulty even with that: they'll talk long and loud about equality, and fairness from *others*, but are strangely unwilling to put it into practice themselves. As George Orwell warned in 'Animal Farm', the slogans of equality and fairness soon become weirdly twisted: "All are equal" shifts to "Some are more equal than others"; the old communard slogan "From each according to ability, to each according to their need" changes subtly into "From each according to facility, to each according to their greed." If unchallenged, childishness rules—and those who genuinely care about fairness and equality often get trampled in the rush.

At college there was a supposedly international socialist group who typified this self-dishonesty almost to extremes. They shouted loudly about democracy, but were notorious for rigging elections and meetings; they pontificated about 'the working class', when none of them had done a day's work in their lives; they demanded 'non-violence' from others, but were far from non-violent themselves. "All property must be liberated!" was their rallying cry—or, more accurately, "All property must be liberated—but don't you dare touch *my* stuff!" And they did *not* react kindly when anyone pointed out the glaring inconsistencies between their theory and their practice...Who do you know who is similarly inconsistent in their ideas of 'fairness'? What problems do you have in relating with them?It's hard to see our own inconsistencies, for obvious reasons! But if you have friends who you can trust to be honest with you without being hurtful, ask them what inconsistencies they see in

> *your* behaviour: what do you learn? How easy is it to face up to what they tell you? How easy is it to accept that this *is* what you do?

It's bad enough when a whole family finds itself focussed on pandering to one member's childishness. But the childish among us are often completely unaware of it, because—as we saw with the Queen of Hearts, a while back — everyone's running around covering it up for them, for fear of even more abuse. When a whole society or sub-culture gets into this state, some groups describe it as a 'patriarchy': but it's more accurate, and more honest, to describe it as a 'paediarchy'—"rule by, for and on behalf of the childish". A society which claims to be concerned only with 'fairness' and 'equality', but in which childish people are actively rewarded for 'playing foul': time to take a look around, because it's everywhere around us...

Playing foul

Placating childishness doesn't work: the childish ones—including all of us, at times—simply *take*, in the certainty that it's their 'right' to do so. (One of the characteristics of a paediarchy is a strong emphasis on 'rights', and very little mention of responsibilities — except for *others'* responsibilities, of course.) Responding to childishness with further childishness—"*He* gets away with it, so why can't I?"—only increases the overall amount of childishness, and also of fighting, from which everyone loses. For the same reason, responding aggressively—fighting back— just drags everyone down, and solves nothing. Ignoring the childishness — "It's only a phase, she'll grow out of it" — sometimes works: but in many cases it doesn't, because what the childish one is after is *attention*, and will simply crank up the childishness until they *do* get that attention. And punishing childishness rarely works, because they have no idea *why* they're being punished: since whatever they did was, from their perspective, entirely fair, 'punishment' is, by definition, others being unfair to *them* — so they'll often come back even angrier, demanding revenge... Facing others' self-centred childishness can be a big problem: especially when they're completely unaware of the true extent of their 'playing foul'.

> Oh, the joys of shared student houses... There was one girl I particularly remember, who routinely ranted about her supposedly abusive parents (who happened to be paying her entire way through college, and plenty more besides), blaming them — and, later, us — for all the many problems in her life. When she wanted to watch our shared television, no one else was allowed in the same room—it was an invasion of her privacy, she said. We had a rota for cooking: she never cooked for anyone else, but claimed her share of everyone else's food as her right — several times I came home to find she'd eaten my supper, though she never offered to replace it. And so on, and so on—no fun at all!
>
> What's your experience of people like these, who carry their self-centredness almost to the extreme of an art-form? How *do* you relate with them? Given the frustrations, the temptation to respond in kind is always strong: how do you *not* fall into the same kind of childishness yourself?

Childish behaviour is to be expected from children—that's why it's called 'childish', after all. At first, children simply don't know how to look after themselves, or how to relate with others in a complex society—and they can't be expected to. So parents do — in most cases — take responsibility for their children. Walking down the street, a child finishes its ice-cream, and hands the wrapper to mother: it's now *her* problem — as far as the child's concerned, she magically makes the wrapper disappear. Unless the child is shown how to take responsibility for its own mess, it'll never learn: the teenager turns round to hand its ice-cream wrapper to mother, finds she isn't there—so dumps it on Mother Earth instead. Somebody else's problem, not mine; hey, where the hell has all this disgusting litter come from? Somebody else, not me: it's never *my* fault—how dare you suggest that it could be? Douglas Adams described this succinctly when he said that the best way to make something invisible was to surround it with a "somebody else's problem" field—it's always somebody else's problem, somebody else's responsibility, so we don't bother to look...

Another common form of childishness is what we might call 'faked incompetence': "I'm too lazy to do it, so I hope someone else does—if I show them I can't do it, they'll have to do it for me..." The old gender-stereotypes play their part in this, of course: some men use it to duck out of their share of the housework—"You're so much better at it than I am, dear"—and some women say exactly the same about checking the oil, the water or the tyres on the car. But it's by no means gender-specific, as we saw in the last example, with the student 'accidentally' breaking crockery every time she washed up; and I remember one journalist shouting that he'd given up on computers—they were too complicated for him, he was going to go back to using a quill pen!

There's another side to this, as we'll see later; but who do you see who feigns inability or incompetence at some task, to trap others into doing it for them? What do you *feel* when you find yourself doing it for them, time and time again?

When do *you* indulge in this same belief that "power is the ability to *avoid* work"? What do you *feel* when others do what should have been your work for you? How do they respond to you when you feign incompetence or inability?

Childishness is a problem. But placating it doesn't work; responding in kind doesn't work; fighting back doesn't work; ignoring it doesn't work; punishing it doesn't work. All of these lead straight into those loops of wyrd, where the same theme is repeated over and over again in endless variations — especially where people are covering up for others' childishness, and hence covering up the only way out of the loop. There *is* a weird way out of this: there's always a choice to change things, within the

54

weavings of the wyrd. But we may not be too keen about the twist...

Each thread of the wyrd passes through everyone, every-where: what's going on 'outside' of us, in others' behaviour, is also always present in us. *We're* childish too; *and* child*like*, if we can allow ourselves to be so. There's little or nothing that we can do to change others' behaviour directly: but we *can* change our own. And as we do so, their behaviour tends to change too—we don't *cause* the change as such, but it happens in parallel, as our choices echo up and down the threads of the wyrd.

So the twist is that the best way to face childishness in others is to come to face our own: to admit to the ways in which *we* 'play foul'—or condone others' doing so—and shift instead to learn genuinely to 'play fair'. Uncomfortable and embarrass-ing at the best of times, but it *does* work... for everyone.

The quest for the Inner Adult

These days there seem to be any number of references to 'reclaiming the inner child': Inner Child courses and workshops, Inner Child therapy, articles in self-help magazines, whole racks-full of books on the subject in the bookstores' self-development sections. Reviving the inner childlike state from the midst of adult gloom is certainly a good idea: but not so good if all we 'reclaim' is our inner childishness, as was the case with one woman I know well...

The concept of the 'inner child' is lifted—often inappro-priately—from Transactional Analysis theory, which describes all interactions between people in terms of three complex stereotypes: the Parent—the over-responsible, 'father/mother-knows-best' critic—the Adult, and the Child.

> In your interactions with others, in what ways do you play the Parent: taking responsibility for others, criticising others, acting as if you're the only one who knows what to do? How do others respond to you, or *with* you, when you do this?

> In what ways do you play the Child: evading respon-
> sibility, meekly accepting criticism, doing what you're told
> without thinking about it, rebelling against the Parent —
> or, alternatively, being inventive in a childlike way? How
> do others respond to you, or with you, when you play
> this type of role?
>
> In what ways do you play the Adult: mediating,
> rationalising, persuading? How do others respond to
> you, or with you, when you play this role? What happens
> if, in this role, you try to stand between an arguing
> Parent and Child?

In some ways the Parent stereotype is just a grown-up version of the Child: the original childishness transmutes into adult arrogance; childish thoughtlessness changes to reliance on externally-defined rules — the edicts of the Law, the Bible, the Koran, the Company Handbook or whatever—as a *substitute* for thought, and a tendency to be 'judgemental' without awareness of context. There's more responsibility than in the Child: but even that is often given grudgingly, unwillingly, and with much complaint about unfairness... The classic 'codependent' relationships involve two or more people oscillating between the Parent and Child stereotypes, often constantly bickering, and constantly moving between the two stereotypes in search of power-over or power-under the other, to offload responsibility or fears onto the other. Some codependent relationships may seem relatively stable in a kind of "you scratch my back and I'll scratch yours" way — the gender-stereotyped roles of the 'traditional' marriage easily fall into this pattern, for example — but the moment any party tries to move out of the 'game', all hell can break loose!

The Adult, by comparison, is more like a mature version of the Child's child*like* qualities: the willingness to explore, to risk, to create, in a much more complex social and conceptual world. And it's much rarer than either the Parent or the Child, for the simple reason that *both* tend to attack the Adult: the bleak reality is that, caught up in their power-games, both Parent and Child often *want* to fight, and to hurt someone—and the openness and honesty required of the Adult role makes it a very easy target... But there's no way out of a codependent loop unless the wider awareness of the Adult is allowed to drift in—sometimes from outside, but preferably from within the people themselves—to point out the choices that are being hidden (or hidden *from*) in the twists of the wyrd. So as one friend put it, "It's not my Inner Child that I need to find—it's my Inner Adult!"

> I'm in the middle of yet another flaming row about work: Mary's stuck in the Parent role, nagging and demanding that I do things *her* way; and I'm stuck in the Child role, torn between bowing to her authority and rebelling against it. Suddenly yet subtly I become aware of a kind of inner voice, telling me to slow down and *listen* to what Mary is saying. Initially I rebel against this 'inner adult' too—I want to do things *my* way, dammit, and no one's going to tell me otherwise!—but I find myself doing what it says: I shut up, and listen. Within moments, Mary stops in mid-sentence — mid-rant! — and the anger vanishes from between us: an argument that looked likely to go on all day, and probably all week, is resolved in minutes, *both* of us feeling comfortable about what we'd now agreed to do. Like the dancing, creative, magical Inner Child, that weird Inner Adult is always there, always willing to help in any way it can—*when* I remember to listen for it, and let it speak!
>
> What's your experience of the Inner Adult? In what kind of circumstances have you heard it speak? In the midst of an argument, perhaps, as in that example? Or elsewhere? How easy—or not—was it to accept what this inner voice was saying? More to the point, how easy—or not—was it to *act* on that advice? What did the Child or Parent in you have to face by doing so?

Most of what we'll see in the practical work here is concerned with 'reclaiming'—or becoming aware of, perhaps for the first time—our own Inner Adult. That work includes developing an understanding of the differences between selfishness, self-centredness and self-awareness, and slowly exchanging — wherever we can — our naturally childish and Parent-ish self-dishonesty for a rigorous honesty with ourselves and others. None of this is likely to be easy... but it can make a vast difference—a vast improvement—to our relationships, not just with others but also within ourselves.

As with the Inner Child, the characteristics of the Adult include a full acknowledgement of the *self*: things like self-love, self-trust, self-respect, self-awareness, self-responsibility. Finding these alone can be hard enough... But at the same time the Adult also needs a full acknowledgement of *others*, and both *by* and *with* others: a love (in many different senses) of others, trust *shared* with others, respect of others as well as of self, awareness of others' needs *and* one's own, and responsibility about, or to, or with (but never 'for') others. And that's even harder, because it requires a full understanding of the interweaving of 'I' and 'not-I'.

One of the reasons the Celts eventually lost their battles with the Romans was that they were *too* 'childlike'—too focussed on 'I', with too little awareness of 'We'. Culturally and militarily they emphasised individual prowess, individual skill, with a poor grasp of tactics *as a group*; in the end the Roman army, using the classic power-under tactic of 'divide and conquer', broke through — because no *individual*, however skilled, can withstand indefinitely the might of the disciplined many. (A few centuries later, though, when Roman discipline had all but collapsed, the Germanic Celts had their revenge... and with the sack of Rome, the once-mighty Roman empire was no more.)

So 'personal development' alone is not enough: it needs to be complemented by *inter*personal development, an awareness of what is possible — and *only* possible — by working together as 'we'. By sharing, in every sense, we resolve the childish need to be at the centre of the universe, to *be* that centre — because through the weird experience of 'we', we also *share* that centre, as 'I and We and I'.

5

I AND WE AND I

What am I? I am... something... I... whatever 'I' is, I suppose. "I think, therefore I am"? Not really: it would be just as true to say "I relate, therefore I am" — and certainly far closer to many people's experience. "I am a rock, I am an island"? Makes a good song, but it doesn't work out that way in practice: in fact, it would probably make more sense to say that I'm the sea—part *of* the sea, *in* the sea, an expression of the sea as a whole. The sea of wyrd, that is... and in that weird sense, 'I' is not that which changes: 'I' is that which *chooses*.

So we can choose to think of 'I'—or experience 'I'—as a thought, a relating, a rock, an island, an amorphous sea, or anything else: it's up to us. Each choice of 'I' is a thread, a path with many possibilities and an ultimate ending — and many, many interesting twists upon the way...

But if that's 'I', what is 'We'? If We is what happens between us, between your 'I' and mine, then where—if anywhere —is the boundary of We, the boundaries between I and We and I? Weird... wyrd... 'wyrder', perhaps?

Which I is We?

"'I' is not that which changes: 'I' is that which chooses." Yeah. Sure. If you say so. No problem.

Hey, *wait* a minute... that's not right! What about the times when it *isn't* my choice to change: like when I have to do what others tell me to do? Or the different things I find myself doing when I'm with other people? Who's doing the choosing there— because it certainly isn't me... is it?

I'm at a summer festival, way out in the country, with a few hundred other people. It's hot — very hot — and the river is cool and inviting. No one swimming is bothering to wear any kind of costume — in fact fewer and fewer people seem to be wearing any clothes at all. After the swim I don't bother putting my clothes back on: it feels odd, strange, *wrong* at first; then by the end of the long hot day it seems equally strange—unnatural, almost—to be putting a few light clothes back on again, for the cool of the evening. And I notice a sign at the festival exit: "Clothing tips for leaving the site." *"Clothes!"* I'd all but forgotten that 'out there' everyone—including me—*does* usually wear clothes in public: indeed, almost anywhere but here I'd be in deep trouble if I didn't! Yet here, for this brief time, I'm in a different community, with a different set of rules: and I find that *I've* changed to match. Weird...

In what circumstances do you find yourself changing your 'normal' habits, your usual 'I'? What changes? How much do you *choose* to change, and how much is it a change that 'just happens' because you're in a different place, or with different people?

Who are you with at these times? (Are you at a party, perhaps? A conference? On holiday? A football crowd? A mob of shoppers in the 'Sales' season?) Perhaps more to the point, who are *you* at these times?

We *do* change in different circumstances, and with different people: our behaviour certainly changes, though whether that's truly 'I' is another matter... The issue is more about choice, about whether we *choose* to change our surface 'I' in response to the changes in our surroundings — and the answer to that question would have to be 'Sometimes'! Sometimes we do consciously choose to change, to 'fit in' with what everyone else seems to be doing—which in itself can cause problems, for us or for others; and sometimes we change more 'by default' for much the same reasons, but without really being *conscious* that we've chosen to do so.

> A simple illustration of this: note the differences in your behaviour when you're with your family; your friends; your work-colleagues; clients; shop-assistants; the cleaner; government officials; police. Who are you when you're with each of these groups of people? What is your 'persona' — literally, the mask 'through which you sound' —in each case?
>
> What happens when someone you know well from one context appears unexpectedly in another: bumping into a client when you're out with friends, or meeting someone from work when you're away on holiday? What happens to your sense of self when you're in this sort of mixed-up context? (A sense of "Which 'I' is me?", perhaps?) In what ways do you become confused about the 'proper' way to respond to them?

Even when we 'must' change our behaviour to suit others — pandering to a bullying boss, perhaps — it *is* still a choice: there'd be different consequences for choosing to do otherwise, of course, of which we're no doubt all too aware — but the choice *is* ours. That's important, because if we say they've 'made' us or 'forced' us to change our behaviour, we've surrendered *our* power of choice *to* them. They haven't 'taken' it from us — though no doubt in many cases that's what they'd want us to believe... A central part of reclaiming our power *with* others is in becoming more aware that the power to choose our 'I' actually resides in us — and nowhere else. The hard part is in taking responsibility for that fact: it always seems *much* easier to hide from responsibility with that ever-popular excuse, "Oh, sorry, I wasn't myself there...", or — even more popular — to blame others instead!

The temptation to duck that responsibility is always

strongest when there's a lot of weird energy flying around. 'Being in love' (or, as the veteran feminist Glen Tomasetti wryly put it, being caught up in 'romanticised lust'!) is one obvious example; so too is the bizarre behaviour — and even more bizarre childish language—many people indulge in when they're around infants! But perhaps the strangest twists in behaviour occur in religious or supposedly 'spiritual' settings: in some cases people literally abandon themselves to whatever happens to be going on... infamous examples of which include the ritualised murders committed by the original assassins—Arabs known as 'hashishin', caught up in an hashish-induced 'religious experience'—and thugs—devotees of an obscure Indian cult known as 'thuggee'. I remember one well-known Indian guru being very careful to point out that the 'weird energies' that his followers experienced around him—and which they inevitably attributed to him—were, strictly speaking, entirely their own: he provided conditions under which people could become aware of their own power—conditions which were as safe and stable as he could provide, which was by no means easy—but he could not and would not take responsibility for what was, he reminded them, *their* choice of what to do with that power.

'We' is the interweaving of 'I' and 'I' (or, when many people are involved, at least as many 'I's as there are people); 'We' is a kind of compound-'I' created by many people's choices interweaving and echoing along the threads of wyrd. In the guru's example, he was being responsible for his own 'I', and for its part—*his* part—in the 'We' being created at that gathering: but precious few other people there were doing so... If no one (or almost no one) is taking responsibility for their own 'I'—as is often the case with any large crowd—then which 'I' is 'We'? Without awareness, and without responsibility, 'We' could be *anything*: often that which is least conscious, and most suppressed and denied—as we can see all too clearly in many large crowds... But we can begin to have choice—and a better awareness of our own choices—by noticing how *we* change in the company of others: by listening to 'We', we gain a better understanding of 'I'.

Listening to We

'Listening' is far more than just hearing what someone says: it's about being aware of the whole of the communication, and being an involved — and often active — part *of* that communication. ('Communication' itself literally means a 'shared oneness', an acknowledgement of the interwovenness of each other on the threads of wyrd.) Words themselves can easily go 'in one ear and out of the other': it's the communication as a *whole*—the words, the tone and pitch of voice, the 'body language' and everything else—to which we need to pay attention in listening. The first part of listening to 'We', then, is that we need to become more aware of the *dance* of 'We'.

In 'body language', every movement—or even absence of movement—is an expression of self, a phrase in a choreographed dance. When we're with others, this becomes a ballet, an interweaving *with* each other in a literal, physical expression of the wyrd. Often the movements are subtle, minimalistic; sometimes they're wild and free; but they're always there — and are always seen, or heard, or sensed.

What are *your* dances with your colleagues, your friends, your family? With whom are your movements subdued, stiff, formal — even timid? With whom, and when — if ever — are you able to be wild and free? Whose movements are stiff, formal, subdued with *you*? What are *your* choices in this dance? What are theirs?

You're also, often, alone on the stage of life: what does your 'solo dance' look like? When you listen to your own body-language, what do you learn?

In some ways this is easier to notice when there's *only* the dance, and nothing else. Even when there's no verbal component to the communication, there's still always communication...

I wander down a crowded street, and find myself swerving to the side as a man walks straight out of a shop, looking the other way; then I find myself slowing down automatically, in a weird kind of sympathy, as an old woman painfully crosses the street in front of me. In principle, all I'm doing is walking down a street: and yet there *is* a kind of dance that's happening here—a dance that involves everyone as 'We'.

What is *your* dance when you're in a street-full of strangers? What moves are *your* choice? And which moves do you make as a response to *others'* moves in this wider dance? What do you *feel* when you change your intended moves—change your choices—in order to accommodate those of others?

Adapting ourselves to others is still a *choice*; especially, adapting ourselves for the approval of others, or to keep others 'happy', is still a choice. And if we're not aware of the choices we make — if we've abandoned our awareness to the 'senses taker' of habit, for example—then we have, in effect, lost that choice. If we abandon that choice, we in effect abandon 'I' — and then can't exactly be surprised if we repeatedly find ourselves engulfed in whatever 'We' happens to be passing by... So another central part of listening to 'We' is learning to listen, very carefully, to 'I'.

One of the weirder paradoxes of 'We' — and one that illustrates well the nature of the wyrd—is that whatever is *not* being expressed by someone invariably ends up being expressed elsewhere by someone else. It's as though unexpressed anger, for example, has to come out *somewhere*: a kind of automatic, unconscious version of what's known in psychology as 'projection', but projected out to the wyrd in general rather than onto a selected individual who can be blamed for it. By becoming aware of what *is* our choice, if we find ourselves doing or feeling something that is *not* our choice, then it's probably coming not from us but from 'We', our interaction with others through the wyrd. The computer consultant Gerald Weinberg, borrowing from fellow-consultant Nancy Brown, describes this awareness as 'listening to the inner music': when we're with someone else, and there's a kind of discord in the inner music, it's time to bring it into conscious awareness—and, if appropriate, conscious action.

> I'm talking with a staffer at a client's office, and something's odd. He's talking about his poor relationship with some of his own staff, but his body-language is completely relaxed; then he talks about his excellent relationship with his boss, and yet he's tense, nervous, his voice slightly strained — and *I'm* unaccountably feeling angry. Something wrong here... I pluck up the courage to mention that I'm feeling angry about what he's saying, and I don't know why: there's a moment's stunned silence, and then he tells me the truth — he's terrified of his boss, but has been too frightened of possible repercussions to be able to admit it to anyone. Ah... *that's* what it is... *now* we have a chance to resolve where we've been strangely stuck with this client!
>
> Where have you noticed a similar discord between what was being said and what *you* felt? Were you able to say what you felt? If so—or, equally, if not—what did 'speaking your truth' ask of you in those circumstances? If you did speak up, what happened?

But this works only when we're rigorously honest with ourselves about what *is* our 'stuff', and what isn't... If we're not, we'll end up projecting, onto others, what are actually our feelings that we want to pretend we don't have: for example, we'll say that *they're* the ones who are angry, not us—because it's too dangerous for us to admit, even to ourselves, that in reality *we're* the ones who are angry. That dishonesty—that *self*-dishonesty—is where the whole mess starts: it always seems *much* easier to blame others than to face the responsibility for our own issues ourselves...

This is why sociologist Hugh Mackay describes true listening not just as an act of generosity, but an act of *courage*. To be rigorously honest about our own web of beliefs and assumptions—what Mackay calls 'the cage'—is embarrassing, disturbing, even frightening, and always real work: as Mackay put it, "If you're not sensing the strain involved in stepping outside of the cage to listen, then you are probably not listening fully, openly, non-judgementally."

Making a mistake at this point, and projecting my own issues back onto the other person, is a *really* quick way to turn a confusion into a flaming row! The only way out, when this kind of discord happens, is for me to state what *I* feel—and nothing else. Especially, I have to be *very* careful to phrase it so that it doesn't sound like a criticism. In that instance, I said something like, "Excuse me, but I'm getting confused here—I don't know your boss that well, but I'm feeling... sort of... angry... when you were talking about her, and I have no idea why. Can you help me on this?" By putting the responsibility—if any—for the confusion on me, I've made it safe for him to open up, and be clear about the 'We' that's happening between us. But to say this, I have to face all sorts of fears of my own: Am I imagining all this? Have I been projecting my own stuff onto him here? Is he going to clamp down tight—or even explode? More to the point, have I blown it with this client by telling *my* 'truth'?

What's your own experience of this? With whom do you feel safe enough to be fully honest about what you feel? (If the honest answer to that last question is 'no one —not even myself', you'd be far from alone in this! But notice that you *were* able to be honest about that at least: what difference does that make?)

But if what I'm 'listening' out for in myself, in these situations, is actually someone else's feelings—someone else's anger, perhaps—then what on earth is 'We'? If I'm finding myself angry because someone else is, but isn't admitting it, then where—if anywhere—is the boundary between my 'I' and theirs? Weird? Too right it is...

The circles of We

At this point it's obvious that we need some kind of model or analogy, to clear away some of the muddiness of these confusing experiences! So let's go back to the beginning, to that analogy of the Möbius loop as a boundary between 'I' and 'not-I'. Because of the twist in that loop, the inside becomes the outside becomes the inside again; there is a definite boundary, and yet at the same time there is no boundary. That's wyrd...

Let's hang on that analogy for a while. First there's 'I', all alone—literally, 'all-one'—a single circle, or a single loop:

Along comes someone else. From my perspective, that's another person, a 'Thou'; but from *their* perspective, they're also 'I', so now we have two circles, two loops:

And that's what we'd have if it *was* true that "I am a rock, I am an island": two entirely separate 'I's, never communicating in any way at all. But we do know, from those weird experiences, that there is always some kind of interweaving or overlap. The threads of wyrd pass through every point; every choice echoes up and down the threads; there is a boundary between 'I' and 'I', and yet there is no boundary. That area of overlap, we could say, is what we experience as 'We': an area where we *both* experience that we have choices—*if* we allow ourselves to do so...

So in the classic concept of dependence, one person has all but abandoned their 'I' in favour of what they believe 'We' to be:

That 'included' space feels protected — for a while... and

also apparently in control of the other person, because there's so much overlap. The assumption is that because the entire focus is on 'We', there *is* only 'We'—neither 'I' exists, or needs to exist, since each is submerged into the shared sense of 'We'. But since there is *always* 'I', and 'We', and 'I', with no boundary between them, and yet always a boundary, it's as unrealistic as the 'island I' concept. No matter how much we might like to abandon our 'I' into someone else's care—in effect, to try to return to the 'centre of the universe' feeling back in the womb—we *are* different from everyone else: and if we try to pretend otherwise, there's going to be trouble eventually. By the time we get to classic codependency, the two parties are oscillating between the 'enclosed' and 'outside' positions:

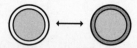

The inner 'I' of the pair is enclosed, protected, yet trapped —there's a sense of being stifled, a need to break out; the outer 'I' feels clung to, is forced to take responsibility for both, and loses the sense of comfort and protection that occurs—for a while—in the 'enclosed' position. So the two end up continually changing places, via any—or many—of the classic 'push-pull' dynamics: clingy, then withdrawn; responsible, then childish; overpowering, then manipulated; demanding commitment, then fleeing from commitment; and so on. What's interesting is that while each 'I' is unstable—sometimes very unstable—their 'We' is not: it remains constant, or at least relatively so. Despite all the turmoil, the characteristics—the threads of the wyrd—that are emphasised in their 'We' remain much the same throughout: all that changes is which 'I' of the two is acting out each characteristic...

Who do you know whose relationship works in that way: that their 'We' is relatively stable, but each 'I' orbits around it in endless instability? Have you been in that kind of relationship yourself? If so, what kind of aware-ness did you need, about your own 'I', the other person's

'I', and your 'We', in order to change that pattern of instability?

The same codependent Parent/Child pattern also happens on a familial and societal level: adolescents rebel against their parents' authority, and become parents themselves; some self-declared Parent-organis-ation — the Church, the State, the Party, Big Brother or, at present, the Big Sister which feminist historian Anne Summers describes as 'God's Police' — defines itself as the 'protector' of the people (at a price, which is subser-vience...), people submit, and then rebel, and the same old revolution creates its own new Parent-figures. In what ways do you find yourself dragged into these larger-scale codependencies? How — if at all — can you break free, to express your own choices as 'I', yet still be part of the greater 'We'?

There's a real human need for 'We'—that spiritual need to be part of 'that which is greater than self'. In dependent relationships — and especially in codependent relationships — what's missing is awareness: the apparent need to hold onto 'We' at any cost is allowed to take priority over almost any awareness of the *personal* choices of 'I'. That's what creates the tension, because every now and then one or other party will notice that what they're doing is not what they choose; but since their definition of 'We' must remain unchanged, the other party finds that their behaviour is *automatically* changing to compensate. That person then realises that this isn't what they want either, but equally clings to 'We': so round and round the garden we go...

Independence — "I'll never be in relationship again!" — looks like an alternative, but isn't, because it happens to be impossible—the wyrd makes certain of that... *Inter*dependence, however, *is* a genuine alternative:

Each 'I' is seen as having the same size, the same priority— "The needs, concerns, feelings and fears of [each person] are of

exactly equal value and importance"; there's a full acknowledgement of both 'I' and 'I'. That each has choices that may vary
from the shared choices of 'We' is also fully acknowledged: in a
classic magical perspective, the old Christian symbol of the
'vesica piscis' (or fish-bladder shape) between them, is created
because the circumference of each one exactly touches the
centre of the other. The commitment to 'We' is still there, but it
is, if anything, stronger than in a dependent relationship; and it
changes dynamically, both as the choices of each 'I' change, and
as their shared choices for 'We' change.

Most of all, a stable and constructive 'We' depends on
awareness: awareness by each 'I' of their own choices, for
themselves and for their 'We'; and awareness also of the natural
weirdness in the interweaving threads of 'We'.

The interweaving of We

'We' is the interweaving of 'I' and 'I'—a kind of compound-'I'
created by and between us. 'We' is not that which changes; 'We'
is that which 'I' and 'I' *chooses*. And it has characteristics of its
own: so much so that a company, for example, is legally a
separate entity, a 'person' in its own right, and *defined* as a chosen
type of relationship between people. A company's 'purpose
statement' is a formal statement of the choices—the function
and direction—that make up that 'We'; and if we take up a job
with a company whose purpose is unclear, or which clashes with
our own choice for 'I', there's going to be trouble... usually for
us, since the company's 'We' is considerably larger, and naturally
tends to subsume others' choices into itself. In fact *any* large
group tends to develop its own 'We', its own direction, its own
habitual choices: the 'We' of a football crowd is usually noisy
and territorial, while a crowd of shoppers out bargain-hunting in
the sales-season has a 'We' that's usually quite a bit quieter, but
can be *very* possessive...

So we need to understand the boundary between 'I' and
'We' and 'I'. The problem is that there isn't one as such: there is a

boundary between each, but the boundary blurs, because our *own* boundaries are blurred, and overlap with those of everyone else.

To experiment with this, choose a quiet corner in your favourite people-watching café (or imagine doing so, if you prefer). Relax; close your eyes, and allow yourself to become aware of the space around you. Feel the limits of your physical boundaries: become aware of your fingers, your toes, your scalp, your stomach, your backside resting on the chair. And pull your awareness of 'I', steadily inward, tighter and tighter, until it forms a small ball — the smallest space that 'I' can occupy. (Where does this tighter awareness settle? Around your heart? Within your skull? Just above your stomach? Or where?)

Then slowly, steadily, expand your sense of 'I' again, out beyond your skin, out beyond the table you're sitting at, until it fills the whole space of the café—you can still hear people talking, sense people moving, but they're now *inside* the space occupied by 'I'. (Notice that this is in *your* choice, under *your* direction: if at any point it feels too disturbing or uncomfortable, quietly withdraw your sense of 'I' back towards your physical 'I', and wait until you do feel more comfortable—more certain of your sense of 'I' — before starting again.) Keep expanding, until the traffic outside is enclosed in 'I'; keep expanding until the whole town or city is inside your 'I'; and keep going; and keep going...

At some point, begin to contract 'I' again, slowly, steadily, until you return 'I' to a comfortable, manageable, 'normal' size. (What space do you now occupy? Is the boundary exactly at your skin? Or larger? Or smaller?)

And with that awareness, where exactly in that whole process was the boundary of your 'I'? It overlapped with the 'I' of many other people: where — if anywhere—were the boundaries between 'I' and 'I' and 'I'?

The boundary—whatever it is—denotes the limits of what

we might call 'personal space': which takes us straight back to that 'I'm the centre of the universe' problem. If I expand my sense of personal space right out to infinity, then I'm again 'the centre of the universe': everything is me, everything is mine. But it includes, or overlaps, or interweaves, with everyone *else's* personal space—which also, in principle at least, stretch out to infinity. Reality Department requires us to share, whether we like it or not: so what we sense as our boundaries denotes the limits of 'me, mine', outside of which we feel comfortable sharing, but within which we don't *want* to share — or don't feel *safe* in sharing.

Still sitting in the café, choose a table where people have to come close to you regularly—to get to the counter, for example—and once again become aware of the *feel* of 'I'. Focus for a while on an image of a time when you felt entirely safe; notice the *feelings* that accompany that state. When you're reasonably certain that you could again recognise that state by the feelings that arise within you then, remind yourself instead of a time when you did *not* feel safe—not so much fear, or danger, as a sense of uncertainty, of unsafety—and note carefully the feelings that accompany *this* state.

Relax; this time you don't need to close your eyes, but remain as aware of yourself as if you had. Pick out someone as they come through the door, and feel your own response to their presence as they move past you. At some point, as they come closer and closer, you're likely to feel a shift within you—that sense of 'unsafety', as their 'I' comes too close for your own comfort. How far away from you does this happen? How much does it change with different people? (A hint: some people will never get close enough to you here for you to feel unsafe, and with a few others you may even feel unsafe as soon as you pick them out.) As soon as that sense of 'unsafety' occurs, 'disconnect' from them by refocussing on your own sense of 'I', and start again with someone else. What do you learn, about yourself, and your previously unconscious interactions with others?

Like 'I' itself, every boundary is a *choice*: do I, or We, choose to feel open to—overlap with—this person's 'I', or not? At this moment, in this circumstance, are their choices — or what I sense as their choices — compatible with mine? The point at which the answer changes from 'Yes' to 'No'—or 'No' to 'Yes'— is what we *feel* as our boundary. When someone else's choices, for whatever reason, happen to pass that point, we then have another choice: to pull in our 'personal space' to a smaller boundary; to accept the feeling of 'unsafety', and work with the fears that arise with it; or to blame the other person entirely for the transgression, and try to force them to change *their* choices, so that we don't have to take responsibility for ours. In these paediarchal days, where so many people are taught that safety is their 'right' but never their responsibility, guess which of these options is more popular? Time to look more closely at boundaries!

6

BOUNDARIES

The wyrd is the interweaving of everything, everyone, every-where, everywhen. Twisting, turning, arriving everywhere in its own weird way, it links, connects, weaves without cease—until it comes across a barrier: which is us. Or, more precisely, the boundaries that we try to place around ourselves, to define and describe our sense of 'I'.

We *need* those boundaries. Without them, *anything* goes: everything and nothing is real, everything and nothing happens at the same time, in the same place, or through everyone all at once. A good recipe for instant insanity... which is why we choose to invent something we call 'reality', which in reality doesn't necessarily exist anywhere but in our own heads. Even in science, we don't so much 'discover' scientific fact as invent it— a point long known to philosophers and historians of science, such as Thomas Kuhn, who coined the term 'paradigm shift' to describe the way in which a whole view of science can change at once, or James Burke, who documented what he called 'the days the universe changed', or the wry anarchist Paul Feyerabend, who argued that the only valid scientific principle is "Anything goes." With very few exceptions — such as the inevitability of Murphy's Law—every perspective on reality is a *choice*: and often an arbitrary one at that.

But it works. As long as we have some way to prop up our

illusion—or, less politely, delusion—that our chosen definition of what is real or not *is* 'reality', then life is literally 'reasonable': predictable, safe, sane, if sometimes a little boring. The wyrd being what it is, though, we'll still keep coming across people who make different choices to ours, with a different definition of reality—and *that's* when the fun starts...

Coming to terms with the natural chaos of the wyrd can be hard enough at the personal level; but it can be even more difficult at the interpersonal level, precisely because the chaos occurs *at* the boundaries we each choose to place between 'I' and 'We' and 'I'. Wherever our boundaries differ, we each show each other that our 'reality' is only an illusion: and that's frightening. Yet to be without *any* boundaries is usually even more frightening: few people can manage more than a few moments of 'being at one' with Pan—at one with the interweaving of everywhere—without giving way to panic... And that's why we need to understand what those boundaries are for—and to understand our own responsibilities with and for them.

Boundary, barrier and wall

The wyrd is the interweaving of everywhere: it has no boundaries, and in many ways it allows no boundaries, since everywhere is already included within everywhere else. This *isn't* easy to understand... especially since almost everything in our society puts up boundaries to prevent us from understanding it...

Let's start again, and look at it from a different direction. The term 'boundary' is another of these concepts that's been lifted from a specific context in transpersonal psychology, and then thoroughly mangled and misused in much New-Age-style pop-psychology: in some New-Age-inspired feminist theory, for example, the concept of a 'boundary' has become little more than a childish tool for blame — "How *dare* you overstep my boundaries!" But in its original context, the term applied to personal choice, personal power and, especially, personal responsibility: "To establish boundaries is to know and respect what I want, and to take responsibility for same"—very clearly an Adult perspective, rather than the self-centredness of the Child.

In effect, a 'boundary' is a metaphor for what we might otherwise call a 'reasonable' limit on the way we choose to interact with others and the world at large. I like to keep my house reasonably tidy, and I don't like others making an unreasonable mess: that's a boundary. If someone agrees to meet with me at a particular time, I want them to let me know if they're going to be delayed more than a reasonable amount of time: that's a boundary. If I agree to do something for you, I expect it to take no more than a reasonable amount of time and effort: that's a boundary too. Right now a colleague has been phoning me every few days for months, pestering me to help him with a project in which I don't want to be involved: but it's up to *me* to be explicit about my boundary, and tell him so — rather than blame *him* for 'overstepping my boundaries' in that respect. I don't like it, but it *is* my responsibility... And what seems 'reasonable' to me isn't necessarily going to be the same as what seems 'reasonable' to you, or to that persistently pestering colleague of mine — which is where all those boundary-problems arise in the first place!

> "To establish boundaries is to know and respect what I want, and to take responsibility for same": how well do you *know* what you want? How much do you respect those choices? How much do *you* take responsibility for those choices?
>
> Notice how much easier it is to 'pass the buck' to others — "How dare you overstep my boundaries!" — rather than take responsibility ourselves for being clear about where our boundaries lie...

During one of our regular arguments on this topic, my friend Catherine expands the boundary metaphor into three distinct layers: 'boundary', 'barrier' and 'wall'. A *boundary*, she says, is a choice which is changing all the time, depending on who, what, when or where we are or are with—much as we saw in those experiments in the café. It's volatile, based on feeling and sense; it's moveable, negotiable, often conscious; it's created by me *for me*, and it's usually quite easy for me to accept my responsibility for its creation and maintenance.

> To illustrate this, cast your mind back to the café, to when you were exploring the boundary between 'safety' and 'unsafety' that you could *feel* as different people passed by. When that transition happens, it certainly does feel as if someone's 'overstepped our boundaries': it *does* feel unsafe. Yet by becoming conscious of this, we can also become aware that it's also a *choice*: we can move the boundary, or change its form—as you did in that experiment, by 'disconnecting' from each person the moment that sense of 'unsafety' occurred.
>
> So repeat the experiment, but this time with the awareness—or belief—that the shape and form of this boundary are *your* choice and *your* responsibility. What difference does this make? Becoming aware of this, what difference do you feel in your sense of *personal* power?

A *barrier* is also based in feelings — particularly unspoken fears — but takes the form of a more intellectualised choice, an injunction, a *moral* restriction rather than a felt one. It's a definite decision about what is right and what is not: hence it often has an air of self-righteousness about it, with much use of 'magic' words like 'ought' and 'should' and 'must' — or, more likely, 'oughtn't', 'shouldn't' or 'mustn't'. It often states what we think *others* should or should not do in relation to us — rather than something we'd also equally apply to ourselves. So "Thou shalt not commit adultery", for example, is a typical barrier — one which most people will at least say they believe in, if not necessarily always apply in practice! A barrier is often less than honest that way, because it's not so much something I create *for* me, as *against* you, against 'not-I'. And the feeling when a barrier is breached is subtly different: rather than a sense of

unsafety, as for a boundary, it's closer to righteous indignation—
"How *dare* they do that!" — a mask of intellectualised anger
covering up a more genuine layer of fear.

> More memories: another would-be partner. Sam's
> pleasant enough, I suppose, but after what happened
> between us the previous time, I just don't want to know.
> But here's yet *another* invitation to go out for a drink
> together, and I just feel a sense of revulsion, a sense of
> 'yuck'... Odd... weird... I just wish Sam would finally get it
> that I *do not* want any kind of 'We' made up of Sam and
> me... at all!
>
> What do you *feel* when someone barges through a
> personal barrier, to do something which you've decided
> is wrong—wrong for you, wrong for others in relation to
> you, or wrong in general?
>
> What happens when you accidentally — or even
> intentionally — barge through someone else's barriers,
> someone else's definition of 'right' and 'wrong'?
>
> What do you *feel* as you do this?
>
> What do you feel in response to their response to
> you for having done this?

Although we create many individual barriers of our own,
we also gain many of our barriers from the society in which we
live: they're the 'rules', sometimes formalised into laws, which
attempt to govern interpersonal behaviour—drive on the left (or
is it on the right?), give way to the right (or is it to the left?),
don't eat with your fingers, don't pick your nose, don't *ever* take
your clothes off in public...

> To illustrate social barriers, what do you *feel* when
> someone drives past you at well over the local speed
> limit? What do you feel when you see someone display-
> ing more flesh than you'd consider 'decent' — a girl
> mincing down the road in a barely-dress that leaves little
> to the imagination, perhaps, or a construction worker
> whose backside is all but falling out of his mis-named
> 'coveralls'?

Although they're far less volatile than our boundaries, our own barriers, and those we inherit from our society, do change slowly over time, according to our 'mind-set' and the local customs—the latter being the literal origin of the word 'morals'. If everyone around me is taking their clothes off in public, I'll probably do so too, despite what I may feel at first... And I'll change my mind on almost anything if someone can show me a reasonable argument as to why I should do so... perhaps... if it feels right... maybe...

That's one of the key points about a barrier: even though it's based in emotions, it's essentially rational (on the surface, at least) and can usually be induced to change by rational means—laws and customs change when the change 'makes sense', or when the old law no longer makes sense in a changed society. But that's also the key difference between a barrier and a wall: a wall is *not* rational, but is driven by a kind of existential fear. A barrier becomes an absolute wall as a result of continual attempts to breach the barrier, or to force change in the barrier —for example, by pestering, or demanding that the barrier 'is' a negotiable boundary, insisting that I 'should' accede to others' wishes, no matter how much I may feel it to be wrong.

Like a barrier, a *wall* is created by me against you, against 'not-I'; but unlike a barrier, which delimits a kind of conceptualised definition of 'I'—what I ought or ought not to be—a wall is part of my *emotional* definition of 'I'. An apparent threat to breach one of my walls is not merely a threat to my ideas, my beliefs, but a direct threat to *me*, to what I feel is my very existence. So a wall is not something that can be argued about, but is rigidly defended, often with a huge emotional loading—and cannot be changed by any rational means.

> Perhaps one reason I don't want Sam to get too close is my own underlying fear of unwanted sex — nothing's ever happened to suggest that the risk is real, but I *feel* a kind of sexual *pushiness* every time Sam's anywhere near me. To say that I don't like it is an understatement... so there's nothing that Sam could say, or do, that would

make me change my mind...

What are some of your own walls? What do you *feel* if there's any threat to breach one of your walls?

What happens when you accidentally bump into one of someone else's walls? You're likely to have all too clear an idea of what they feel... but what do *you* feel when that happens? Does it seem like you're being unfairly blamed for doing something which you haven't actually done?

Like barriers, our walls do shift slowly, through time: but they're so fiercely defended that we usually have to find some way to trick ourselves into letting them change. They may *seem* to collapse temporarily in specific contexts — under the influence of alcohol or other drugs, for example, or under extreme social pressure — but they're often reconstructed afterwards, and defended even more fiercely (or desperately) than before. The only way in which long-term changes are made to our walls is through what's called 'personal growth' — or, more accurately, 'self-transformation', because our sense of self is certainly transformed as our walls begin to change.

But why change at all? If we need those boundaries and barriers and walls in order to stay sane, in order to cope in a complex society, why can't we leave them as they are? The simple answer is that they get in *our* way: the primary blocks we come up against, in our search to express who we are and what we want to do, turn out to be our own boundaries. Those rigidly-defended walls may seem like our fortress against an unfair, unsafe world: but without full awareness of what they are and why they're there, they're just as likely to be our prison instead. There's always a choice, says the wyrd, but there's also always a twist...

My fortress, my prison

The wyrd has no boundaries: but *we* do — or at least we need them, even though they cannot actually exist... Our choices for 'I'

— our boundaries, our barriers, our walls — form the bars of what Hugh Mackay calls 'the cage': it keeps us safe, sane, stable, and seems to keep away what we fear, but it also restricts our ability to dance with the weavings of the wyrd—and with each other.

No matter how much they get in our way at times, it's important to understand just how much we *do* need those boundaries—we won't be able to stay sane without *some* kind of boundary to draw a line between 'I' and 'not-I'. In the absence of a clear, firm boundary, 'I' becomes lost, and in some cases quite literally wanders from personality to personality in the same physical person—as in multiple-personality syndrome—or even between different physical people. The latter may sound more than just weird—crazy, even—but it's well-recorded in one type of schizophrenia. I've even seen it first-hand when I visited a friend in psychiatric hospital: we were talking quietly in her ward, when a young schizophrenic woman wandered past and said, out of the blue, to no one in particular, "If I was adopted, I'd want to know who my real mother was"—and wandered on again. My friend was shocked: she'd never spoken about it, but that was exactly the reason for the emotional collapse which had landed her in hospital... The same 'unbounded telepathy' is also quite common in people who've over-used certain drugs such as LSD and marijuana: an occultist friend suggests that those drugs 'tear holes in the aura' — in other words they fragment the boundary between 'I' and 'not-I', sometimes beyond repair. And that's what 'telepathy' usually is: a muddled mixture of vague memories and blurred images without any distinction as to whom they belong — so perhaps the many people I've met who've said "I'd love to be telepathic" wouldn't be quite so keen once they understood what *real* telepathy is like...

> Which leads us to an interesting philosophical question: are our minds ever really our own? How much do we share them with others? How much do we *want* to share them with others? These questions aren't as trivial as they sound—though the answers may indeed be weird...

It isn't easy to do, because the process of watching itself tends to get in the way: but experiment with watching what seem to be 'your' thoughts, feelings and memories as you go through a day. How often do you spot a thought or memory that seems at first to be one of your own, but doesn't connect with anything else — that is not part of your present or past as you know it? (A hint: don't 'try' — just allow them to present themselves to your awareness.) So where do these 'foreigners' come from? Where do they go? By what paths do they weave their way through you? Weird indeed...

At the other extreme, a combination of unacknowledged fears and a loss of faith in the natural weavings of the wyrd leads to the creation of barriers and walls that really do form a prison of the mind — and it's every bit as destructive as the 'unbounded' state. Fundamentalist religions of all flavours are particularly prone to this problem: the word 'religion' literally means 'to re-bind', but can easily become 'to entrap' instead. So whenever we meet someone who says that they have '*the* truth' — or particularly that they *alone* know 'the truth' — then it's time to be very cautious: as we saw with the Red Queen a while back, they're probably incapable of seeing — let alone admitting to — their own self-contradictions, hence *we're* likely to end up as the ones who suffer the chaos of their cage...

Do you know anyone who has rigid, dogmatic beliefs about how other people 'should' relate? If so, how easily do you relate with them? Do you do so only according to the precepts of that person's belief — or do you still have choices of your own in how you relate with them?

Do *they* always relate with — or to — others in line with those claimed beliefs? If not, what difficulties does this cause? More to the point, *who* has to face those difficulties?

So a fair few of our walls are constructed not so much against others as against our own contradictions — or, less politely, our own hypocrisy. Wherever we've done something that's outside of 'the rules', as defined by our own barriers, or society's—which, courtesy of the wyrd if nothing else, *everyone* has and does at some stage—we're likely to build a wall of denial against the feelings of guilt or embarrassment, or our fear of responsibility and retribution. We don't want others to know that we've 'done wrong'; perhaps more to the point, we don't even want *ourselves* to know. So it gets quietly 'forgotten', until someone accidentally brings it up again—in which case we're likely to blame *them*, 'projecting' onto them whatever behaviour we've concealed, in order to deny what is actually our own self-hypocrisy or self-dishonesty.

> "*I'm* not angry!" I say loudly, aggressively, to Mary, in one of our all-too-regular rows at work. "Why are *you* angry?" Yet it's obvious to anyone standing by that she wasn't, and isn't; but she soon will be if I carry on projecting like this much longer... This time she's aware enough of her own boundaries to *not* respond in kind: she stops, head tilted to one side in wry amusement, and waits until I can accept what Reality Department is showing me about who's playing the 'angry' game and who isn't. That's when the embarrassment hits... it's no fun at all to have to face my own hypocrisy, even though it's what I most need to see...
>
> It won't be much fun for you either, but it's worthwhile taking a careful look at some of your own 'trigger issues' about which you explode when others accidentally come too close. What are you concealing from *yourself* in each case?

Fear is weird, and fear is part of the wyrd—so it knows no boundaries. Fear of ourselves—fear of having to face our own responsibility—causes problems; so does fear of others. That fear can easily become so large that it dominates all thought, creating what we might think of as a fortress, but is actually a prison in which we've entrapped ourselves—and for which we'll almost invariably blame others. Back in my student days, the house in which I rented a room was burgled; I apparently disturbed the burglar when I came home unexpectedly early, because whoever it was ran out the back door as I came in the front, and very little was taken. Yet the landlord reacted dramatically: every outside door was fitted with a new double-deadlock and bars, every inside door fitted with locks and latches, every window in his ground-floor apartment fitted with steel shutters and massive iron grilles—reducing the previous brightness to a dull gloom—and so on. Within days, the place looked—and felt —more like a penitentiary than a personal home. Defence—or self-chosen imprisonment? Defending possessions — or 'possessed' by fear of losing them? Good question...

> What do you fear? How much do your fears restrict your apparent choices? And how much do you blame others for *your* choice to restrict your choices?
>
> For example, many women say they're afraid to go out at night, for fear of assault. Yet police and hospital statistics show that, despite the public image of women as victims, they're actually at far less risk than men are: even in the home, men are more than twice as likely as women to be assaulted, by an intruder, a 'friend' or relative, or even their own partner. That's fact: yet fact doesn't necessarily count for much where walls of fear are concerned...
>
> There's *always* a risk, always a chance that it — whatever 'it' is—will happen, not to someone else, but to *me*. Increasing the barriers, making the walls ever more rigid, may seem to reduce the risk—yet the risk never goes away, and every tightening of the boundaries curtails our freedom even more. So how do you balance the limits *you* place on *your* risk and *your* freedom?
>
> And it's also worthwhile exploring how much the fears behind your own barriers and walls are self-confirming: for example, if you tend to assume "all men are bastards", or "all women are bitches", how much do you notice only those incidents which confirm these bars of your 'cage', and ignore those that don't?

Our cage is constructed from far more than just our fears, and it's also as much formed from the outside as well as from within. Language, for example, can be quite literally a barrier—a fortress, but also a prison. Different languages allow us to express some concepts or experiences easily, but other concepts or experiences only with great difficulty—the fictional language Pravic, in Ursula Le Guin's novel *The Dispossessed*, was designed to make the expression of complex thought simple, while Newspeak, in George Orwell's *1984*, was designed intentionally to make it almost impossible. The various computer languages with which I battle at work each make some tasks easy, and others nightmarish! And every group of people—nation, clique, profession, family, friends—develops their own chosen way of expressing themselves, their thoughts, their fears, their feelings: a way which includes and excludes, at the same time. Crossing those boundaries can be surprisingly difficult...

> In what ways do your national language, your regional dialect, your accent, help include you as part of an 'in-group', and exclude others? In what circumstances have you found yourself shut out — even physically so — because of your language, your dialect, your accent? In what ways do you feel different from others because of the way you speak? In what ways do you find it safer to be with others who speak the same way as you do?
>
> In what ways do you use language to include or exclude others? Through jargon or 'shop-talk', perhaps, or by intentionally speaking in an ambiguous way?
>
> In what medium of 'language' do you find it easiest to express yourself? In writing? On the phone? One-on-one conversation? Or through dance, drama, drawing; or photography or film? In what medium do you find it hardest? Explore the many boundaries and barriers and walls of language for a while...

To expand or contract our boundaries, to raise or lower our barriers, to build or dismantle our walls, to tighten or loosen the bars of our cage—they're all *choices*. For each of us, to establish boundaries is to know and respect what I want, and to take responsibility for same; whenever we're with others, to establish boundaries is to know and respect what each 'I' *and* our 'We' wants, and to take responsibility for our share in those choices. And that means that there's almost always a requirement to *negotiate* boundaries, with others, and even with ourselves.

Negotiating the boundaries

"To establish boundaries is to know and respect what 'I' and 'We' and 'I' want, and to take responsibility for same": in a way, most of what follows is about negotiating boundaries, and accepting responsibility for our part in those choices, but we may as well make a start here!

An alternate name for 'boundary' is 'choice'—a boundary *is* a choice, or an expression of a choice: for example, I feel safe with you if you're standing at that distance, and no closer. What's interesting is that it's far easier to define boundaries in negative terms — 'No!' — and it's often the only aspect of boundaries that's mentioned in most descriptions. But the habit of saying only 'No' soon degenerates into the 'blame-game', and it easily becomes sarcastic and destructive: "What part of the word 'No' don't you understand?" Yet like 'No', 'Yes' is just as much a statement of a boundary: a boundary of *in*clusion rather than *ex*clusion. And it's also a statement of commitment, and acceptance of responsibility—which is perhaps why those who make so much noise about 'No means No!' seem afraid even to allow the word 'Yes' into their vocabulary...

> To what do you say 'Yes'? To what will you commit yourself?
> Go back through some of the boundaries and barriers and walls that you've identified already: most of those will be be defined in negative terms, in terms of 'No!' Turn them round, so that the boundary still remains exactly the same, but you're now saying 'Yes' — a *commitment* to what you *do* choose to allow, rather than

> a shying-away from what you won't. In what ways does your perception of the boundary—and of your relationship with 'not-I' (whatever it may be)—change as you do this? What fears come up in *you* as you shift the description from 'No' to 'Yes'?

In a sense we have to say 'Yes' to *something*, whether we like it or not: without some kind of 'Yes', there is no 'We'—and often not much 'I' either. And people who can only say 'No' are intensely frustrating to be around: for example, I remember how an extremely irritated student described one young woman who'd been to a personal-development course which had placed great emphasis on boundaries—with the result that she now said 'No', at random, to almost any move by anyone. "She'd ask me to look at her work," he said, "and as soon as I sat down next to her she said I was 'intruding in her space', and hence *I* had to move to a seat on the far side of the room, and talk with her from there. She would sit in the middle of the floor, talking for hours on the phone, and no one was allowed past—that was 'intruding on her space' too. So was being anywhere near her in our very small kitchen, or simply walking past in the passageway: she was *real* good at putting up her hands and saying 'No! Stop!' and then you always felt somehow you were to blame for something you hadn't even done — certainly hadn't intended doing then, though sometimes I feel like doing it to her now..." That wasn't so much the woman's genuine boundaries as the 'blame-game', the self-centredness of the Child: what's missing is *negotiation*, an acceptance that *others* have just as much right to *their* boundaries — or simply to co-exist in the same physical space.

Privacy *is* always difficult in a crowded culture, and the bounds of privacy are always different in every group. Some families are very 'touchy-feely', to the extent that some members end up feeling engulfed, constantly intruded on—perhaps like that young woman—and desperately needing 'personal space'; other families are very touchy about *not* being touched, which can, however, often lead to a genuine psychiatric disorder known as 'touch deprivation', and an inability to 'get in touch with themselves' in almost any sense.

We *need* touch; we also *need* privacy; those two needs are mutually contradictory, and hence create *lots* of problems when people start projecting the blame for those contradictions onto everyone else... In relation to others — whether in families, groups, partnerships or whatever — the movement in our boundaries, and movement between the layers of boundary and barrier and wall, is driven by an oscillation between the desire for union—for 'We'—and the desire for separation, for 'I' alone, or literally 'all-one'. (We could equally say it's driven by an oscillation between fear of isolation and fear of engulfment, but it'd be nice to say it in a positive way for once!) But if there is no genuine touch—as opposed to an assumed sexuality, perhaps, or the push-and-shove of cities—and a constant sense of 'unsafety' —simply because people are packed so closely together—there are always going to be difficulties: and something, or someone, has to give way. And the result of any 'negotiation' needs to be *seen* to be fair — which, given the rampant childishness which typifies our society, it usually isn't... so there's a real need to consciously involve the Inner Adult in the negotiations!

> How do *you* manage to feel 'reasonably' safe in a crowded society?
>
> One common answer is that if there isn't enough space for privacy, we can usually make do with *time* instead: 'time out' from work, from habitual patterns, from people with whom we have difficulty, and even — with some difficulty — 'time out' from ourselves... So how do you negotiate a 'time out' with others? How do you negotiate a 'time out' with yourself—such as keeping to an agreement with yourself to take a much-needed break?
>
> A 'time out' is, in effect, a boundary that creates 'personal space' through time. What do you *feel* if that boundary is breached—that you ask for 'time out' in an argument, for example, and the other person just keeps arguing? What are you trying to achieve if the *other*

person asks for a 'time out', and *you* keep arguing? And what do you feel when you break one of your own 'time out' agreements with yourself?

Negotiation isn't easy. It always involves *listening* as well as talking (or demanding...): and genuine listening is a real risk to our boundaries, our cage—because there's always a real risk that *we'll* have to accept changes in *our* choices, changes to the comforting bars of our cage. That's never comfortable, and never 'safe' in the way the Child, or even the Parent, wants — which is why the Inner Adult, with its more adult grasp of the tortuous twists of Reality Department, is so important in this.

But there's one thing more that, whether we like it or not, is always involved in every negotiation of boundaries: namely the wyrd. There *is* such a thing as 'fate': some issues *are* always going to be ours, and ours alone. Ignoring this is not a good idea... and trying to fight against it simply doesn't work: it was from much practical experience that the Greeks assigned the name Atropos —'she who cannot be turned'—to one of the Sisters of Fate... Perhaps we can never truly 'bargain with the fates': but with awareness, we *can* negotiate a more constructive relationship with the wyrd—and to do that, we need next to understand and accept what *is* our 'fate', and what is not.

7

A PROBLEM OF FATE

Few people like the idea of fate. Fixed, immutable, implacable, with no option for choice or chance or challenge: just fate, and nothing else. Some people, perhaps, would seem to accept this bleak 'fatalistic' view of the world—perhaps because they see so many others try to combat the fates, and fail in futility instead. But most of us will fight against what we see as the unfairness of fate—whether it works or not—so as to at least have the sense that we're doing *something*. And that's certainly what most approaches to personal-development seem to advise: for example, one well-known figure in the field claims that his book "will act as a magnificent and devastating battle-plan whereby you will win back absolute control of your life!"—which it can't, because, courtesy of Murphy's Law, control itself is a myth... Fate can be a problem.

At first sight it seems we have only three choices about fate: we can abandon ourselves to it—which leaves us with no choice at all, and hence no power either; we can try to fight against it—which we can't, and hence tends to be an interesting waste of energy in support of an illusion; or we can try, very, very hard, to pretend that "it doesn't exist really and it's all a load of superstitious hogwash and I don't believe it and I'm not going to believe it so there"... at which point Fate comes quietly through the back door and gives us another great big kick in the unfortunates—

because there *is* such a thing as fate, and it doesn't like to be ignored!

But there is another choice—a wyrd choice—which goes straight through the middle of that dilemma (trilemma?): understand what fate is, and how it works, in order to help it work *with* us. So yes, some of what we've seen so far could have been gleaned from the usual approaches to personal issues: but it's here that we start to move off into what can only be called a weird direction...

Lessons in the weaving

Return for a moment to the Gryphon's comments, way back in that imaginary garden: "Everything that happens to us is a lesson," it said. "If you don't understand what the lesson *is*, you get to do it again. And again. And again..." Sometimes the 'lessons' are comments on our own choices—feedback about the many choices we make which *aren't* helping us express our 'I'—and sometimes they're issues that seem to follow us around regardless of what we choose. Whatever it may be, our aim is, as the Gryphon suggested, "to get the lessons to lessen"—because each time we grasp a bit more of it, it doesn't come back so hard!

Every thread—every possibility—passes through everyone, everywhere; and everyone has to face them all to some extent at some time. For each of us, most issues seem to come up just once or twice in a lifetime, often in a quiet, almost unnoticeable way, and rarely re-appear: sometimes they'll only present themselves in our life in the ways in which we see them occur in *others'* lives. But other issues, other threads, will certainly *feel* like ours alone—they'll seem specific to us and to few, if any, others! Although in fact the same threads do pass through everyone—and hence anyone and everyone may be our allies in helping us face these issues—they are, in effect, our own special 'lessons', our very own course in the weird 'university of life'—in which we all get bent to some degree! So for me, for example, it's obvious that for some threads—such as "how to convert a long-distance relationship into a tangible one without wrecking it" and "how *not* to set myself up as doormat and/or scapegoat" —I'm missing something in the 'lesson', because they do indeed keep coming back, again and again...

> No doubt you have your own 'lessons' too: what are they? What issues, for you, are 'the lessons that *don't* lessen' — the ones that keep coming back, time after time?
>
> And *why* do these issues keep coming back? It'd be easiest to blame it on fate, perhaps, but is there something in each 'lesson' that you're missing? What choices are hidden in the twists of the wyrd — hidden behind the bars of your cage?

There's a throwaway line in one of the old James Bond movies that illustrates well what's actually going on here. "We meet again, Mr Bond," says the villain, Goldfinger. "Once is happenstance; twice is coincidence; three times is enemy action!" If something happens to me once: well, that's just the weaving of the wyrd—'blind chance', in the old Greek concept of fate. If it happens to me again: yes, sure, that's coincidence. But three times? Enemy action, for certain!

Yet who's the 'enemy'? Good question... better not look too closely, though, or I might find the *real* answer...

I'd *much* rather say it's 'them'—whoever 'them' might be. I'm their victim: 'they' did it to me. It's all *their* fault, dammit! But, looking back, I can see that I've been treated like a door-mat, or found myself set up as the fall-guy or the scapegoat, a *lot* more than Goldfinger's 'three times is enemy action'—yet in each case it's been with entirely different people, in entirely different places and in entirely different contexts. So who's the 'enemy', then? The only common factor in all of these incidents is me... which suggests that my *real* 'enemy' is me... don't like the sound of that at all!

All right, all right, I admit it: more than a few times it must be truthfully said that I'm 'my own worst enemy'! I'd probably have a lot less trouble with my tax-return if I kept my paperwork in something more systematic than my usual 'sedimentary filing-system'; and I'd probably have a lot less trouble with Mary — and far too many others — if I actually *listened* sometimes to what they're saying...

If 'three times is enemy action', then in what ways do you *know* that you're 'your own worst enemy'? How do you get in your own way, so to speak? In what ways do you find yourself blaming others for what are more likely to be the wyrd's feedback on your *own* choices? What happens to your relationships with others — and with yourself—as a result of this? (And no, it isn't comfortable to explore this...)

But this is true for *everyone*: it's not just us. All around us— *everywhere* around us — there are people who, by any objective standard, are their own worst enemies. They make mistakes — the *same* mistakes — time and time again, until eventually they find a way for the lessons to lessen. The mistakes are often different for different people: even though we each have our own 'preferred mistakes', between us all we find some weird way to make—and re-make—every mistake there can possibly be... no wonder it's such a chaotic mess out there! Slowly understanding just how true this is, we begin to grasp the meaning of the word 'compassion'...

The wyrd weaves through everywhere; it also weaves its way *back*—which is often just what we don't want to happen! Every choice has its echoes in the wyrd, with the result that our 'preferred mistakes' will often have predictable echoes. Since this is the wyrd we're dealing with, the *form* those echoes take will vary—sometimes imperceptibly, but often radically—yet the *fact* of the echo will not. This general principle is known throughout the world under a variety of different names: in the common, if rather simplistic, Western interpretation of the Indian concept of 'karma', for example, every action has its equal and opposite reaction, and every inaction leads to an equal and apposite re-enaction, another 'lesson'; whereas the witchcraft tradition, by contrast, argues that whatever we send out to others—for good or ill—comes back *threefold*. Either way, they all suggest it's a good idea to be careful of what we say and do!

> What's your experience of 'karma', or of the witchcraft notion of the 'threefold return'? Both suggest a fairly simple linkage of cause-and-effect: in that sense, if you think that something that happened to you was an effect of your karma, what was the cause? The wyrd is a little more twisted than cause-and-effect: in what weird ways did your karma—your wyrd—weave its way back to you, no matter how much you might have tried to block it?
>
> What choices did you have in this? If you can't change the *fact* of that karma, what choices did you have about the *form* that it takes? There's always a choice, there's always a twist: but that means there's always *some* choice about the twists too...

"Issues weave through me on the threads of wyrd: are unchanged by how much *I* am unchanged"—that was a comment in *Positively Wyrd*, which also applies here. Whether I like it or not, *I'm* responsible for the threads that make up these repeating patterns. (That's not the same as saying that I'm to blame for them—we'll be looking at the distinction between blame and responsibility later—but it certainly means that I can't blame others for them either!) And my personal work on those threads, those issues—how I accept them and work *with* them—changes the visible choices for everyone. I change my wyrd, and the wyrd as a whole—change what happens to me, and to others—through changing myself, and by my example: *not* by trying to 'make' others change!

We always have choice, though there's always a twist... But there's an even more twisted layer to this, because not all of these repeated patterns can be traced back to our own choices, our own 'preferred mistakes'. It's a layer which the mythology of wyrd describes as 'geis'—a layer in which we discover that there really *is* such a thing as fate.

Wyrd and geis

The word *geis*—pronounced variously as 'gesh' or 'gayas', and with the plural *geasa*—roughly translates as 'bond': a commitment, a promise. Just who the bind is made by, or to, though, is rarely clear...

In one sense, the term is used to describe the milieu into which we were born, our 'place in life', over which—in principle at least—we had no apparent choice: the bond, but also the promise, of threads such as our genetic inheritance, our family, sex, race, place of birth, education, historical period and so on. Each of these do affect—often strongly—the relative ease for us of some choices compared to others: given my body-shape, for example, I've never had any realistic chance of choosing to become a champion athlete! If I'd been born as a girl a hundred years ago, I'd have had little chance to study, and even less chance of being taken seriously if I did; if I'd been born as a boy at that time, my most likely fate would have been to die as cannon-fodder in someone else's war. Such is our wyrd: and it's worth reflecting on just what we *have* been 'given'—or *not* given—as the background to our own lives.

> What have you been given as the background to *your* life? What have you inherited, or learned, or gained, from your family? What advantages — and there are always some — have you gained from being born male, or born female, as a member of your racial group and social background? What has happened — or not happened—to you because you were born *when* and where you were born? What options were opened to you because of the educational and other choices that others took on your behalf, in what they saw as your 'best interest', without your informed involvement?
>
> And what have you *not* been given? It's easy enough to notice the things that you think you missed

> out on — a more stable home environment, perhaps, or the apparent advantages you see held by the other sex — but there are others that are harder to see simply because they're *not* there.
>
> War or plague or poverty, for example, or physical handicap, or no access to education or health-care: what advantages have you gained from these *not* being part of your own background?

An interesting question, though: if that's what we've been given, who's doing the 'giving'? Christians, Jews and Moslems alike might argue that these things are in the gift of God alone; those who believe in the continuation of 'I' from life to life, such as Buddhists or Hindus or the ancient Celts, might agree in some ways, but would suggest that 'our' choices in previous lives — whatever that might mean—also play their part in this. Just how much we choose our parents, for example, is arguable indefinitely! We may not be responsible about our past, or what happened before our (current) past, or for what others chose for us before we could choose for ourselves, but we're always responsible for our choices *now*.

The Celtic version of geis is complex and multi-faceted. In one sense it's a bond or taboo lasting well beyond death: the Celts legally could, and did, borrow in one lifetime under bond to pay it back in the next — a somewhat extreme idea of a mortgage as a literal 'death-pledge'! But in another sense it's also a challenge, or a dare, which inevitably places the bondee in a double-bind. This is well illustrated by a key segment of the Irish legend of Diarmid and Grainne. The lively young chieftain's daughter Grainne had agreed to be married to the great hero Cuchullain, whom she'd never met: but at her wedding-feast she's realised that it's not what she wants to do—at all. Either as 'love at first sight' (as some versions of the legend insist) or as an escape from her ill-chosen promise, she picks out the young warrior Diarmid; and while the others are drinking, demands that he rescue her from her situation—or elope with her, which comes to much the same thing. "I put you under bond," she says; in Celtic terms, she places a geis upon him—uses his sense of honour to pass the problem to him.

And he cannot refuse: the concept of honour is so deep in that warrior society that to do so would be to have failed *as a human being*. So he's caught in a double-bind: he cannot refuse to go with her; yet to do so is to betray his own oath of loyalty to Cuchullain. Despite her betrayal of others, the formal statement of the bond means that it *is* now his problem: and the only way out is to break through an unbreakable barrier—either his own, or that of the society in which his lives. So whatever he does now, it's wrong: and the results of his choices will echo every-*when* within the wyrd, to haunt his soul through the lifetimes— and, as myth, will weave its way throughout the 'collective unconscious' of all humanity. In that sense, geis is a weird variant of the old notion that the sins of the fathers are fetched even unto the seventh generation—except that, as Celtic legend shows, its results are nothing like so simple, or so limited, as to affect a mere seven generations of only one family...

> "You must, but you mustn't; you mustn't, but you must": what's *your* experience of being caught in that kind of double-bind in which, whatever you do, you know it will be wrong? What were the circumstances that led to that fate for you? What did you choose? In what ways have your choices come to 'echo everywhen within the wyrd, to haunt your soul through the lifetimes'?

Whatever form it takes, the commitment required by the bond demands the completion of an apparently impossible task. So a geis is also an ending, a closure of the wyrd—or in Greek terms, the fate associated with hubris, with over-reaching oneself too far into 'the pride that comes before a fall'. Every thread of the wyrd has its ending: the difference is that, through the weird twists of geis, we can even *know* what that ending would be— though the warning can often be too twisted to make sense until it's far too late!

Every wyrd has an ending...

This is the fatalistic aspect of wyrd: in the Nordic myths, even the gods were subject to their wyrd, meeting their end in the Gotterdämmerung, the cataclysmic Ragnarök which marks the end of the world. The same fatalism comes up often, too, in early Anglo-Saxon poetry, which merges older myths and the then-new Christian symbolism in some very strange ways. Alluding to the death of Jesus on the cross, the poet-author of the seventh-century *Dream of the Rood*, for example, comments: "I have endured many terrible Wyrds upon the hill." Elsewhere in the same poem is a similar comment: "The corpse grew cold, that fair house of the soul; then men began to fell us to the ground—that was a terrible Wyrd!" Anglo-Saxon scholars often translate *wyrd* as 'trials' or 'experiences', but it somehow loses the intensity inherent in the aside made by another early poet: "Lo, we suffered many dreadful wyrds that night..." The ending implied by a 'dreadful wyrd' is not necessarily a death: though it's definitely an ending of some kind — a death of the soul, the death of hope, the death of what might have been.

There's a strange Welsh word, pronounced 'heraeth', that could describe one common response to this aspect of wyrd: it's almost untranslatable, but approximates to "a longing and a grieving for that which never was, which cannot be, and never will be". I sometimes find myself mourning for lost possibilities in past relationships, or the sense of loss in the hope of relationship with Nicky, which seems so much blocked by the weavings of the wyrd: for what past or present issues are *you* still caught in 'heraeth', in 'a longing for that which can never be'? How much does this hopeless grieving for the past, or for the impossible, affect your choices in the here-and-now?

Every thread of the wyrd has its ending; a geis describes and delimits that moment of ending, when the twists and turns of the thread finally fold back upon themselves. And a geis usually carries some kind of weird warning of its presence: so great is the tension created by the tangled predicament that it's as though the fabric of reality itself is twisted, and creates a characteristic echo throughout the wyrd. If we know what we're looking for, we can recognise this: and that means that we *do* have some choice as to how best to respond.

The twist is that these echoes are described in symbols—"a sword and a rope over water"—and often make no sense if we try to interpret them literally. There's one famous historical example of this, in the story of James, Duke of Monmouth, a seventeenth-century pretender to the English throne. As a child, a geis was identified for him: he was warned that he would meet his end at the Rhine. So throughout his long exile in France, in the middle of the century, he was careful never to cross that river: as long as he didn't do so, he would be safe—or so he thought. But in 1685 he led a rebellion in southern England; and after the battle of Sedgemoor, where his army was finally defeated, he was captured hiding in a drainage ditch, and was executed soon after. So where does the geis come in? Those drainage ditches on the Somerset levels around Sedgemoor are known locally as 'rhynes': the geis was indeed explicit, but perhaps not explicit enough...

"We have no geis that we know for you," says a character in Marion Campbell's weird historical novel *The Dark Twin*. In the midst of the chaotic maze of symbols and images which fill my dreams and my inner life — suburban trains, a deer, a twisted ring — the only geis I know for myself concerns a ferry, or travel over water. I have no idea what form it will finally take: I'm expecting a typically wry weird twist, like the story of the Duke of Monmouth, when it finally comes...!

This is perhaps asking a bit much at this stage, but do you have any known symbols which describe *your* ending, or the ending of something which means a great deal to you? If you know this, how much does it affect your choices? In what ways does it already affect your relationships with others?

A geis is an end-point in a thread of wyrd: it describes something that we're certain will never happen — or, if we're forewarned, often try to make sure can never happen — but which somehow, in the weird twists of fate, always finds some way to transpire. Faust makes his pact with Mephistopheles: he will be free if he never once in forty years says the words 'Linger, thou art fair'—and yet, with only moments left before final freedom, Faust finds himself saying the fateful phrase. No matter how much we'd want to blame others, some things *are* our wyrd: everyone is trying to avoid the end, yet everyone has their geis...

...but there's always a choice!

There may always be an ending: but sometimes, listening to that strange sense 'impending wyrd', we can know in time to change to another thread, another choice of action, and hence avoid it— for a while, at least! And even if we cannot avoid the ending, we *do* still have choices about how we face it—and about what we do in the meantime. Not all of our wyrd can be said to be truly our choice: and yet within those weird twists there are *always* choices available to us. Our 'lessons' *are* ours, and it's up to us to find a way to make them 'lessen' — not just for us, but for everyone.

There's one example that immediately comes to mind. A few years ago I was on a training course, one of whose themes was about 'making a difference'. There were about thirty of us on the six-month course, from all different backgrounds, and all different age-groups. One of the others was a man named Alan: an odd character, struggling hard against the harshness of his wyrd—which included a minor physical deformity—and trying as best he could to make something of his life. In his mid-forties, he'd never had any kind of intimate relationship—not even a date, as far as we could gather—and he spent his nights working as a taxi-driver, and his days studying in private, though he was at last beginning to have a social life in the form of amateur theatre. The course ended, as these courses often do, with each of us making a statement about 'our purpose in life', and we each went on our separate ways.

I forget what Alan had said his 'purpose' was, but it soon didn't matter: six months after the course ended, he was dead, murdered in his own taxi by a couple of kids, in an adolescent robbery that went horribly wrong. A futile waste of a sad and lonely life...

And yet... and yet...

Our group reconvened over Alan's death: we agreed that it had been a shock, in this quiet city, and yet it hadn't been a surprise — somehow, almost all of us had been expecting it. A group of strangers, including one of my friends from the course, met by chance in a café: it turned out that every one of them knew Alan, or had been involved in the incident—one was a social worker assigned to the boys in the past, another was a lawyer working on the case, another had known Alan from the theatre, and so on. Weird... I'd first known about the murder when I saw Alan's face on the front page of the newspaper; yet in the months that followed, his photograph was *often* on the front page of the newspaper, in any article on risks to taxi-drivers, or juvenile crime, or the problems of social workers — even once, by accident, wrongly captioned in an article about psychiatric patients who'd died on the streets. Weird indeed...

Alan *had* 'made a difference', even continues to make a difference to the lives of others—but in his own way, and more in the manner of his dying rather than in the manner of his living. Most of us would probably prefer to 'make a difference' while still alive: and yet in some weird way it seems that even *that* is in our choice. There's always a twist, perhaps, but there *is* still always a choice...

> Do you have any sense of your own 'weird purpose in life' — the purpose of *your* wyrd? In what direction do those repeated 'lessons' seem to be pushing you?
>
> To fully resolve those 'lessons' from the wyrd means accepting that they *are* part of our wyrd, and that our

> most constructive response would be to learn to work
> *with* them, rather than fighting in futility against what is
> evidently our fate. What would accepting that demand of
> *you*, and of your relationships with others? What would
> you have to give up — your pride, perhaps, or your
> certainty? — in order to work *with* the weavings of your
> wyrd?

We each have our own wyrd; and each wyrd, interweaving though it always does with every other, has its own endings, and its own geasa. So we could say that our 'weird purpose in life' is to learn how to resolve our geasa constructively: for ourselves, for others and—if we happen to believe in such things—in all our other lives past, present and future, anywhen within the wyrd. It's not easy—but probably easier than having the same 'lessons' come back again and again, never lessening in their impact on our lives... And it does need to be understood as a *quest* rather than an achievable goal: we do what we can, but "let us live a little while we may"!

So the next five chapters explore a variety of ways in which we can better understand how our wyrd interweaves with others' —and what we can constructively do about it. Some of it may be heavy going at times — there are some important threads which few of us want to face—but it *will* help us to find the tools with which we can learn to work *with* our wyrd, and share that power with others wisely. Time to open the toolkit, then— and to find out more about the subject and the object of this exercise!

8

SUBJECT AND OBJECT

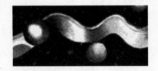

Quite soon after earliest infancy, we discover that there's a definite boundary between 'I' and 'not-I' — or, more to the point, that there *is* such a thing as 'not-I'. We're not the centre of the world, and certainly not its sole content: there *is* 'Other' out there. Yet we still want things to happen—or not happen—out there. Problem...

A weird problem... yet one that most people try to 'solve' by avoiding the weirdness—with the chaotic results that we see around us. There are two standard approaches: treat everything 'out there' as *objects*; or regard everything 'not-I' as *subjects* of 'I'. But for many purposes *neither* of these approaches works well: and if we try to use either of them—as most people do—as our primary or even our sole 'solution' to the problem, they can be immensely destructive, especially of our relationships with others. So understanding why these two approaches so easily go wrong, and how to find a balance between them by working *with* their inherent wyrdness, forms an important part of our interpersonal 'toolkit'—weird though some of it may seem at first!

One reason why achieving a balance can be difficult is that one side of the equation is well understood and much studied—and much complained about!—while the other is hardly known at all. So we'll start with the better-known 'object-centred' worldview—but while we're looking at that, keep in mind that there *is* another 'subject-centred' side to the story...

Everything's an object

"I am a rock, I am an island": I am *I*—individual, independent, unchanging, I defend my boundaries against all comers. Just occasionally I might notice that I feel a little isolated from others; but since everyone is the same—*everyone* is a rock, an independent island—there's no other choice anyway. And if I want something to happen out there—well, I'll *make* it happen! Action speaks louder than words: *action*! Do It Now: that's *my* motto!

> Recognise this? Who do you know who take an 'Action Man' or 'Superwoman' approach to life? What difficulties do you have in relating with them? If they acknowledge you as 'you' at all—which often such people don't, or can't—how *do* they relate with you?
>
> How much do you follow this same approach yourself? Looking at it from the other side—so to speak—what difficulties might others have in relating with you?

I work from an 'object-centred' worldview: everything else 'out there' is an inanimate object—or may as well be inanimate, from my perspective. I'm a self-made man: I don't mess around waiting for things to happen, I take control. Whatever I want, I'll get for myself; anything that gets in my way, it won't be so for long. And if you get in my way, you won't be in my way for long either—so *move*!

> It's easy to see why the object-centred worldview so easily becomes objectionable! But it has its validity and its advantages as well as its problems—as you'll see for yourself in a moment. For this example, borrow a chair and a friend, and stand them in front of you; or just imagine them both in front of you. You now want them on the other side of the room. They're both objects: which

means that if you want them to be moved, you move them yourself.

Pick up the chair, and move it to the far side of the room. What problems — if any — do you have with making this happen? What complaints — if any — does the chair make to you about being treated as an object? What is your relationship with the chair-object as you do this? (If your response to those last two questions is 'Huh?', there *is* a reason for them, but it may not be clear until later!)

Pick up the other object—the person—and move it to the far side of the room. What problems—if any—do you have with making this happen? What complaints—if any—does the person make to you about being treated as an object? What is your relationship with the person-object as you do this?

In Jungian psychology this standard 'island-I' model forms part of the 'masculine' archetype: it's certainly stereotyped as 'male' in Western society. But in reality it's no more 'male' than 'female'. It's one way of working in—working *with*—the world: and that's all.

And it's not just the 'objectionable' types who live by this object-centred worldview, because it's also a good place to hide if you happen to have difficulty coping with *people*. Objects don't answer back; objects don't make demands; objects don't bully; they're always the same, they're predictable, practical, above all *safe*. Mostly...

The object-centred worldview is well-understood because it *works*—or at least, produces concrete results—in the material world, if not necessarily anywhere else. It analyses, breaks into component parts, reduces to a formula—a set of mathematical or logical relationships rather than human ones—calculates, gets the numbers... it's *quantitative* rather than *qualitative*. And precisely because it *is* quantitative, it can prove that one solution is better than another—in quantitative terms, at any rate. It fully understands "Bigger is better": but it has no way at all to grasp the qualitative notion that "Small is beautiful"...

Which notion makes more sense to you: "Bigger is better", or "Small is beautiful"? In what ways are *both* true? Given that they seem to contradict each other, how can they both be true *at the same time*?

The downside of that worldview is that it *only* understands 'objects'—and bases all its values on that understanding, or lack of it. So a car is *obviously* better than a horse: it goes faster, it carries more load, it's much cheaper and simpler to refuel and maintain, it's far more predictable, and so on. But it's easy for this view to degenerate still further, and treat everything and every*one* as inanimate objects — 'the peasants', 'the rabble', 'the staff', 'the workforce', items to be moved and manipulated in whatever way we choose, because it's assumed that they have no will of their own, no life of their own. And when there's a clash —when the childish fantasy of 'absolute control' meets up with Reality Department's insistence that there *are* others out there, and they do have lives and choices of their own — the object-centred worldview tends to roll up its sleeves, and resort to power-over. *Not* funny... not amusing at all...

Yet even these issues are fairly well understood: the advantages and disadvantages of the object-centred worldview are well-enough known by now. Not so its counterpart, the *subject*-centred worldview — because it's less obvious unless we know what we're looking for. And we need to understand *both* sides of this equation if we're to find a more practical, if wyrd, way to handle that weird boundary between 'I' and 'not-I'.

Everything's *my* subject

"I relate, therefore I am": everything is a sea of relationships, a sea of 'I', which—since it has no centre as such—must obviously revolve around *me*. "The personal is political"—whatever happens to me, happens to everyone; whatever happens to anyone, happens to me. I'm interested in everyone: and everyone *should* be interested in me. There are no 'objects', only subjects, people, relationship: *everything* is personal, and everything is part of me.

> Recognise this? Who do you know who takes this 'subject-centred' approach to life? What difficulties do you have in relating with them? If they acknowledge you as 'you' at all—which often such people don't, or can't—how *do* they relate with you?
>
> How much do you follow this same approach yourself? Looking at it from the other side—so to speak—what difficulties might others have in relating with you?

Everything 'out there' exists in relation to me — perhaps *only* in relation to me. I accept that if I want something, it'll happen if it's *meant* to happen. It's not in my hands to make it happen: nor is it my responsibility to do so. Instead, I *suggest* that things should change themselves: and they do, as part of their relationship with me, and because they know that I *know* what is best for us, best for We. And if they don't change, it's *their* fault, because they should *want* to change—for their own good.

> Like the object-centred worldview, the subject-centred one has its validity and its advantages as well as its problems. So borrow the chair and the friend again — either in physical reality, or in imagination — and stand them in front of you. As before, you now want them on the other side of the room. They're both subjects, extensions of yourself and your will: which means that if you want them to be moved, you have to get them to move *themselves*.
>
> Ask the friend to move to the far side of the room. Make it clear that this is your friend's responsibility: your friend ought to *want* to do this for you. What problems— if any — do you have with arranging this to happen? What complaints—if any—does the person make to you about being treated as your subject? What is your relationship with them as you do this?
>
> Ask the chair to move itself to the far side of the room. Make it clear that this is the chair's responsibility:

> the chair ought to *want* to do this for you. What problems
> — if any — do you have with arranging this to happen?
> What complaints — if any — does the chair make to you
> about being treated as your subject? What is your
> relationship with the chair as you do this?

In Jungian psychology this standard 'sea-I' model forms part of the 'feminine' archetype: in Western society, it's as much stereotyped as 'female' as the 'island-I' model is supposedly 'male'. Its whole focus is relationship, about the quality of feelings rather than numbers of things: since many relationships become all but impossible in large numbers, or large crowds, this worldview doubts that 'bigger' is *ever* 'better', and usually insists that "small is beautiful" — or even that "two's company, but three's a crowd"!

There *is* some validity in describing this as a female stereotype: it's certainly true that the so-called 'women's magazines' intrude on the private lives of 'public figures' in ways that can only be described as pornographic — but in a subject-centred way, rather than the objectification of the so-called 'men's magazines'. And a woman doctor, speaking from much experience, wrote to me about "women's tendency to react emotionally to situations rather than to discuss facts in a sensible practical way — I don't mean that women *can't* talk about facts sensibly but there will always be this emotional overlay, e.g. if [the] washing machine doesn't work it's doing it on purpose!"

Just how much this genuinely *is* 'female' — rather than the product of social conditioning — is open to debate: for example, I've seen many a male programmer behave in exactly the same irrational way, yelling at his computer "What the hell's wrong with you *now*? — you're doing this on purpose!" as it hangs up on yet another bug in his program... It is interesting, though, that in those standard gender-stereotypes, the supposedly 'male' object-centred view 'takes control', while the supposedly 'female' subject-centred view assigns all responsibility for action to the 'Other'; so in *both* cases only the male is deemed responsible, or to blame, for anything — which is in itself another common gender-stereotype.

The subject-centred world-view is a good place to hide if you want to avoid responsibility, especially for the inevitable problems of the material world. Objects don't respond to being pleaded with, or cajoled, or bullied; but there's usually someone around who *can* be pleaded with, or cajoled, or bullied, into dealing with it instead... we really don't have to look far to find people—female or male—who make that a way of life.

Yet it's also true that without that subject-centred notion—or more accurately feeling—that "I relate, therefore I am", there would *be* no relationship, no empathy with others: it dismantles the barriers, re-creates the links between people, everywhere and everywhen. It *is* true that "the personal is political"; it's also true that "the political is personal", in that arbitrary decisions made by unknown, unnamed people somewhere 'out there' may have enormous impacts on our individual lives. That's where this worldview *works*; that's where it *matters*—a lot.

> It's easy to intellectualise about an abstract slogan such as "The personal is political": so, for a change, where do you *feel* it? It's easy to see inequality between the sexes, between the races, between North and South, or whatever; it's easy — too easy — to talk about it; but where do you *feel* it, within *you*?
>
> Often the driving force behind a desire to remedy some perceived inequality or unfairness is a feeling of anger: if so, where, within you, do you *feel* this anger? Is it something that arises from others as such, or from your *relationship* with others? In what ways—if any—do you express this feeling in action?

The downside of the subject-centred 'sea-I' worldview is that it *only* understands 'subjects'—and bases all its values on that understanding, or lack of it. So *my* horse is obviously better than *your* nasty, smelly, noisy, dirty car: I don't have any relationship with your car, and no way to create a relationship with your car, so it *must* be worse than my horse. All too easily this descends into a habit of judging value or truth solely in terms of the closeness of relationship—leading directly on the one hand to favouritism, and on the other to racism, sexism and so on. When an object-centred system of law, which expects "the truth, the whole truth and nothing but the truth", meets up with a subject-centred worldview where 'truth' depends entirely on who's saying it, life can get more than a little chaotic...

And it's easy for this view to degenerate further still, because it regards 'not-I' not as an independent 'Other', but as an *extension* of self, with no real existence other than in relation to 'I'—rather as the Red Queen, back in the garden, claimed that you existed only because the White King was dreaming about you. Almost by definition, the subject-centred worldview has difficulty in maintaining clear boundaries: so unless the *internal* relationship between self and ego is clear—which for most of us, most of the time, it usually isn't—we're likely to project our own inconsistencies onto others. Reality Department's feedback shows us that something isn't right, yet we're sure it can't possibly be us, so it *must* be happening 'out there'... without a clear understanding of the boundary between 'I' and 'not-I', that's a very easy — and convenient — mistake to make. In its worst forms—such as the shrill moralism of the 'God's Police' mindset — the subject-centred worldview regards all 'not-I' as wayward and insubordinate *subjects* of self which may be morally condemned and righteously punished for failing to conform to our expectations: "You *don't* feel that!" it says; "you *can't* feel that; you *shouldn't* feel that; you have *no right* to feel that!" And in the same way that the object-centred worldview may resort to power-over to get its way, the subject-centred worldview can be very skilled at using power-*under*— and also blames that exclusively on 'the Other'. It's no wonder things get into such a mess!

Given the destruction that both the object-centred and subject-centred worldviews can so easily cause, it's easy to forget that they *do* both have their own valid uses — and that, despite those habitual gender-stereotypes, they are *both* available to *everyone*. They can be used — or misused — by anyone, male or female: it's up to us. Each worldview is not so much 'the way things are', but a *choice* which has its own consequences, its own weird twists: and as we begin to grasp this, we begin to gain more choice within the weavings of our wyrd—and the wyrd we share with others.

Everything's wyrd

Both of those worldviews are 'true'—in the appropriate context. Neither is wrong as such: but they become wrong—sometimes very wrong—if they're used inappropriately, without awareness of context. So this is where we come back to the problem of paediarchy, the challenges posed by our own childishness: because without the more adult awareness of the reality of 'Other', we'll tend to fall back, by default, into treating others either as objects to be manipulated and controlled, or as subjects which *ought* to do what we want and which we're entitled to punish if they don't. It *is* hard to give up the childish delusion that we are, and should be, and have every right to be, the centre of the universe: and one of the central themes in our society's paediarchy is that it so clearly condones over-indulgence in either the object-centred or subject-centred worldview, regardless of the damage caused. But the wyrd, in its own weird way, *can* show us when and how to use each one appropriately—*if* we let it...

From a wyrd perspective, everything is both subject *and* object—at the same time. There is 'I', and there is 'Other', and there is a boundary between them, between every 'I'; yet there is also *no* boundary — at the same time. 'I' is not that which changes, 'I' is that which *chooses*: yet this is true for *every* 'I', every 'Other'. Every 'I' is a nexus in the threads of wyrd, a clustering of choices within *every* possibility; and while each nexus is the result of personal choices, the threads of possibility are affected by *everyone's* choices. And there's always a certain amount of feedback from the wyrd about our handling of those boundaries between 'I' and 'not-I': if we treat everyone as an object, we'll find ourself being treated the same way too; if we regard everyone else as our subjects, it won't be long before we meet up with someone else who does exactly the same—or who treats us as an object instead. Yet there are also times when it *is* appropriate to treat others as objects — in an emergency, for example, when the need to get those others out to safety *now* means there's simply no time for the niceties of relationship. And there are also many times — such as in almost every group-activity, every 'We' — when it *is* appropriate to regard others as extensions of 'I': though perhaps rarely, if ever, to the extent of punishing them for failing to do what we expect.

> There've been many times when others have treated you as some kind of mindless object: looking back, in which circumstances was it appropriate for them to have done so? What was the difference in *feeling* between the times it was appropriate, and the (many) times when it wasn't?
>
> There will also have been many times when you've treated others as mindless objects: in what circumstances was it appropriate for you to have done so? (This one won't be comfortable to answer, but explore it anyway.) What was the difference in *feeling* between the times it was appropriate, and the times when it wasn't?
>
> There've been many times when others have treated you as their subject, an extension of themselves: looking back, in which circumstances was it appropriate for them to have done so? What was the difference in *feeling* between the times it was appropriate, and the (many) times when it wasn't?
>
> And, to complete the set, there'll also have been many times when you've treated others as your subjects, as extensions of yourself which *should* have been subject to your will: in what circumstances was it appropriate for you to have done so? (This one won't be comfortable to answer either, but explore it anyway.) What was the difference in *feeling* between the times it was appropriate, and the times when it wasn't?
>
> In each case, what feedback did you get from the weavings of the wyrd? What did it tell you about *your* choices in each case?
>
> If you tried to ignore it, or 'forget' it, why did you do

> so? If you didn't, what action did you take in response to
> what it showed you?

Used inappropriately, the object-centred worldview assumes too much of a boundary between 'I' and 'not-I'; the subject-centred worldview sometimes doesn't even acknowledge that any such boundary exists. Paediarchy runs rampant almost everywhere in our society; and it's an easy habit to fall back into, because we can almost always make out that someone else is to blame... So creating a balance between object and subject isn't easy. It needs awareness and respect—both of self and of others — and a willingness to move beyond the comfort-zone of stereotypes. And it also needs something which most of us shy away from at the mere mention of the word—namely *discipline*.

But 'discipline' simply means 'education', in its literal sense of 'out-leading' — drawing out the student's inner knowing. It depends on careful observation and a rigorous self-honesty: technology and science apply that observation to the 'objective' world of the shared reality, whereas the 'soft sciences', spiritual disciplines and, more recently, feminist research methodology apply the same level of careful discipline to *self*-observation and the subjective world of personal reality. In principle, that is... it often doesn't work out that way in practice, either in science or subjectivity! And discipline is *work* — in the sense we've seen earlier. Once we start to understand that 'power is the ability to *do* work' — rather than avoid it — and that this work centres around awareness and self-honesty, we begin to have choice about subjects and objects: but as usual, we also need to be aware of the twists...

> For example, weave your way past the weird contradic-
> tions of "bigger is better" and "small is beautiful", to
> create a context in which *both* are true.
> Look 'out there', to marshal the objective arguments
> for 'bigger is better': efficiencies from economies of
> scale, for example, or standardisation of results. What
> other evidence can you find? How do you assess its

truth? What *is* 'truth' in this sense?

Then look inward, to explore the emotions and feelings that express the meaning of 'small is beautiful'—the sense of inclusion, perhaps, or the absence of anonymity. What other *subjective* evidence do you find, from within yourself? How do you assess its truth? What *is* 'truth' in this sense?

Now move sideways from the stereotypes: be subjective about the 'objective' world, and vice versa. What are the *feelings* that, for you, describe 'bigger is better'? What are the *objective* arguments for 'small is beautiful'?

Now merge *all* of these viewpoints into one whole, in which the contradictions of 'bigger is better' and 'small is beautiful' can be reconciled—if only in your own experience. How do you ensure that you apply the *same* level of discipline and care to all these ways of viewing the world?

If this seems weird—which it probably does—how do you manage the 'weirdness'?

Sometimes we need a weird twist in our thinking to see what *really* works. From an object-centred perspective, for example, a light truck seems *obviously* better than a horse and cart: until we try to use that truck in the middle of the city... at which point a slightly weird approach can pay real dividends. A few English breweries still use horse-drawn wagons to deliver beer-barrels to nearby pubs, as they have done for centuries; but as the cities become ever more crowded, some companies are beginning a new 'tradition' of horse-drawn deliveries. For example, an office-equipment firm in this city recently switched back to using a horse and cart—or rather a fine pair of greys and a meticulously coach-worked dray — for its inner-city deliveries: it seems a little strange to see computers and boxes of copy-paper stacked on the back of a horse-wagon, but it works. It probably wouldn't work so well in the suburbs, but in that context it actually costs *less* to run than a light truck; no one seems to mind if the wagon stops the traffic, whereas they'd curse like crazy if a truck was double-parked in the way that the horses do; and since everyone seems to want a relationship with the horses, it helps build their relationship with the company too. In what circumstances is a horse better than a car better than a horse? Answer: it all depends...

It's hard to break free from the 'senses taker' of habit: and particularly so with habits of thought, habitual ways of looking at the world. We need to be 'non-attached' to any one worldview, but also 'non-*de*tached': and hence able, in this context, to use either the subject-centred or object-centred worldviews as *tools*— rather than being used *by* them—using awareness of context to assess their appropriacy in the moment. The crucial part is to be willing to *listen* to the feedback we get from the wyrd, from the interweavings of Reality Department—and act on those weird 'messages' that we get back. This is what the Taoists describe as 'doing no-thing', and it's *not* easy — not at first, at any rate, though it does get easier with practice.

> Non-attachment is non-detachment — letting go without letting go. Someone once told me, accurately, if a little unkindly, "You're a bag of flab held together with fears — the moment you let go of control, you collapse in a puddle on the floor." It's taken me a *lot* of practice to be able to let go of my usual wild oscillation between subject-centred and object-centred worldviews, and become more able to use them as tools — 'doing no-thing' to make it happen. The real difficulty has been that a way of seeing, or feeling, doesn't usually let us look at the way of seeing itself — like trying to look inside my own eyes *with* those same eyes!
>
> If you've read *Positively Wyrd*, you'll remember that we looked at non-attachment and non-detachment there: how well have you been able to put it into practice? How much does 'letting go without letting go' make *practical* sense to you now?

And this brings us back to that weird task of finding our 'Inner Adult': because we're most likely to get stuck in the childishness of either the object- or subject-centred worldview when we try to hide from the responsibilities of that task. The next stage of that task requires from us a deeper exploration of self-awareness and self-responsibility, in order to understand our own destructive self*ish*ness; so the next part of our weird 'toolkit' involves a closer look at responsibility and blame.

9

BLAME AND
RESPONSIBILITY

"Round and round in the usual old game... *and it's all your fault!*"
The ever-popular blame-game... see it on any street corner, in
any queue, in any office or boardroom or works canteen, any
time you like...

Blame and responsibility seem to go hand in hand: "*Who* is
responsible for this mess?" yells an irate school-teacher, as he
surveys the aftermath of a few minutes'-worth of over-exuber-
ance from his students. Which is odd, though, because in many
ways they're opposites: responsibility is, literally, 'response-
ability', the ability to respond in the present; whereas blame is
mostly concerned with the *avoidance* of responsibility—assigning
it to someone else or somewhen else.

Without responsibility, we have no power; without power,
we have no choice. It's as simple as that. So the more we try to
avoid responsibility by blaming, the less power, and less choice,
we have; the more we allow others to offload their responsibilities onto us by blaming us, the less power, and less choice, that
we *all* have available to share. So we need to separate responsibility and blame, and distinguish clearly between them: but that's
not quite as simple as it sounds...

Blaming the world

A simple question to start with: *why* does it always seem so much easier to blame — blame anyone, or anything — than to accept responsibility? It's weird...

It's been a bad day: I've had yet another one of my infamous rows with Mary at work, straight after having to deal with one of our more obnoxious clients; Kaye's blaming me for having mislaid a file that Mary says is crucial, but I know it's *her* fault that it's gone missing. And now, rushing out from the supermarket, trying to make up for lost time, I've just tripped over and dropped the whole lot on the floor. Broken eggs and broken bottles everywhere; coffee and honey and cooking-oil all mixed up with toilet tissue and breakfast cereal and Gawd only knows what else. Chaos! Panic! "Why does this always happen to me? Why is the universe conspiring against me?" I wail; but strangely enough, nobody's listening...

Stop for a moment, Chris, says an inner voice: try listening to *yourself*... might just see what's going on behind that maze of blame... So yes, I stop for a moment: the panic eases, softens. All right, yes, it's true, it *doesn't* "always happen to me": it just happens on rare occasions — like right now. And it probably wouldn't have happened if I hadn't been so busy blaming everyone else that I forgot to look where I was going. Right. There's still one heck of a mess there on the floor, but at least I'm able to respond to it now...

So go back to an incident of your own which had that same feeling of "why does this always happen to me?" Sometimes, as we've seen, there *is* an element of geis, of something which *does* "always happen to me" — but it's much more likely to have been tied up with getting lost in blame. If so, how — if at all — did you recognise that you were lost in blame — using blame to avoid your *own* responsibility? How — if at all — did you reclaim that responsibility, to deal with the task in hand?

> If you 'passed the buck' to someone else, what hap-
> pened? And how did you *feel* about what happened?

Life seems so much easier, being a victim: it's always
someone else's fault, and it's always someone else's responsibility
to fix it. Being a victim, we can blame others in the past in order
to avoid responsibility in the present: "If only they hadn't done
that to me, I'd be able to..." The catch with 'playing victim' is
that we then *need* someone else to play the Parent and do the
fixing for us: and if *everyone's* busily playing victim—locked into
'a culture of complaint', to use Robert Hughes' term — then
nothing is ever going to get fixed...

A victim is literally 'a conquered one': it's an accurate
enough label for someone who's in shock, or actively recovering
from some traumatic incident, but most of the time, bluntly,
self-styled 'victims' are more likely to be playing the blame-game
for all it's worth—if only to gain "that special attention which is
the prerogative of the miserable". What they rarely seem able to
see is that the only way out of the situation about which they're
so loudly complaining is to acknowledge their *own* responsibility
in the affair: but since that's what they—*we*—are usually most
avoiding, there tends to be an awful lot of 'round and round the
garden' before any change starts to happen...

> I'm sitting in the café on a quiet Sunday morning, when
> in storms Julie, wanting someone to talk at. "That's
> *another* lousy man I've had to get rid of out of my life!"
> she says, gesticulating wildly. "He insulted me, so I
> slapped him—I mean, what else could I do? And, d'you
> know, he not only had the nerve to get cross about it, but
> he even *threatened* me: 'I'll hit you back if you do that
> again'—that's what he said! I mean, I ask you! Why do I
> always get these creeps, Chris? That's the third time this
> year... Are *all* men bastards, or are there *any* good ones
> out there?" And a thought crosses my mind: once is
> happenstance, twice is coincidence, three times is
> enemy action... but who's 'the enemy' here? Men — or
> Julie's own reliance on blame?

She sees another friend across the way, and moves over there to pour out her tale of woe once more. But just as I breathe a sigh of relief, in walks Geoff — who does exactly the same. "*Bloody* women! Blood-sucking leeches, the lot of them!" What is it this time, Geoff? "Sarah — *you* know. All those things I gave her: I mean, she took them from me, and now she's gone. Gone off with Barry. Hope she does the same to him, the swine... Took *everything* I gave her, and never a word of thanks!" Did she *ask* you for any of it, Geoff? Did *you* ask her for anything in return? "No, I just gave it to her, didn't I, but so what? I don't know what you're on about: I mean, she *took* everything, didn't she? Bitch... Are there *any* good women out there, Chris?" And a slightly nastier thought crosses my mind: Geoff, meet Julie; Julie, meet Geoff; you've got a lot in common, you'd get on like a house on fire... literally...

Who do you know like Geoff or Julie, so busy blaming the world that they don't notice the part *they* play in creating their own mess? Why is it so easy for us to see what's really going on, but so hard for them to do so?

Stop for a moment, though, and turn this round: how much do *you* play the same blame-game as Julie and Geoff? (It'll be embarrassing to explore this, but do it anyway.) From *this* side of the mirror, it'll be hard for you to see what's going on, but much easier for others to do so; so perhaps you can use those others as 'allies', to show you how *you're* contributing to your own problems. Who could you do this with? Perhaps more to the point, who would you feel *safe* to ask to do this for you?

No one is immune from the blame-game; everyone does it to varying degrees at varying stages of their life. Ultimately, no *one* — no one individual — is ever to blame, because *everyone* is to blame: the threads of wyrd pass through us all, and we're all shirking some part of our responsibilities somewhere in there. It's not exactly comforting to face that, but at least it's honest — which blame rarely is.

The whole purpose of the blame-game is to 'export'

responsibility to others: that way, we hope we'll be able to avoid the work that being 'response-able' always involves. But Reality Department rarely lets us get away with it—although sometimes the ways with which it works back to us can be more than a little weird... One form of the blame-game begins when we 'project' onto others what *we're* feeling, but don't want to admit to, or are too embarrassed or too frightened to admit to: "What's wrong with you? Why are *you* angry?" I ask, when it's obvious that the only one who's angry is me, but I don't want to admit it. Another form of the game starts by assigning responsibility to others for what are *our* actions, our choices: "You *made* me love you! You can't leave me," I wail, carefully avoiding the possibility that my clingy dependence is not something anyone would want as part of their 'We'...

> "Why aren't you with that group any more, Chris?" asks a friend; "you were very involved with them: what happened?" "Oh, they pushed me out—did the dirty on me after all my hard work — didn't you know?" In reality, they'd done nothing of the kind: *I'd* wanted out, for a number of reasons — over-commitment elsewhere, habitual 'issue-hopping' and a short attention-span—but it's much easier to blame them than to face the embarrassing fact that *I'd* broken my promised commitment to *them*...
>
> Look back at some of your own examples of where you blame others: watch out for the feeling of embarrassment that you'll want to shove down quickly in angry blame, but which always hides the facts of your own choices in each incident. What do you learn about your choices? What other feelings are hidden behind that wall of blame?

Running away from responsibility, it always seems easiest to blame *someone*. If we run out of others to blame, well, we can always blame ourselves... But that's no solution either: since the threads of wyrd pass through everyone, blaming others is, in a weird sense, blaming ourselves, and blaming ourselves is also a way of blaming others. The real problem is not who to blame, but blame itself.

Blaming ourselves

One of the traps when we first recognise the dangers of blaming others is that we'll switch over to blaming ourselves instead — and we'll have plenty of 'encouragement' to do so... "See! You *admit* it! It *isn't* all my fault, is it? So it *must* be all *your* fault — go on, go on, admit it!" And perhaps the most popular tactic in the blame-game is the old 'all-or-nothing' trick: if you're willing to accept responsibility for anything at all, you *must* be willing to accept the blame for *everything*. It's a massive disincentive against honesty: but it does mean that once we *do* start to be a bit more honest with ourselves, it's all too easy to take on far more responsibility — and certainly far more blame — than is actually appropriate.

> Back in primary-school days. One of the pupils has pushed another's shoes into the toilet: the teacher wants to punish the culprit, so we're all stuck here until someone owns up. We wait. And wait. And wait. Two hours pass: it's obvious no one's going to admit to it. I look around once more. Oh well, *someone's* got to do something, I suppose, so it may as well be me... The teacher frankly disbelieves my 'confession', but beats me anyway — on principle, perhaps — and lets everyone else go. Do I get any thanks from the real culprit, or anyone else, for my self-chosen martyrdom? Not likely! What I get instead is a great pile of mockery — and everyone else's blame for anything they can dump on me... *Not* a wise choice...
>
> Go back to some incidents of your own where you were 'over-responsible' — for example, where you took on the responsibility for something which you didn't do, and found yourself landed with the blame instead. What did you *feel* when your well-intentioned actions went so wrong? What did you — or do you — feel towards those who were so quick to use your self-blame to dump all

> their blame on you?
>   Looking back with the advantage of hindsight, you're likely to have had *some* kind of warning from the wyrd that this kind of self-blame was not a good idea: and that 'warning' was likely to have been linked to a particular feeling. Can you yet recognise this feeling of 'impending wyrd', which you can use to warn yourself in future?

Another word for self-blame is *guilt*: and trying to take on the guilt of others—trying to emulate "the one who died to take away the sins of the world" — is rarely wise, not least because those others rarely notice anyway... So self-scapegoating is a problem; but there are other kinds of self-blame which are rather less honest. Sometimes it takes the form of 'playing victim' to *oneself*, and blaming our *own* choices in the past in order to avoid responsibility in the present: "If only *I* hadn't done that to me, I'd be able to..." Another form is a variant of that old game of trying to gain "that special attention which is the prerogative of the miserable": if no one else will blame me, so that I can complain about how unfair all this blaming is, I can probably get the same attention by blaming myself... "Oh, woe is me! Oh, I have been so foolish! Look at what I have done wrong now!"

> I know that, at school and elsewhere, I often tried to 'buy being liked' by blaming myself for everything that went wrong, for anyone: I didn't *like* some of the 'attention' I got for doing this, but at least it was attention... And it took me many years to stop blaming others for what they then 'did to me' as a result of *my* habit of self-blame — and recognise that it *was* in my choice to end the hurt, simply by ending the dishonesty of blame.
>   In what ways have you 'played victim' to *yourself*, in order to gain attention, or to avoid responsibilities in the present? What did you feel about yourself when you did this? Feeling uncomfortable about that, how much did you blame others for 'doing it to you', when in fact you *knew* it had been your own choice?

Blame helps no one. Once we start to look more closely at our own involvement in each interaction with others, it slowly becomes obvious that we *can't* blame others: as the wyrd will often show us with startling clarity, 'they' are just people, doing what people do, and making mistakes just like everyone does. But it's then essential to remember that exactly the same applies to us: we're human too, we make mistakes too, just like everyone else—and blaming *ourselves* helps no one either.

What *does* help is taking responsibility — the *appropriate* degree of 'response-ability'. Not too little—running away from responsibility — but also not too much: especially as some common ways of appearing to be helpful or over-responsible— such as the 'gatekeeper' and the 'judge'—are really little more than a subtler version of the blame-game.

The gatekeeper and the judge

A while back, we looked at how we sometimes shirk our responsibility through 'faked incompetence', pretending that we're not capable of doing some task — such as the boring household chores, or tackling the frustrations of a new computer system. But it *is* true that everyone starts out incompetent at those tasks: and we can't do better than that unless we're genuinely encouraged to find our own power and responsibility within them — which we certainly won't be able to do unless we're *allowed* to learn. What happens instead, in yet another version of the blame-game, is that someone demands that we 'should' or 'ought' or 'must' do some task or learn some new skill — and then acts as 'gatekeeper', preventing us from learning how to do the task while at the same time complaining at us, or blaming us, for having supposedly refused to do it. Because the gatekeeper holds back essential information, we *can't* do the task properly—or even at all—and hence often give up in frustration: which is then taken as 'proof' that we've faked incompetence, and ducked our responsibility. The gatekeeper probably feels equally frustrated—"Dammit, it's quicker to do it myself!'" — but often finds it easier to blame others than to notice their own involvement in the situation...

> Mary's landed me with the task of bringing Kaye up to speed on the new computer system. I must have shown her how to use it a dozen times today: but here she is again, with yet *another* question. How on earth am I supposed to do my own work with Kaye interrupting me all the time? "Look, it's simple: you click here, then you select the next record, highlight it, then do *this*" (I quickly type in a short key-sequence) "then cut-and-paste to the other file — okay?" And I'm already starting to walk back to my desk before Kaye has a chance to say 'No'...
>
> Five minutes later, she's back again, looking more frustrated than ever; and I'm fit to explode — "Why can't you work it out for yourself?", I want to scream at her; "it's *obvious*, dammit!" Just in time, though, a gentle hint comes drifting in from the wyrd: "*How* long have you been working on that system, Chris? Six months? And *how* long has Kaye been using it — six hours, perhaps? So perhaps what's obvious to you might just possibly not be obvious to her, eh?" Uh-oh... I've been playing 'gatekeeper' again, haven't I? Better show her *properly* this time — *without* blaming her for not knowing what she simply doesn't *know*; and this time find out first what *is* obvious to her, in order to find out what isn't...
>
> In what circumstances, and for what tasks, do you find yourself playing 'gatekeeper'? Childcare? Household maintenance? Something at work that you think of as your own specialty, that you're certain no one else could — or should — do as well as you? While appearing to help others learn those tasks, in what ways do you actually prevent them from doing so — and blame them for it? To resolve this problem, 'do no-thing' about it: let those quiet inner whispers from the wyrd warn you when you're doing it — and take action when you hear them!

The 'judge' is another variant of this: like the gatekeeper, it blames others for failing to do what it in effect *prevents* them from doing — but masks the dishonesty of the blame with a great deal of righteous indignation.

> Sounds like Mary's had real problems with that client again: she's in one of her fortunately-rare 'judge, jury and executioner' moods, and everyone's running for cover. She'll soon find *something* wrong to get angry about: and this time it's Kaye who's not been quick enough to get her head down. "That's just *not* good enough, Kaye!" says Mary. "You *know* that this form *must* be laid out in the way that I've said!" Kaye mumbles something... and Mary snaps back, "So what if it doesn't fit! That's *your* problem! Just *do* it!" She drops back into her 'sweet-and-reasonable' voice — "Just do as I ask, will you?" — and sweeps back to her office, putting on her smile-mask for the client as she does so. Out here, everyone else stops holding their breath — and we turn to the shell-shocked Kaye, to help her recover from The Judge...
>
> Not pleasant... but it'll probably be even less pleasant to turn this round, and face what's *really* been going on in those times where *you've* played The Judge... What was your righteous indignation there being used to hide — from others, or from yourself?

There's a weird twist to this. Most people's idea of a judge seems to be that of someone in authority, with the right to have power over us: but the problem is exactly that, namely 'power-over'. In a more practical sense, 'judgement' is about the development of skills and awareness — appropriacy, rather than abstract 'truth' — so the functional role of a 'judge' is not to judge as such, but to help *others* develop their own judgement: power-*with*, not power-over. So the more authority we gain, the more responsibility is placed on us to mediate *with* others, and the *less* right we have to judge others — which is not quite how most people in 'authority' positions tend to see it... Yet successful leaders, and successful relationships, depend on awareness of that twist.

I remember, a few years back, watching a classic example of

how *not* to do it—*playing* at 'judge', rather than *being* that role. It was at a kind of conference, somewhat political, but there were also schools delegates there—even some from primary schools —so part of a formal agreement signed by each delegate was a commitment not to use 'offensive language'. Unfortunately, one of the organisers—taking an overly subject-centred attitude, as tends to happen at such events — decided that 'offensive language' included *any* comment which in any way disagreed with his own personal politics: so he felt that he was not only within his rights, but righteously correct, to publicly eject from the conference anyone whose words—or presence—he disliked. A few people questioned his behaviour: this too was deemed 'offensive language', and he demanded their instant removal too. Quite soon the discussions became quite heated—some of it using a great deal of offensive language! — but eventually the organiser's 'judge'-game was brought to a halt: especially as the event's main theme was supposed to be 'freedom of speech'...

> "I disagree with every word you say, but I will defend to the death your right to say it": how easy is it for you to follow this old maxim about freedom of speech? To what extent do you want to control others' thoughts as well as their actions — or for them to control *their* thoughts to conform to *your* beliefs, which comes to the same thing?

Maintaining true freedom of speech is always going to be difficult. The political-correctness movement, for example, started with the laudable aim of creating 'non-offensive language', to reduce habitual disparagement of minorities. But it soon fell into that trap of playing The Judge, issuing ever-more-tortuous tirades of blame, and demanding increasingly harsh 'anti-vilification' laws to vilify 'offenders', until eventually it became clear that its tactics were, in reality, even more oppressive than the original supposed 'offensive language', and the whole movement collapsed into self-parody, where it remains to this day. A single thread of wyrd, complete with the weird twist —its geis—through which it comes to its end... The *aim* of the movement was right, and responsible; where it went wrong—the choice which was never faced—was in its dependence on blame.

Dancing with responsibility

Responsibility is not something which can be dumped on others, but is a dance with *ourselves*—a dance with our own choices, and our own 'mis-takes'. One shift in perspective that's important to make is to recognise that responsibility is about *our* responses—and no one else's. If I take offence at something you've said, it's *my* response to your comments—not something you've done 'to' me—so I need to understand that the 'response-ability' to act on that response lies with *me*, not you. Anything else is blame, which doesn't work: all it does is build more walls.

The aim here is to move from 'you-statements' — "You insulted me!" — to 'I-statements' — "I feel offended by what you've just said." That shift in perspective usually feels weird at first — 'I-statements' can sound pompous and stilted, and can seem much more difficult to say, mainly because we're accepting that the responsibility *is* on us rather than on 'the Other'. Weird though it may feel, it *does* work: a 'you-statement' builds walls of projection and blame, but an 'I-statement' opens a doorway, and creates a space for negotiation. I still don't *like* what you've said: but you're not an object, so I can't force you to 'take back your words'; and you're not my subject, so I can't demand that you change yourself to suit my whims. You're you; I'm me; 'We' has a disagreement; let's talk about it...

"You insulted me!" Try watching the way you interact with others: notice how many 'you-statements' you use in a single day; notice how many walls you build or reinforce that way...

So shift your perspective, and try to reframe those 'you-statements' into 'I-statements' — statements about what *you* feel, not what you think the other person did. Notice how much easier it is to blame others instead... so what is it that 'I-statements' demand from *you*? At first, it's probably safest to practice this in private, such as in a personal diary; but aim to find the courage to put it into practice in public. When you first do so, don't be surprised if the initial response is one of mockery and disbelief—which will hurt. But if you can, persist, bearing always in mind that this is *your* 'response-ability': then notice the weird 'negotiations' that begin to happen...

What we're doing here is working with projection and export—both our own and that of others. The purpose of the shift to 'I-statements', weird though they feel, is partly to provide enough awareness of our own self to enable us to identify the *degree* of our responsibility—and hence our appropriate 'response-ability' — and also to prevent us from responding in kind when others blame us. With that awareness, we watch the feedback: both directly from those others, and also from the more tortuous twists by which we get feedback from the wyrd.

Projection and export depend on blame—in many ways *are* blame — and also depend on playing dishonest games with boundaries. The first part of the game is a switch to a subject-centred view, to dissolve genuine boundaries and drag in some 'other': "It wasn't me that broke the plate—it was my hand," says a friend's small son. The 'other'—whatever or whoever it may be—is then assigned the *entire* blame for the incident: "It was my hand that did it!" exclaims the boy. And the export is completed by switching back to an object-centred view, slamming the boundary shut by making the other 'Other' again: the boy looks down at his hand, and slaps it, saying "Naughty hand! — you musn't *never* do that again!" — so it's now the hand's responsibility, not his...

Disentangling these weird webs of projection and blame can take a lot of work—and lot of honesty. "We've been trying to get the co-op going for ages, but nothing seems to happen," says Kim. "Last week one man said, 'I don't know where my commitment is with this. I don't think we've any chance to get anything together till next summer.' And it felt like it just cut everyone off at the knees: an abandonment, a betrayal. He didn't turn up to last night's meeting, but I had to go into the pub then to make a phone-call: and there he was, glaring at me with eyes of hate—that's what it felt like, anyway. But I know I'm angry with him: so is this 'hate' I perceive genuinely his, Chris, or something I've projected onto him? I just don't know..."

The way to resolve this is simply to *ask* — build comm*uni*cation—starting with an 'I-statement'. Not quite as simple as it sounds, though: for example, if the other person doesn't want to communicate—share 'response-ability'—then we have to accept that this *is* their choice, no matter what we may feel about it...

When someone 'refuses to communicate', what do you *feel*? In what ways do you try to *force* them to 'communicate'—even though it can't be true comm*uni*cation? What does it take for you to move beyond blame, to allow them to communicate in *their* way—and also accept that a refusal to communicate is itself a communication?

There are a few tricks that can make this shift to 'response-ability' easier—even though, in the usual weird way, they actually demand more from *us*. One of the most useful—though often most challenging — is to assume that people's intentions are good, even where their actions seem to be otherwise. For example, since everyone had agreed not to use 'offensive language', back at that political conference, it would have been useful to assume that if they then used 'offensive language', it was by mistake—a 'mis-take'—rather than by intention. If I take offence at what's said, that's *my* response, not something they've done to me; and it's up to *me* to say so, and accept the feedback that I get.

Even where they're nominally 'wrong' — such as by breaking an agreement about not using 'offensive language' — my only 'right' is to negotiate, not blame. Once is happenstance: however well-intentioned we may be, 'mis-takes' *do* happen. Twice is coincidence: sometimes we *do* have to repeat our objections before they're heard—and it's up to us to ensure that they *are* heard. So it's useful to assume that it's only when it gets to be three or more times that it's likely to be intentional — at which point we may indeed need to suspect a possible 'enemy action'...

Even then, it's wise to be wary about thinking in terms of 'punishment': it's true that some people, and some situations, can be abusive, but it's not going to help anyone if we just add to the abuse with an over-zealous 'mis-take' of our own. Uncomfortable though it may be, it's time we looked more closely at the problem of abuse—and our own 'response-ability' within it.

10

USE AND ABUSE

We're not alone: we share this world with others—many, many others, human and otherwise. And there are many things that we simply cannot do on our own (one of the more obvious being reproduction, which at *some* point must still involve both a male and a female of the species!), and many others which we'd prefer not to do on our own. Some of our 'use' of those others can be difficult for us to face: for example, like every animal, we survive by killing and eating something else—even vegetarians and other herbivores do this, although the fact of the killing is often sidestepped because plants show no easily-visible emotions...

We *use* others, and others use us: it's a fact of life — a normal and necessary part of life — and we don't have much choice about it. Where we *do* have choice is in *how* we use, or are used: and also a choice as to whether our use of, or by, or *with* others oversteps a subtle boundary, and becomes abuse.

Abuse isn't something that 'just happens'. It isn't even something that 'just happens' *to* us. It's *always* linked to a choice on our part: true, it's often the result of a choice to evade responsibility, or of a habit of evading choices, but even that, as we've seen earlier, is still a choice. The wyrd passes through everywhere, everyone, everywhen: every thread, every moment, is made up of *choices*—and those inevitable, inexorable twists... So it's up to us: whether we use, or abuse, is up to us—and we're always responsible for that choice. That alone can be hard enough to face: yet facing the other side of that coin—that it's just as much up to us as to whether we're used, or abused—can be the harshest twist of all.

The problem of abuse—and particularly our own involvement in it—is probably going to be the most uncomfortable part of the wyrd that we'll ever face. There'll be parts of this section that you certainly won't want to look at—other than to blame others for it (or me, perhaps). But it *is* important to face this: because it's in this one issue that most of us so easily lose most of our power. Only once we understand what's going on, and our own involvement in it, do we start to reclaim our power —our power of choice, our power *with* others, and our own power-from-within.

Use and power

The boundary between use and abuse is essentially a problem of power—power-with and power-from-within being on one side of the boundary, and power-over and power-under on the other.

> To make sense of what's going on here, you'll need to have a *practical* grasp of the issues about power and fear that we looked at earlier. It might be a good idea to stop for a moment, to go back and review the practical examples in that section, before moving on.

The problem is that we *want* to be used: it's more than just a want, it's a deep spiritual *need*, a central part of that 'sense of meaning and purpose, a sense of self and of that which is greater than self'. Being used—especially, being acknowledged in practice for what we do and how we express who we are—is essential to our well-being: so much so that for many men, and now increasingly for women too, the loss of employment can literally take away their reason for living. But we want to be used *appropriately*; we want to be used with respect, with honour, with integrity; yet we live in a society which barely understands any of those concepts...

How do *you* want to be used? How do you want to use others? In what ways do you *like* being used? What is the *feeling* you experience when you know that your skills, your knowledge, your sense of self, are being used by you and by others appropriately and with respect? Where, within you, do you feel this?

How do you *not* want to be used? How do you not want to use others? What is the feeling when you, or someone else, crosses that boundary from use into abuse?

In what ways *are* you used by yourself, and by others? In what ways do *you* use others — 'borrow' their skills and knowledge, use their time and other resources, or whatever?

Looking wider, in what ways do others — people you know, people you just hear of or read about — use or abuse others? In what weird ways does society condone, or even incite, some kinds of abuse? Find your own examples, but there's a simple clue: look closely at the common usage of the word 'power'...

As we've seen earlier, power is best understood as the ability to do work, as an expression of choice. Since it's closely linked with personal choice, the only real source of power is from within ourselves — our own 'power-from-within' — though it can also arise as 'power-with', from our interweavings with others — in effect, from the choices made by 'We', rather than only by 'I'. Anything else is likely to be abuse... it's as simple as that. Any attempt to shuffle responsibility onto others without their explicit consent is abuse; any attempt to prop ourselves up by putting others down is also abuse — and that includes getting together as a group to put others down, which is not power-with, but a collective form of power-over, or more often power-under. These are all extremely common...

So the fact of abuse shouldn't be a surprise: in the terms I'm using here, many aspects of our society — such as those countless advertising campaigns which depend on fear — are inherently abusive; and with paediarchy running rampant, and true self-honesty being the exception rather than the norm, it could hardly be otherwise. Most relationships have a few threads of abuse running through them somewhere; some relationships —personal, professional, familial or whatever—may have more than just a few of those threads... But there's a simple reason for this: *we're all human*. And human abuse, and human violence, arise from a perfectly human mistake: evading 'response-ability'. *No one* is immune from this mistake; so no one is immune from abuse, or is free from responsibility for abuse.

And despite the well-meant wishes of so many would-be social engineers, we'll never eliminate abuse. For it not to exist would require every aspect of the world — every adult, every child, even every animate and inanimate entity — to be fully responsible and fully 'in control' of themselves at all times: it's not an achievable goal... Like use itself, abuse is a thread of the wyrd — a major thread — which passes through everything, everyone, everywhere, everywhen: we can never *control* it as such —but we *do* have the choice to direct how it impacts on our own lives, and the lives of those around us. For example, we can play 'victim' if we so choose: but as we've seen, it doesn't actually help *anyone*, especially ourselves. A wiser choice, perhaps, would be to accept, and aim to work *with*, that weird comment that "The world breaks us all—but afterwards some of us are strong in the broken places." Yet it's up to us: there's always a choice, there's always a twist — though sometimes the twists of abuse can be very tangled indeed...

Context and consent

One of the weirder twists is that there's no such thing as 'abusive behaviour': what makes a given action—or inaction—abusive is the *context*, not the behaviour itself. For example, hitting someone obviously sounds like abuse: but if you're in a full-blown panic in a burning building, it's quite possible that the *safest* action for a rescuer, both for you and for themselves, would be to hit you hard enough to knock you out — because then they can get you to safety without your panic getting in the way... And sometimes the *absence* of behaviour is abusive: if you're in desperate need of help, and I sit back and do nothing, smiling smugly at your predicament, that would be abuse — it certainly couldn't be called power-with, at any rate! What matters is the context, and the *consent* to be used in that way. As long as there's clear consent (preferably conscious consent, though at times, such as with children, or in some kinds of emergency, it isn't always practicable or possible), *anything goes*: it's entirely up to us what behaviour we choose to *share* with others.

> Most sports involve a kind of 'play-fighting', a weird cross between competition and co-operation. And some people seem to *need* to play-fight, and to wrestle: as long as it remains a game, by mutual consent, anything goes—and it's *use*, not abuse, because it helps all those involved to find, and extend, the limits of their power and their 'response-ability'.
>
> "Yeah, I really *like* fightin' with me old man," said Lisa to me the other day, "'S'great fun! And we both really get into it, too! The other day," she said, grinning, "he trod on me foot by mistake and I couldn't duck out the way, an' he caught me a great big wallop on the face. Gave me a great big bruise, too... We're always yellin' and screamin' at each other — we have a great time, but Gawd knows what the neighbours think!" Which is a valid point, because in another context exactly the same kind of 'fighting' could have a very different edge, and be all too real.
>
> In what ways do *you* 'play-fight' with others? What do you *feel* when you play that edge between co-operation and competition, between sharing and selfishness?
>
> The game collapses as soon as anyone takes it too seriously—stops seeing it as a *game*—and tries to 'take control', to gain power-over others, or manipulate their defeat through power-under.
>
> What do you *feel* when the game collapses in that way? What do *you* feel towards the 'giggle-wrecker' — the one who took the game too seriously, and spoiled it

for everyone? When you've been the one who made that 'mis-take', what do you feel towards yourself? And how much do you try to cover up those feelings by blaming others instead...?

Another key part of the context is the distinction between fear and respect. The image comes to mind of a stereotyped 'little old lady' character driving a huge bulldozer down a suburban street: she has enormous power at this moment, and enormous 'response-ability'—and the choices are hers, not ours. Watching her smooth but inexorable progress down the street, what do *we* feel? Respect for her skills?—that's power-with, and acknowledging her power-from-within. Or a hint of unacknowledged fear? — which might lead us to want to take control (power-over), or to mock or belittle her (power-under) until she gives up. The key here is *trust*: when we don't trust, it's fear; when we do trust, it's respect—or possibly foolishness...!

"The key here is *trust*": what's *your* response to someone not trusting you, or respecting your skills and abilities? When others don't trust you, and try to take control, or to mock or belittle what you've done, what do you *feel*? Are you likely to respond in kind, with your own attempts at power-over or power-under?

Now turn this round: what are others' responses to you when you don't trust them, and try to put them down? Notice how quickly the abuse can echo back and forth... Yet in what conditions do you *not* get a similar response in kind? What happens then to that apparently endless cycle of mutual put-downs?

Twist this a little further: what's your response when someone *does* acknowledge your skills and abilities? When others *do* trust you, and *don't* try to take control, or to mock or belittle what you've done, what do you *feel*? Are you likely to respond in kind, with renewed respect of those others' skills and abilities? How difficult do you find it to trust their apparent respect of you? If you don't trust, what do you do — and what happens then?

So notice the choices you have here: we *always*

> have the choice to change a situation for better or worse
> —the twist is in what it asks from us!

And a further twist in the context of use and abuse is gender—social stereotypes about sex-differences. There are *some* differences—as a friend put it, about both use and abuse, "He was stronger, but I was more persistent!" — yet in reality the differences between the sexes are much less than the differences between individual women, and between individual men. One of the most serious mistakes is to stereotype abuse as something that only men do: abuse is a *human* fault, not a gendered one. An earlier generation of feminists — writers like Germaine Greer and Betty Friedan—acknowledged this: they promoted women's power and women's responsibility, yet were equally aware of women's potential for abuse. But it's a point which, in their rush to blame men for everything, has been conveniently forgotten by more recent cuckoo-feminists... a mistake which, by the usual weird twists, is more likely in the long term to drag women back down into powerlessness again than anything men could do — because responsibility and power are inextricably interwoven, and cannot exist without each other. ('Cuckoo-feminism'? It looks like the real thing but hatches out into a childish monster that destroys everything for which feminism once stood.) The subject-centred stupidity we call 'sexism' goes both ways, not one: and it always hurts *everyone*, not just the ones who are blamed...

Stereotypes can be useful, but help no one if they're taken too literally: so in many of my examples I've deliberately shown women using power-with in positions of authority—their *use* of others — and also resorting to power-over and power-under in their abuse of others. In facing their own role in abuse, men do have the advantage of knowing that they're at least responsible for *something*; but for some decades now, women have been taught to believe that they're never responsible for anything they do, and particularly not for anything done 'to' them. So you may find this next section particularly hard to face—especially as you may not see much relief until well into the following section... But abuse—and our own involvement in it—is something that we *must* face if we want to find our own power, and especially our power to share *with* others: because whenever we're abused by ourselves or others, or abuse others or ourselves, *that's* where most of our power is lost. That's the twist: that's the choice... it's up to us.

Facing abuse *does* take courage, so stick with it as best you can: but *do* be gentle with yourself. Stop for a while, if the going seems to get too rough; and then come back to it again when the courage returns—as it always does. Just keep going, keep going, one step at a time...

Threads of abuse

We use others, and ourselves, to get what we want and need—that's how we survive. Sometimes it *is* just 'survival'... But an awareness of how the wyrd works, in order to work *with* it, can help to change that into being *alive*—and a central part of that awareness is in knowing how to change abuse into mutual, respectful, *use*.

Use takes many different forms, but always has the same intention: to create something which is *shared*, and in which everyone 'wins'. In much the same way, abuse takes many different forms, yet always has the same intention: to offload responsibility or fear onto others—the aim is to 'win' by making others lose, but in reality, courtesy of the usual weird twists, *everyone* loses.

And abuse is much the same for both men and women: women tend to be a bit more personal and a bit more subtle than men, but it comes to much the same in the end... This makes sense in terms of those gender-stereotypes: a stereotyped 'masculine' abuse would be object-centred, and follow the 'hunter' stereotype of small numbers of large, visible actions—which are easily identifiable, and easily labelled as abusive; whereas a stereotyped 'feminine' abuse would be subject-centred, and follow the 'gatherer' stereotype of large numbers of small actions, each one individually deniable, apparently trivial, and easily dismissed as 'ordinary relationship problems', but often adding up to greater overall damage than the 'masculine' forms.

> Stereotypes about 'masculine' and 'feminine' abuse can be useful, but as usual we need to be wary about taking them too literally. In particular, its important not to make the mistake of assuming that 'masculine', in this sense, means 'male', or that 'feminine' means 'female'—they're stereotypes, and nothing more. For example, think back to your own experiences of childhood bullying: open carefully that closet of memories about the pupils you feared the most... Which of the girls typified 'masculine' abuse, hitting others, using direct threats and intimidation to get their own way? Which of the boys typified 'feminine' abuse, mocking and deriding others, or—that most feared of all forms of bullying—spreading rumours about you?
>
> This time we won't look at how you did the same: that will probably begin to be all too obvious anyway... if memories about that do re-emerge, don't push them down again, but just notice them, accept them, and quietly move on...

Physical abuse can be a serious problem, but at least its effects are visible. Non-physical abuse is often much more difficult to tackle, precisely because its effects are *not* so visible—which also makes it much more difficult to get help, or even to heal, because there's so little that's visible on the surface. We *can* make some comparisons, and there are some well-known metaphors for this: we might talk about a 'cutting remark', for example; an insult is 'a slap in the face'; a man was 'broken' by his supervisor's constant put-downs. But because non-physical abuse *is* so difficult to describe, I tend to look more at how long it takes someone to return to constructive creativity ('constructive' because some people's creativity is turned towards further abuse...)—in other words reclaiming power-from-within and power-with, rather than turning that power against oneself or against others as power-over or power-under.

In those terms, like everyone else, I've suffered my share of both kinds of abuse—physical and otherwise—from others. For example, I've been beaten up by a man who wanted to hurt his ex-girlfriend, and found me an easier target; but that took only days to begin to heal, whereas it took me many months to begin to recover after a woman deliberately brought me to the edge of a nervous breakdown in order to give herself an illusion of superiority. And one of the worst forms of non-physical abuse —the most difficult to respond to or to defend oneself against —is 'third-party abuse', giving a false or incomplete story to set up a third party, such as a teacher, a supervisor, a welfare official, or another family member—"I'll tell my big brother on you!"— to carry out abuse on our behalf: most stories must be taken on trust, so the real abuser—*us*, if we're the ones who provided the false story—can easily evade all responsibility, and blame others for the entire incident...

None of this is simple. It's rare that there's a single easily identifiable 'abuser' and 'victim': what there is instead is a weird web of interactions and 'mis-takes', weaving its way through many different people, and often spanning many generations. "I sometimes wish my father *had* hit me in those adolescent arguments of ours," said a sad friend, going back over her childhood issues. "At least it would have released that awful *tension*, constantly holding back his anger... it killed him in the end..." Codependent relationships are often mutually abusive, with each party oscillating between abuser and abused; Transactional Analysis theory also recognises the role played by an 'enabler' who appears to take no active part in the battles, but condones the abuse — or self-abuse — by at least one of the other parties, and helps to maintain the blame-game.

So the usual approach to the problem of abuse — find someone to blame, and then punish them—is often worse than useless: *everyone* is to blame, and punishment is just another form of third-party abuse... What *does* work is to shift from blame to responsibility: be honest about our *own* part in each incident— courtesy of the interweavings of the wyrd, there's *always* some— and find our own power to respond, to change the weaving of that thread for everyone. That's what 'response-ability' means.

Any practical approach to the problem of abuse has to begin by accepting its inevitability as part of the human condition: we're all human, and everyone makes 'mis-takes'... To learn how to minimise abuse, and to help others and ourselves recover from it, is *everyone's* responsibility. But it *is* true that most abusive behaviour comes from habits passed down through the generations: and it's unreasonable to blame others, or ourselves, for what they, and we, have been taught. Yet if the sins of the fathers (and mothers) are fetched even unto the seventh generation, then it's also true that if we manage to face more than a seventh of our familial 'bad habits', we're doing better than the average—and that at least is an achievable target!

So let's make a start at this. We already know a number of key points: for example, we know that true power — power-from-within, power-with—cannot co-exist with abuse—power-over and power-under — and it's up to *us* to choose which we want. (There are some weird twists that can get in the way, of course, but the choice *is* still ours, and is always there.) And we know that abuse generally arises from a felt sense of power*less*-ness, and from a socially condoned delusion that it is possible to 'export' this sense of powerlessness to others, and that to abuse others in this way *is* 'power'.

What we *feel* is not an issue here: feelings such as anger, sadness, love and joy arise from the fact of being human, and pretending that we don't feel what we feel usually causes damage, to self and often also to others. What *is* at issue is how we *respond* to those feelings — literally, our 'response-ability'. Whatever we do 'to' others eventually weaves back through the wyrd into our own lives: so it's a good idea to learn to take that responsibility seriously—yet also not *too* seriously!

Our feelings are ours, not anyone else's; nor are they

anyone else's responsibility. Uncomfortable as it may well feel, no one has a 'right' to not be afraid, or to not experience feelings such as embarrassment or shame: and any attempt to offload responsibility for fear or other feelings onto others is not only counter-productive, but is actually a form of abuse. We can be responsible *about* others' fears, but we cannot be responsible *for* them — a subtle but crucial distinction; and since one of the most common sources of abuse is a 'pre-emptive strike' against an imagined threat, we also have 'response-ability' to learn to distinguish clearly between real and imagined threats, and to respond appropriately to each.

The aim here is simply to explore our *own* involvement in abuse, whether to us or by us; and what we *don't* do matters as much as what we do. In a sense, as we'll see, what others do or don't do eventually becomes almost irrelevant: like all the threads of the wyrd, the threads of abuse pass through everywhere, everywhen, everyone, but the only place we can change them directly is within us, and the only behaviour we can change directly is our own. That's *our* 'response-ability': nothing more, but also nothing less.

Although abuse can occur in *any* context, and in any form, the standard legal summary is the 'Duluth Wheel', developed by the Duluth Domestic Abuse Intervention Project, in Duluth, Minnesota. This divides abuse into eight categories: coercion and threats; intimidation; economic abuse; emotional abuse; abusing privilege; isolation; third-party abuse ('using children' in the original); and minimising, denying and blaming. Unfortunately, the original version can only be described as sexist, because it was written solely for men, with women as the only examples of 'victims': but with one small change, to make it gender-neutral, we can use it for our wider and weirder purpose here — we'll need a little imagination and a little courage, but that's all.

Use the examples in the eight boxes that follow to explore your *own* involvement in abuse: go through your memories to remind yourself of your and others' behaviour which would fit that category of abuse, and your own responses to and interactions with that behaviour. The temptation here may be to rush it, or to blame others (or even to skip the whole thing entirely!) but *don't*: because the more carefully you do this, the more you'll be able to see how you lose *your* power in abuse, and the more you'll be able to reclaim it.

In each of the examples, I've used the generic term 'Other' to indicate the supposed 'victim' of the abuse. But if we keep it generic, we'll probably learn nothing: so the key point here is to *make it personal*. Read each example several times, each time substituting a different person—a former partner, perhaps, or a work-colleague. Don't just use 'her', or 'him': use their *name* as you read it. And always use your *own* name at least once, to explore abuse done *to* you...

When looking at abuse done *by* you, notice how easy it is to hide by blaming others: "Look, she started it, she hit me first." When this happens, bring the focus back to *you*, and your 'response-ability': imagine someone saying to you, "Yes, we accept that that's your experience, and we neither agree nor disagree: we're asking you what *you* could do to change the situation to something better for *both* of you if it happens again."

When looking at abuse done *to* you, you'll probably find instead that there's a tendency to blame yourself: "He always tells me it's my fault, so I suppose I must be to blame." When this happens, bring the focus back to *you*, and *your* power, to find alternatives which are responsible rather than blaming: "Yes, we accept that that's what you were told, and we neither agree nor disagree: we're asking you what *you* could do — what power *you* have — to change the situation to something better for *both* of you if it happens again."

None of this is likely to be easy or comfortable, but you won't be able to understand your 'response-ability' — and hence your own weird power *with* others — unless you work your way through this. Be gentle with yourself, be careful with yourself, yet "feel the fear, and do it anyway"!

In each of these categories of abuse, there's an attempt to 'control' the Other directly — through power-over — or to manipulate the Other — through power-under — to 'control' *themselves* on our behalf. Some categories are more object-centred, others more subject-centred; some are more 'masculine', others are more 'feminine'; but ultimately it's all the same. In each case I've also summarised the opposite of that type of abuse — a constructive approach to the same issues — though we'll look at them in more detail in the next section.

The first, and most physical, category is *coercion and threats*; its opposite is 'negotiation and fairness'.

> Coercion and threats include: physical assault of any kind — including any hit or slap — to the Other; making and/or carrying out threats to do something to hurt the Other; threatening to leave the Other, to commit suicide, to report the Other to welfare, police, employers, teachers or other external 'authorities'; making the Other withdraw complaints; and making the Other do illegal or other 'forbidden' acts.
>
> What is *your* involvement in such behaviour? Who is 'the Other' here? Seeing your own involvement in these types of abuse, how could you respond differently? What is *your* 'response-ability' here?
>
> The opposite is negotiation and fairness, which includes: seeking mutually satisfying resolutions to conflict with the Other; accepting change; being willing to compromise with the Other.
>
> What is *your* involvement in such behaviour? Who is 'the Other' here? Seeing your own involvement in these types of constructive behaviour, how could you create the same in the abusive situations above? What is *your* 'response-ability' here?

The next category is *intimidation*; its opposite is 'non-threatening behaviour'. Like coercion, it's often mis-stereotyped as 'male': for example, one friend described to me her mother's 'normal' behaviour in exactly these terms...

WYRD ALLIES

> Intimidation includes: making the Other afraid by using looks, actions, gestures; smashing things; destroying the Other's property; abusing pets and other animals as a threat to the Other; and displaying weapons (for example, brandishing a kitchen-knife). What is *your* involvement in such behaviour? Who is 'the Other' here? Seeing your own involvement in these types of abuse, how could you respond differently? What is *your* 'response-ability' here?
>
> The opposite is non-threatening behaviour, which includes: talking and acting so that both self and the Other feel safe and comfortable expressing themselves and doing things, both in their own ways and with each other. What is *your* involvement in such behaviour? Who is 'the Other' here? Seeing your own involvement in these types of constructive behaviour, how could you create the same in the abusive situations above? What is *your* 'response-ability' here?

Next we come to *economic abuse*, whose counterpart is 'economic co-operation'. Because of the still-prevalent stereotypes about economic roles, this is another category of abuse that has strong gender-overtones: but as before, it works *both* ways...

> Economic abuse includes: preventing the Other from getting or keeping a job; making the Other ask for money; giving the Other a restricted or conditional 'allowance'; taking the Other's money (including trapping the Other into a 'provider' role); and concealing nominally shared resources from the Other (such as not letting family Others know about or have access to family income). What is *your* involvement in such behaviour? Who is 'the Other' here? Seeing your own involvement in these types of abuse, how could you respond differently? What is *your* 'response-ability' here?
>
> The opposite is economic partnership, which includes: making money decisions together; and making sure both self and the Other benefit from mutual financial

> arrangements. What is *your* involvement in such behaviour? Who is 'the Other' here? Seeing your own involvement in these types of constructive behaviour, how could you create the same in the abusive situations above? What is *your* 'response-ability' here?

And the next category — whose opposite is 'respect' — is *emotional abuse*. This is often type-cast as 'female' rather than 'male', but it is, interestingly, reported as the type of abuse most feared by schoolboys from other boys. This is often the most difficult type of abuse to face, because it can take such subtle forms: it's characterised by subject-centred 'magic' words like 'should' and 'ought' and 'must', which are all too easily abused to export blame and responsibility — and as John Bradshaw warned, 'resentment' is, in effect, "a demand that the Other should feel guilty"...

> Emotional abuse includes: putting the Other down; making the Other feel bad about themself; calling the Other names; making the Other think they're crazy; playing mind-games (such as setting up a double-bind for the Other); humiliating the Other; attempting to control the Other's feelings, or to force the Other to control or deny their feelings; and making the Other feel guilty. What is *your* involvement in such behaviour? Who is 'the Other' here? Seeing your own involvement in these types of abuse, how could you respond differently? What is *your* 'response-ability' here?
>
> The opposite is respect, which includes: listening to the Other non-judgmentally; being emotionally affirming and understanding, both of self and the Other; accepting and acknowledging the needs, concerns, feelings and fears of both self and the Other; and valuing opinions of both self and the Other. What is *your* involvement in such behaviour? Who is 'the Other' here? Seeing your own involvement in these types of constructive behaviour, how could you create the same in the abusive situations above? What is *your* 'response-ability' here?

The next category is even more subject-centred: it assumes

a right or *privilege* — literally, 'owning the law' — to control the Other's behaviour. Its opposite is 'shared responsibility' — power-with, in other words.

> Abusing privilege includes: treating the Other like a servant; excluding the Other from major decisions that concern them; acting like the 'owner' of the Other — assuming 'authority' from social stereotypes; and attempting to be the one to define male and female roles, or other social or familial roles. What is *your* involvement in such behaviour? Who is 'the Other' here? Seeing your own involvement in these types of abuse, how could you respond differently? What is *your* 'response-ability' here?
>
> The opposite is shared responsibility, which includes: mutually agreeing with the Other on a fair distribution of work and responsibilities; and making family and other group decisions together. What is *your* involvement in such behaviour? Who is 'the Other' here? Seeing your own involvement in these types of constructive behaviour, how could you create the same in the abusive situations above? What is *your* 'response-ability' here?

And the next category is so subject-centred that it refuses to allow 'We' to be anything other than its own 'I' — and hence tries to force the Other into *isolation* from anything 'not-I'. What's missing, of course, is the opposite, which is 'trust and support'.

> Isolation-abuse includes: controlling what the Other does, who the Other sees and talks to, what the Other reads, where the Other goes; limiting the Other's involvements and interests outside of the relationship; and using jealousy or envy to justify actions against the Other. What is *your* involvement in such behaviour? Who is 'the Other' here? Seeing your own involvement in these types of abuse, how could you respond differently? What is *your* 'response-ability' here?

> The opposite is trust and support, which includes: supporting both self and the Other's goals in life; and respecting self and the Other's right to their own feelings, friends, activities and opinions. What is *your* involvement in such behaviour? Who is 'the Other' here? Seeing your own involvement in these types of constructive behaviour, how could you create the same in the abusive situations above? What is *your* 'response-ability' here?

The next category is what the Duluth group called *using children*, but is more generically the use — or *ab*use — of nominally-uninvolved third-parties such as children on the one hand, or 'authorities' on the other, as a tactic in intimidation or emotional abuse of the Other — and particularly the use of those third-parties as a shield while abusing the Other. With children, the opposite is 'responsible parenting'; with others, the opposite is simply being responsible—and honest.

> Using children for third-party abuse includes: making the Other feel guilty about the children; using the children to relay messages; using visitation (after divorce) to harass the Other; and threatening to take the children away—to isolate the Other from the children. (As you explore this category, expand it to include similar types of third-party abuse, such as using others to relay messages, at school or at work.) What is *your* involvement in such behaviour? Who is 'the Other' here? Seeing your own involvement in these types of abuse, how could you respond differently? What is *your* 'response-ability' here?
>
> The opposite is responsible parenting, which includes: sharing parental responsibilities; and being a positive non-violent role model for the children. (Again, expand this category outward into other contexts if you can.) What is *your* involvement in such behaviour? Who is 'the Other' here? Seeing your own involvement in these types of constructive behaviour, how could you create the same in the abusive situations above? What is *your* 'response-ability' here?

And the final category is *minimising, denying and blaming*, whose opposite is 'honesty and accountability'. Perhaps the most extreme example of this that I know was described to me by my friend Rob, an engineering technician. He and another man had been working late one night, so he gave the friend a ride home; as they were standing in the kitchen, the man's wife started to berate him about something—Rob didn't remember what—and at some point the man said "I'm not going to argue with you about this, you don't know what you're talking about." As he turned to walk away, the woman grabbed a heavy cast-iron skillet from off the worktop and, as Rob put it, gave the man "a great big whack round the back of the head with it, which laid him straight out on the floor." As the man lay there, groaning, the woman dropped the skillet, ran over to him, and screamed "You stupid idiot! It's all your fault! You shouldn't have said that!— now look at what you've made me do!"

> Minimising, denying and blaming includes: making light of the abuse and not taking the Other's concerns about it seriously; saying the abuse didn't happen; shifting responsibility for abusive behaviour; saying that the Other caused it; and attempting to convince the Other that they deserved to be abused. What is *your* involvement in such behaviour? Who is 'the Other' here? Seeing your own involvement in these types of abuse, how could you respond differently? What is *your* 'response-ability' here?
>
> The opposite is honesty and accountability, which includes: accepting responsibility *for* self, and *about* the Other; acknowledging past use of abuse; both self and Other feeling safe in admitting being wrong; and communicating openly and truthfully with the Other. What is *your* involvement in such behaviour? Who is 'the Other' here? Seeing your own involvement in these types of constructive behaviour, how could you create the same in the abusive situations above? What is *your* 'response-ability' here?

That's abuse. But the opposite of abuse is not just 'use', it's how we get to be *able* to change abuse into mutual, respectful use. That's what we call *assertiveness*—asserting 'I'—and after the rough ride we've been through, in looking at abuse, it's what we urgently need to turn to next!

11

ASSERTING 'I'

"I have a right to be here, no less than the trees and stars." So says the *Desiderata*: but it neglects to mention that it's not just my 'right', but perhaps even more my responsibility. Often it seems that life just *is*—"Life is what happens while we're busy making other plans," as John Lennon put it—yet to a surprising, perhaps terrifying, degree, life is, as another old adage puts it, what *we* make of it, what *we* choose. It often won't feel like that... and it certainly won't unless we choose to assert, clearly—and as much to ourselves as to others—our choice of 'I'. "Who am I?" you say? Well, I can't choose for you... and it would be abusive of me, and of you, if I tried to... so assert yourself, choose for *yourself*! What would *you* choose as 'I'? And what would you choose as *your* part of each 'We' you share with others? It's up to you...

'I' is a choice

Everyone has their own choice: what matters is that it *is* a choice —and also whether it's a *choice*, rather than the result of evading choice and blaming the results on others. If what happens arises from a genuine choice, from asserting 'I', there's an entirely different feel to it—powerful in an equally genuine sense—even when it seems to go 'wrong'. A few weeks ago, for example, the canteen manager arrived at work with her arm strapped up, and obviously in some pain. She's a small, vibrant woman, but I knew that her partner-relationship was a very physical one — she'd been gossipping gaily with her staff about their 'sexercise' — so I made a quiet comment. "Oh no," she said, laughing and wincing at the same time. "This is what comes of trying to tackle a woman who's built like a brick shithouse! I must've kissed the ground more often than any other time in the three years I've been playing women's football — it's a lot rougher than the men's!"

To her, the risk—and reality—of bumps and bruises was far less important than the fun, and the empowerment—both power-with and power-from-within—that she gained from the game. That was her *choice*: 'I' is not that which changes, 'I' is that which *chooses*—and every choice has its consequences, or at least its interweavings, within the wyrd.

> What do you choose for your 'I'? What are some of the consequences, or interweavings, from those choices?
>
> There's always a choice, there's always a twist: what twists are you willing to risk? If you're not willing to take *any* risks, you're rather limiting your choices...
>
> One of our greatest barriers is fear: and the only way past it is to look within, to find the courage — the literal 'heart-madness' of *trust*—to take risks, to "feel the fear, and do it anyway". In the rough-and-tumble of a contact-sport such as football, what do you fear? Where do you *feel* that fear? What do you feel when you *choose* to face the risk, and do it anyway?
>
> Fear reduces when we face it, and accept the reality —rather than only the fear—of the risk: so when you *do* take a risk, note what *doesn't* happen as well as what does. Looking back at your past fears which you faced this way, what do you *feel*?
>
> Yet it's also essential to remember that, inflated though they may be by our fears, most risks are real: if and when it *does* express itself in your version of Reality Department, what do you *feel*? Rather than running from the fears and feelings, from where within you do find the

courage to pick yourself up and start again? What help—
power-with—do others give you in this? (Perhaps more
to the point, what help will you *allow* others to give you in
this?) Looking closer at the threads of your own wyrd,
what do you learn about your choice of 'I'—and about
the geasa which weave their inevitable way through
those choices?

'Consequences' is perhaps the wrong word, because the
wyrd has no sequence as such: whatever patterns we may
perceive—such as the 'common-sense' concept of causality—
arise as much from what *we* choose to see, and not-see, as from
anything else. What we think of as cause-and-effect is no more
than an *apparent* pattern in time: but the wyrd interweaves
through everywhere and everywhen, hence any event is simply a
'co-incidence'—and any meaning it may seem to have depends
on how we choose to *interpret* that event. In a very literal sense,
it's *all* coincidence, an endless 'coinciding': things happen
because they happen to happen, and everything and nothing is
the cause. Weird... but that's the nature of the wyrd.

Yet there *are* patterns to be seen: there *are* parallels within
the wyrd, there *are* 'sequences' that can seem like cause-and-effect.
So events *can* have meaning for *us*—if not necessarily for anyone
else. And those events gain their meaning only if we *choose* to let
them do so—the 'meaning' being a glimpse of where each thread
leads, and the possibilities open to us by choosing to claim it as
part of our 'I', and following its path for a while. The twist is
that to not-choose—to try to stay still, to hold on to what we
have—is still a choice: we have no choice but to face choice itself.

So there's *always* a risk: *nothing*—not even doing nothing—
is 'safe'. And there's no way we can analyse everything, or even
anything, in enough detail to be able to predict — and hence
control — the final outcome: since the wyrd contains the
interweaving of everything, everywhere, everywhen, the
possibilities within even the simplest of events are, quite literally,
infinite. What *does* work, though, is what the Taoists called 'doing
no-thing', or — in terms of the wyrd — *allowing* ourselves to

become aware of what the wyrd itself tells *us*. Once we allow ourselves to recognise it, there's a clear sense of 'impending wyrd' that enables us to refine our choices, and to *dance* with those apparent risks—rather than hiding in some desperate all-or-nothing gamble...

> And that's another choice: to *listen* to that strange whisper of 'impending wyrd', or to ignore it. I can't count the number of times I've had a clear warning, a clear message, about a more appropriate choice, a better way to go—even about something as simple as a traffic-jam —but have ignored it until too late: by which time the choice is gone... Almost all of us have perfect retrocognition — otherwise known as 'hindsight' — but perfect precognition might be a lot more useful! Yet that weird sense of 'impending wyrd' can also provide us with what one friend described as 'precognitive recovery' (the art of *not* being in the wrong place at the wrong time!): what's *your* experience of this? On the probably rare occasions when you've trusted that *feeling* of 'impending wyrd', what happened — or, perhaps more to the point, what *didn't* happen?
>
> The choice to 'do no-thing' is closely related to that sense of 'impending wyrd': taking action at what we *allow* ourselves to know is exactly the right moment, at that subtle balance-point between doing nothing, and doing too much. What's your experience of this? How do you allow yourself to *know* that subtle point of balance, between not trying hard enough, and trying too hard — between oblivious enthusiasm, and the inward-turned anger of apathy? And how hard—or easy—is it for you to trust that inner knowing?

'I' is a choice; to assert who we are, and what we choose, is a choice. It's perhaps the most important of all the choices we make, because without committing to that, we have no certainty to 'I' — or its boundaries. Trying to control others — either through aggressive abuse (power-over), or else by trying to entrap others through the more covert 'passive' abuse (power-

155

under)—or refusing to assert ourselves in relationship at all—as in the old 'anything for a quiet life' scenario—helps no one, least of all ourselves: the only way out is to become assertive, and *live* the expression of our choices. Courtesy of some 'New Age' confusions, the term 'assertiveness' has unfortunately become something of a cliché: but it certainly won't feel like that once we start to put it into practice... To be assertive demands of us a full understanding of the distinction—yet also the arbitrariness —of the boundary between 'I' and 'not-I'; it demands of us that we understand our own choices, and accept full responsibility for and about those choices; and it demands that we accept that others *do* exist, and that they *do* have right and responsibility for *their* choices, just as much as we have for ours. Sounds easy? Not exactly... but at least we do have one definite place to start: namely that subtle boundary between 'not-I' and 'I'.

'I' is a boundary

I make my choices; you make yours; everyone else makes theirs. And wherever those choices overlap, there's a boundary — a boundary of sorts, if often a weird one...

So here we come back to those boundary-issues that we looked at earlier: to assert myself, to claim and express my 'I', is exactly the same as asserting my boundaries—namely 'to know and respect what I want, and to take responsibility for same'. If I don't know what I want, there may not be much for 'I' to assert... if I don't respect what I want, it'll be no surprise if others don't respect what I want either... and if I don't take responsibility for knowing what I want, respecting what I want, and doing something about it, then it's unlikely that anyone else will... All of these may *seem* obvious enough, and simple enough: but for most people, in practice, they are *far* from simple—and society's rampant paediarchy can make it harder still.

> "You gotta be yourself — be more like I tell ya!" — that classic double-bind, described in song by Joan Armatrading. Do you know what *you* want — rather than

what other people tell you that you *ought* to want, you *should* want, you *must* want?

Given the social confusions and social pressures, it's sometimes easier to start from what we *don't* want rather than what we do: so what do you *not* want in your life? By the nature of the wyrd, every thread passes through us somewhere, so we can never entirely exclude *anything* from our lives: but to a surprising extent we *can* choose how we express or experience each thread. So in that sense, what threads of wyrd do you *not* want to express as part of your 'I'? What threads would you *not* choose to experience as the main themes of your 'I'?

That's your choice: now comes the twist... Given that you now know at least *something* of what you want and don't want in your 'I', in what ways do *you* respect that choice? In what ways do *you* take responsibility for that choice?

Neither of those is easy: so in what ways do you evade responsibility for expressing *your* choice of 'I'? In what ways do you export to others the responsibility—or the blame—for what are actually *your* choices for 'I'? As you begin to notice the extent — perhaps frightening extent — to which you do this, in what ways could you begin to reclaim that 'response-ability' to assert your own choice of 'I' — 'to know and respect what I want, and to take responsibility for same'?

In a society as complex as ours, we *cannot* do everything: we have no choice but to rely on others to some extent in most aspects of our lives. Whether we like it or not, there's always 'We' as well as 'I'—which means that there are always likely to be confusions about boundaries, about where my 'I' ends, and yours begins. The wyrd, helpful as ever, will often provide us with its own weird reminders of this...

Another quiet Sunday morning—my favourite time of the week. Off to my favourite café for a leisurely breakfast, reading the paper, catching up on the local gossip: *just* what I fancy! Into the familiar gloom, and — but... hey! Wait a minute! There's someone sitting at *my* table! How *dare* they! Behind the counter, Kel sees my horrified expression, gives me a wry shrug in sympathy, and points me to another table. But it's not *right*: breakfast tastes wrong, coffee's different... none of this would have happened, I'm sure, if *they* hadn't been sitting at *my* table — it's all *their* fault! I'm grumpy, irritable, resentful... yet "resentment is a demand that the Other feel guilty — a common form of covert abuse", as that weird Inner Adult reminds my decidedly childish Inner Child! Uh-oh... oops... Better take a closer look at Reality Department...

Do I *really* think I own that table? They're not regulars here: could they *really* have known that it's my favourite table — or even that I was going to come in today? If I *need* to 'own' that table, I'll have to demand, or cajole, or bully them to move: is that what I *really* want to do? Is it *that* important to me? Some other time, some other place, just possibly yes; but right here, right now, the answer's a clear 'No'. So how about asserting what I *did* come here for: a leisurely breakfast, read the paper, catch up on the local gossip? Sure enough, here comes Kel, grabbing a break to give me the latest news: *great!* Weird how things can change so fast, isn't it?

What's *your* experience of this? When the wyrd's given you something other than you wanted, and you lose yourself in resentment and blame, what kind of weird reminders do *you* need to get back on track, and able to assert what you *really* choose?

All abuse arises from boundary-problems — from dishonesty to self or others, or from a refusal to take responsibility for self, for asserting 'I'. We *always* have 'response-ability' for our boundaries, even when someone oversteps them: Transactional Analysis theory, for example, makes it clear that 'playing victim' *invites* abuse — and is itself often a form of abuse, in which the self-styled victim *needs* someone to blame in order to prop up their own "ain't it awful?" attention-grabbing game. Caught in the webs of codependency — needing others to take the responsibility, or the blame, for us — most of us oscillate, without much awareness, between passive and aggressive: the *only* way out of the loop is to become clear about our boundaries, and to take responsibility for asserting our *own* 'I'.

On the aggressive side of the cycle, we'll find ourselves ignoring others' boundaries, and treating them as objects, non-entities which we have a *right* to use — or abuse — according to our needs. By the usual weird twists, there are plenty of opportunities for well-meant confusion, especially when we can pretend that our aggression is on behalf of others: some of the worst offenders in recent times, for example, have been those feminists who've been so obsessed about women's rights that they've fallen for the old "the end justifies the means" trap, and set out to enforce new laws which assign all rights to women, and all responsibilities — and blame — to men. Another common delusion is the notion that violence and abuse by women is *always* self-defence: the reality, as is indicated by that all-too-common experience of seeing frustrated mothers in supermarkets hitting their 'uncontrollable' children, is that all abuse is *ego*-defence — 'defence' of a self-*image*—which is not the same thing at all...

"I'm only defending my rights!" I say, angrily. Well, yes, that's probably true — but I'm doing it in a way that's riding roughshod over everyone else's... I may *think* I'm asserting 'I', but to everyone else it's just plain aggression — which might well explain why they've responded in the way that they have...

Embarrassment-time again, perhaps, but take a closer look at what you've done in the past that you've claimed was in self-defence: what were you *really* 'defending'? Were you genuinely defending yourself—or simply exporting your fears, dumping them 'over the boundary' onto someone else? Notice the feelings that arise as you explore these memories — minimising, justifying, blaming, "It's all *their* fault!"... those all-too-common kinds of covert abuse...

The past is gone: there's little or nothing that you can do now about what you've done in the past, and you'll help no one by blaming—especially yourself. But you *do* have 'response-ability' for the present, and the future: when boundary-issues like these come up again,

> what can *you* do to assert your 'I' *without* falling back into old habits of aggressiveness or blame?

But if we don't at least *state* our boundaries, then others will inevitably ignore them—not necessarily out of malice, but often because they simply don't know that they're there. This can be a problem, because many people do have some weird ideas of what constitutes 'use': and if we don't *tell* others how we want to be used, they're likely to assume—quite reasonably—that we *want* to be used in the way that they want to use us. We can be responsible *about* others, but we cannot be responsible *for* them; so our boundaries are *our* responsibility—and no one else's. If we choose to play 'doormat', and refuse to take responsibility for our 'I', we really can't complain about the resultant feedback that we get from the wyrd...

> "It's not *fair!*" I wail—but I don't have the courage to say so to anyone else, so it's hardly surprising that it isn't 'fair'... Playing passive, as that infuriating Inner Adult quietly reminds me, *evokes* aggressive: so if I genuinely choose to break free from yet another co-dependent setup—rather than playing my usual game of looking for someone else to blame—then it's up to *me* to assert those boundaries about what I believe is fair...
>
> If you've long been in the habit of playing 'doormat', passively taking all the knocks as other people blunder through your boundaries, from where within you can you find the courage to trust that you *do* have the right—and responsibility—to assert your boundaries, your choice of 'I'? As you begin to do this, notice the feedback that you get from the wyrd: there'll be those usual weird 'challenges', of course, testing your commitment to the changes you make in your choice of 'I', but what happens as you hold to that commitment?
>
> Notice, too, that often the strongest challenges to that commitment will come not from others, but from *you* —"It's too hard, it's not *fair*" and so on... in what ways can you call on your own Inner Adult for aid in this?

If we've constantly been trampled on by others, it's important to start off by saying 'No' — and assert clearly, and strongly, that 'No' does indeed *mean* 'No', and nothing else. (It's then important to *only* use 'No' to mean 'No' — and not as 'Maybe', or 'Perhaps', or 'Push a little harder and you may get to Yes'... there are plenty of weird confusions that can arise from *that* popularly dishonest game...) But on its own, 'No' is not enough: if it's overused, it builds walls rather than boundaries — and then we're *really* stuck, in a cage of our own making... In any case, the wyrd often has trouble with 'No': as several writers have commented, "There is no image for 'not' in dreams," and if we say only what we're 'against' in others, the wyrd — helpful as ever — tends to provide us with exactly that, to give us something to say 'No' to! So at some point we have to say what we're 'for': we have to *commit* ourselves to a boundary, by saying 'Yes', claiming that particular thread of the wyrd as part of our 'I' — with the usual weird results.

> "He was *always* late," says the young woman in the bar, "and I *always* waited for him — getting angrier and angrier, but I never said anything. He was supposed to bring me here today, and he was late again; but this time, for once, I came here anyway, on my own, without waiting. And it feels really different — it feels *great!*" Defining a boundary, a boundary of *time*: saying 'No', then shifting to 'Yes'. And at that moment he comes in through the door, and she greets him delightedly: despite his lateness, she's pleased with *herself* — which means she can greet him with pleasure rather than her usual ill-concealed anger...
>
> What happens for you when you become clear about your own boundaries, your own choices? In particular, what happens when you shift from 'No' to 'Yes'?

'What we're *for*' can take a lot of finding, with many mistakes — and many weird loops and repetitions of lessons — along the way. It does take a great deal of work to reach the fluid, dynamic inner certainty described in the Taoist expression that "In me the tiger can find no place to rest its claws"—an inner certainty which *is* echoed, in some weird way, in our interactions with the world 'out there'. But it's our responsibility — our 'response-ability'. Ultimately, it *is* up to us: and no one else.

Those boundaries of 'I' are *our* responsibility: but they're also mostly about *our* choices, not what others choose—which is why it's so important to use those 'I-statements' rather than 'you-statements' to describe them. Above all, though, 'I' is an expression of who *we* are, who *we* choose to be: and the best way to reach that expression—and avoid falling into passivity on one side, or aggressiveness on the other — is to learn to recognise, and understand, the *feeling* of 'I'.

'I' is a feeling

The only way out of abuse—whether done to us or by us—is through asserting 'I'. But when trying to correct for previous habits, it's easy to over-compensate, and end up abusing in a different way: many feminists, for example, exchanged their old power-under for power-over, mistakenly thinking that aggression *was* assertiveness; many 'pro-feminist' men exchanged their previous power-over for power-under, and collapsed into the cowed and complaining role of the 'New Age wimp'; the end-results of those shifts have been to few people's satisfaction... So the key is that asserting 'I' is also a *feeling* — one that is quite different from the feigned 'helplessness' of passivity, or the self-righteous indignation of aggression.

Like many other feelings we've explored here — each associated with, or attached to, its own thread of the wyrd—it's subtle, yet specific: there's no other feeling quite like it, so it can act as a clear indication that we're 'on track' to assertiveness. There are all too many distractions on the way — it's easy to confuse self-awareness and self-centredness, for example—but by watching the feelings, and watching the feedback that we get from the wyrd, we slowly become clearer about what 'I' is, and about what we genuinely want as 'I'.

> True assertiveness creates a balance at the boundary between 'I' and 'not-I', so one way to become familiar with that feeling of assertiveness is to explore not just the meaning, but the *experience*, of 'equality'.
>
> Perhaps the best place to start is by asserting that equality means "equally deserving of respect" — all people are equally human, including 'I' and *all* 'not-I'. *Everyone*: no exceptions. There'll be several people, or classes of people — politicians, used-car salesmen, bag ladies or whatever — for whom you'll find this a little difficult: "Surely I'm not equal to *them*? Surely they're not equal to *me*?" Who are they? Why is it difficult to think of them as *equally* human — rather than superhuman or, in all too many cases, sub-human by comparison with you? What *feelings* does that question bring up for you?
>
> Explore a little further, with that phrase from the *Desiderata*: "I have a right to be here, no less than the trees and stars." Assert, then, that *everyone* has a right to be here, no less — yet no more — than the trees and stars; assert that every*thing*, as well as every*one*, is equal — for a start, the same threads of wyrd pass through all of them, all of us. There'll be plenty of feelings that that'll bring up, too... but somewhere in the midst of them is a specific feeling, one that's assertive and aware of equality — what is it? Allow the wyrd to show you, and remind you, so that you can *know* when you're truly asserting 'I'.

Assertiveness is neither passive nor aggressive: it's not just in the middle, between them, it's somehow entirely *beyond* them. In some ways assertiveness *is* equality: but it's more than just an idea, an idealised concept, it's something that we learn to express by *living* it. What makes it hard at times is that it demands of us a rigorous honesty and self-honesty: a full awareness that we can— and usually should — be responsible *about* others, whoever or whatever they are, but that ultimately we can only be responsible *for* ourselves. We acknowledge our 'response-ability'—including facing what one friend describes as 'the insecurity of apology', when we face our responsibilities towards others; yet we also strive for an acceptance of *ourselves*, a weird combination of valid pride and valid humility without empty regret—an acceptance of 'is-ness'. That's assertiveness: that's asserting 'I'.

As usual, this sense of equality and assertiveness will remain no more than an idea unless we put it into *practice*: so it would be useful to go back through that list of categories from the 'Duluth Wheel' that we saw in the last section, but this time focussing on the assertiveness and awareness of equality that breaks free from control and abuse—or self-abuse. In each case, watch for that *feeling* of assertiveness, that will show you when you're 'on track' to a genuine equality...

The first category was *negotiation and fairness*, whose opposite was coercion and threats. How hard is it for you to reach *mutually* satisfying resolutions to conflict — where you don't ride roughshod over others' needs, yet still fully acknowledge your own? What does it take for you to compromise with others—and create a space in which others are willing to compromise too? If 'I' is not that which changes, but that which chooses, what do you need in order to be able to accept change?

Next is *non-threatening behaviour*, the opposite of intimidation. That's about talking and acting so that both you *and* others feel safe and comfortable expressing themselves and doing things: what do you need in order to be able to do this?

Then there's *economic partnership*, the opposite of economic abuse: making money decisions together, making sure both others and self benefit from mutual financial arrangements. What challenges do these pose for you, creating a balance of equality between you and others, yet still asserting 'I'?

Next comes *respect*, which is the opposite of emotional abuse: how hard is it for you to respect both yourself *and* others — to acknowledge the needs, the opinions, the concerns, the feelings and the fears of others *and* yourself, and to be emotionally affirming and understanding, both of self *and* others—all at the same time? It's useful to avoid the resentful 'demand that the other should feel guilty', and the use of subject-centred words like 'should', 'ought' and 'must'; it's important to listen to others *and* yourself without judgement or blame; but what else could you do to create a *mutual* respect?

The next challenges come from *shared responsibility* —the opposite of privilege, that old pretence of 'owning the law'. What does it take for you to create agreement with others about a fair distribution of work? How hard is it for you to ensure that *everyone* is heard, when making family and other group-decisions?

And there's the need for *trust and support*, the opposite of isolation: this is similar to the issues about respect, but more concerned with dependency — or breaking free from dependency. How do you support your own goals in life, at the same time as supporting those of others? How can you assert others' right—and responsibility — for their own feelings, friends, activities and opinions, while also respecting your own?

Next is *responsible parenting*, which is also about responsible *leadership*. What do you need in order to be able to share parenting, or leadership, with others? How can you *live* assertiveness and equality, rather than control and abuse, as a role-model for children and others?

And perhaps the hardest of all, yet central to all, is *honesty and accountability*, the opposite of minimising, denying and blaming. What does it mean to you, to accept responsibility for self, and about others? What does it ask of you, to acknowledge your own past use of abuse—and to provide a safe space in which others can acknowledge theirs? How hard is it for you to admit being wrong — or to make it safe for others to admit having been wrong? From where can *you* find the courage to communicate openly and truthfully — fully expressing and asserting your choice of 'I'?

Knowing how to assert our 'I' is an essential part of our toolkit: but we share this world with everything else within the wyrd—which means that we also need to know how to assert our own part of each 'We' which the weavings of the wyrd happens to bring our way. To do that, we need to become more aware of two more subtly-different members of the toolkit: sympathy, and empathy.

12

SYMPATHY AND EMPATHY

After the rough ride of the past two sections, you probably feel in need of a little sympathy—or is it empathy? Whichever it is, it's time to turn our attention to these two strange sentiments: because they're our primary links with the wyrd—and with each other.

Sharing the passions

A common sense, a shared passion — that's literally what 'sympathy' means, though in practice it also has a few weird twists and turns of its own. We echo each other, through the wyrd; or perhaps the same weird threads echo themselves as they weave their way through each of us — there's no way to tell which way it really goes.

> Perhaps the best way to illustrate this weird concept of sympathy would be through a classic science experiment. Tie a length of strong cotton or fishing-line horizontally across a small open space — between two chair-legs, for example. Then make up two small pendulums, each with a short length of line—two to four inches or so—and a small weight such as a sinker or a cotton-

reel. Tie one of these pendulums onto a point about one-third the way along the horizontal line; tie the other one on about two-thirds the way along, but do it such that you can change the vertical length of the pendulum. Start off with one line longer than the other, so that the whole contraption should look something like this:

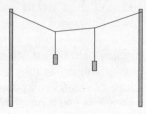

Start one of the pendulums swinging. Quite quickly, the other one will start swinging too, and try to follow the first —after a fashion. Stop them moving, change the adjustable pendulum so that both vertical lines are about the same length, and then start one of them swinging again; this time the second pendulum will start playing copycat almost immediately—moving 'in sympathy' with the first. After a while, though — depending on how much the pendulum lengths differ — the two will move 'out of sympathy', sometimes getting in each others' way, sometimes speeding things up, so that the whole line can be jumping about. And if you start the two pendulums off at the same time, but from opposite directions, they'll quickly come to a complete stop: perfectly in sympathy with each other, but in opposite phase—from opposite points of view, so to speak — they'll exactly cancel each other out.

But there's no way to tell, in any of these interactions, which pendulum really 'caused' the other to move, or to stop: the 'sympathy' is in the *relationship* between them, rather than in the objects themselves. Yet that's how radio transmissions work; that's how sound travels, by creating a 'resonance' of vibrations in the air; and sub-atomic particles can play even weirder games, interacting with each other apparently outside of the 'normal' confines of space and time.

So too, perhaps, with us. With whom do *you*

'resonate'? (For that matter, with *what* do you 'resonate' —such as your car or your cat, perhaps?) What are the 'vibes' that weave you together? What are those shared sights and sounds and feelings that move you?

When you've been perfectly 'in sync' with someone else for a while, and it suddenly stops, what happens? In what ways do you then try to control the situation — either your own behaviour, the other person's, or the relationship as a whole—to try to force it back into that sense of sympathy? How hard is it for you to accept that these changes, unsettling as they always are, arise from the weird nature of relationship itself — and that *everything*, in that sense, is just a passing phase?

Sympathy is not only weird in itself: it *is* the wyrd—or at least the way in which we most directly experience it. Through sympathy, and its close cousin, empathy, we can *know* that we share this world with others. 'We' only exists because of sympathy—in some ways exists *only* when there is sympathy, when the interweaving threads of wyrd resonate between each persona, or mask, or cage, that forms the choices of each 'I'. Yet to share with others is a choice; to align ourselves with others, and their experience, is a choice. So sympathy is a choice: which means, as always, that there's a twist...

Twisted sympathies

Before we can grasp where those twists come in, we first need to understand the distinctions between sympathy and empathy — they're similar, but there are some important differences. Perhaps the most central of these is the difference in context: sympathy brings others' experience, via those threads of the wyrd, into our own context, whereas empathy allows us to sample that same experience *in the others' own context*. In effect, by understanding both sympathy and empathy, and this crucial distinction between them, we can use them to explore our own boundaries and barriers—and those of others—from *both* sides of the fence.

This distinction between sympathy and empathy can take a bit of practice to understand, but it's worth the effort. To illustrate this, I could easily come up with an example or two from my all-too-common rows with Mary — where sympathy and empathy are sometimes conspicuous only by their absence—but it's probably best to go straight back to the café for another session of people-watching!

Sympathy is relatively easy to understand, and to experience: all we have to do is watch what we feel in relation to others. For example, just as you quieten down in the café and start to construct that sense of 'connectedness' that we've explored before, Julie comes crashing in through the door, throws herself down into a cubicle beside some friends, and talks *at* them animatedly—obviously angry about something or someone, as usual. What do *you* feel as you watch her? Notice first your own response to her—your pulse will probably start racing a bit, for example, in defence against her sheer energy — but then look *behind* that: where do you feel her anger within you? Where within *you* do those weird echoes of *her* anger appear? What form does that sense of being 'in sympathy' with her take?

That's sympathy. Sometimes there's a sense of being dragged 'into sympathy' with someone, whether we want to or not—that's certainly the case with Julie's regular rampages, for example—so we have to *choose* to be 'unsympathetic', and shut ourselves off from them, for our own safety and sanity! But we also have the choice to switch into empathy: to reach out into the wyrd to experience those threads in *their* context, from *their* perspective rather than ours — sometimes with very different results.

One way to do this is to place ourselves literally in their context: for example, to hold the same posture and stance as others, or to move in the same way as they do, will often bring up an empathetic response in us—as we saw in the previous book. For example, that man sitting quietly over there in the corner, looking vacantly into space, still nursing the same cup of coffee after more than half an hour: what do *you* feel as you watch him? Sadness, perhaps? Isolation? Loneliness? That's sympathy; but now sit in exactly the same posture as him, holding your cup in the same way, your head at the same angle: in what ways do the feelings change? From apparent alone-ness, perhaps, to quiet contemplation (or 'all-one-ness'); from apparent sadness to a subtle satisfaction? Sympathy is important; but if we rely on sympathy alone, we can make a lot of mistakes...

Without sympathy, we can't ever really be aware of others, or of our relationship with others; yet without empathy we'll never be able to understand why others are the way they are, or why they do what they do, in the way that they do it. One friend commented that her husband had always been disparaging about her fear of driving a car; he was obviously sympathetic and understanding, but annoyed, because it seemed to him to be so irrational — and it made her very dependent on him, especially when they moved out of town. But then she took up motorcycling—and took to it like a duck to water, with none of the fears that had plagued her behind the wheel of a car. Yet while she became less afraid, he became *more* so, with—to her—increasingly irrational fears about *her* safety. In effect, he'd become lost in over-sympathy: he translated her experience of riding the bike into *his* context — and assumed that she had to be feeling as unsafe as he did on a bike. He couldn't quite make the shift from sympathy to empathy: but if he had, it would have solved the problem, because he would then have *known* that from *her* context — *her* point of view — motorcycling for all its known dangers, *felt* far more safe than driving.

The usual notion of 'sympathy' — that I'm sad because I see that you're sad, and somehow that's supposed to be a 'good thing' — is actually more of a hindrance than a help in these circumstances! It's best understood as a well-meant attempt at 'import' rather than 'export', trying to 'make things better' by inverting the usual power-over and power-under delusions: the idea seems to be that there's only a limited amount of sadness in the world, so if I willingly take it from you, you must necessarily feel happier. But it's unfortunately just as much of a delusion as power-over and power-under: and because of the weird nature of *real* sympathy, it can actually backfire badly — so that we're now *both* stuck in sadness, with no way out... Genuine sympathy is important, especially in maintaining relationships: but there are subtle twists to that choice of sympathy — so do what you choose, says the wyrd, but be *very* sure that you choose it...

> What's your experience of the usual idea of 'sympathy'? When you've tried to 'be sympathetic' with others, how well has it really worked? And what did you feel when others tried to 'be sympathetic' with you in that way?
>
> Rather than the muddled confusions of the usual idea of 'sympathy', what *does* work is a more subtle, but much more difficult, combination of sympathy and empathy. We first need to understand *their* choices, through empathy: which may show us that they *choose* to feel sad—to explore their grief, perhaps—and do not want our 'sympathy'! Yet if they *do* want our help, we can choose to move into sympathy with them, sharing the same feelings, the same grief—and be aware that, if we get it right, it will hurt just as much for us as it does for them... which can sometimes be very hard to face. While in that space, though, we need to keep enough aware- ness open to be able to accept that choice and, *at the same time*, choose differently — yet still maintaining the state of sympathy with the other person, so as to bring them with us to that different state.
>
> A subtle juggling-act—and one that demands a *lot* of courage... What's your experience of this? What courage does it ask for from *you* to reach this weirder, yet more successful, state of sympathy?

As usual, we need to beware of gender-stereotypes here— particularly the commonly-asserted claim that only women are capable of empathy. If we really want to argue about gender- stereotypes, we'll discover that many kinds of empathy — a connection and an awareness of the Other, in the *Other's* context

—are historically more 'male' than 'female' anyway: the complex contextual relationship between the hunter and the hunted, for example, or that weird respect of 'the Other' which impels a man to risk his life on behalf of a stranger in a fire or other danger—something which, even now, few women will do. In any case, as more recent feminist authors such as Naomi Wolf and Kate Fillion have warned, what's usually described as 'women's empathy' is, far more often, not empathy at all, but a mangled pseudo-'sympathy' which has more to do subject-centred manipulation and control than with anything else, and which can be immensely destructive for everyone involved.

One form of this is what's known as 'awfulizing' — "Oh, how terrible! How awful!" — which *looks* like sympathy, but in fact is best described as an addiction to adrenalin (specifically, the 'freeze' mode of its 'fight, flight or freeze' reflex), because it provides an *illusion* of meaning and urgency. It's actually an abandonment of 'I', our *own* context, in favour of what looks like the more exciting and interesting — even if perhaps more dangerous or disturbing—lives of others. And it relies, in effect, on a subject-centred form of pornography — meddling in others' lives in order to avoid responsibility for or within our own — which can become more and more intrusive as the addiction grows. One glance at any of the so-called women's magazines or chat-shows—"lives of the rich and famous!" and so on — will provide all too many examples of this... other people's misery used as *entertainment*... There's little real sympathy there—more like an intrusion over others' boundaries that's so pervasive and so entrenched that it's thought of as 'normal', rather than recognised for the abuse that it really is. Unlike true sympathy or empathy, there's little real intent to create power-with, to help the Other overcome their difficulties: in fact there's more a need to *maintain* whatever it is that's 'awful' for the Other, in order to continue 'awfulizing' about it...

What's going on in this ersatz empathy is a misunderstanding of the role and responsibility of 'I': the other's experience is not a substitute for our own, and sympathy and empathy only exist in the *relationship* between 'I' and 'the Other'. If we've abandoned 'I' in favour of someone else's more interesting attributes or experiences, there's no 'I' for there to be relationship *with* — and hence no real sympathy or empathy. Living vicariously could hardly be called 'living', either...

> I'm out of the city for a change, up at a country-dance. As the music starts, a large group of dancers move onto the floor — and space themselves out in lines, all carefully copying each other, all carefully keeping a safe distance apart, all carefully avoiding responsibility for the path of the dance. Sure, there are a few real dancers there, weaving a pattern with the threads of the music, but as for the rest... a line of empty puppets, moving jerkily in sympathy to a weird puppet-master's strings — nary a sign of any 'We' to be seen, and little enough of any 'I'. No wonder the acquaintance who's brought me here raves about it so much: it's the only form of 'social' dance that could support her fear of intimacy, her terror of touch...
>
> In what ways do *you* abandon yourself by playing 'copycat' — claiming others' threads instead of your own — in an empty kind of 'in-sympathy' with others? Why do you do this? To gain their sympathy, perhaps? Or a sense of sharing, however hollow it may be? Becoming aware of this, what can *you* do to retain your own sense of 'I' as well as your relationship with others — and thus make that sympathy and empathy real?

Another kind of 'pseudo-sympathy' that causes many a problem is that subject-centred expectation that others *should* be 'in sympathy' with us — and should thus know exactly what we want, when we want it. Since they often aren't, and *can't*, it's easy for us to blame them for *our* refusal to take responsibility for our needs — which usually leads us straight into the unpleasant tangles of abuse and counter-abuse...

> Stuck at a junction: there's a huge pickup truck beside me, and I can't see past it. So I edge forward: but as I do so, the truck jerks forward too, blocking my view again. I

edge forward once more; immediately, the truck pulls forward again — I can't see a thing, and this is getting dangerous... Suddenly, without any warning, the truck roars forward, straight across me, its boat-trailer only just missing the front of my car; the passenger leans out, screaming obscenities, fingers gesticulating — and that was the only signal I ever saw! As far as they're concerned, it's entirely my fault, of course: I should have been 'in sympathy' with them, and *known*, without any indication, that they wanted to turn across my lane...

What are some of your own experiences of this? What do you feel when someone expects you automatically to be 'in sympathy' with them — and blames *you* when, unsurprisingly, you're unable to do so?

And what are some of the circumstances in which you've done the same: expected others to *know* (magically, perhaps?) what you want and need — and have blamed them for failing to do so? If sympathy is about *relationship* with the other — rather than a subject-centred 'passing the buck' — what 'response-ability' do *you* have to change this?

Sympathy and empathy are the means by which we become 'in touch' with others, sharing threads of the wyrd that pass through 'I' and 'We' and 'I'. But this only works when there's a full understanding of the boundaries between 'I', and 'We', and the other's 'I' — and a full understanding, too, that to connect with others, in sympathy and empathy, is a *choice*.

Choosing sympathy

It's sometimes difficult to see that we *do* have choice in this: more usually, it'll seem that either we're in sympathy with others, or not, and there's not that much that we can do about it. And it's certainly unwise to pretend that we feel what we don't feel, or that we don't feel what we do: so where does choice come into it? The short answer is that while we can't control what we feel, we *can* direct our response to what we feel: but to do that means that we first have to be *aware* of what we feel — and also when what we feel actually *is* our own feeling, rather than one that's drifted in, through sympathy, along the threads of wyrd.

That sounds a bit weird, perhaps, but we've met something similar already: those 'foreign' memories that we learnt to watch out for, back in the practical work on boundaries. And this time we have, if not an explanation as such, then at least a better understanding of what's going on: like those two pendulums on the string, we can find ourselves drifting in and out of being 'in sympathy' with others, which means that we'll find ourselves sharing 'foreign' feelings much like those 'foreign' memories—or perhaps find ourselves unable to 'connect' with others, no matter how sympathetic we might be, because we're 'out of phase' with them. With awareness, we *do* have the choice to change this.

Back to the café again! Most of what we've done there before has been about boundaries: this time we're looking more closely at the threads that *cross* those boundaries, weaving together 'I' and 'not-I' as 'We'.

So find a convenient quiet corner, and relax; close your eyes, and allow yourself to become aware of the space around you. Feel the limits of your physical boundaries: and then explore the blurred edges of 'I' — the warmth or coolness around your hands, the way your hair extends outward into 'uncertain-I', the way your breath moves into and returns from a space you share with others.

Then expand this blurry bounded-yet-unbounded sense of 'I' outward into that shared space, carefully, yet respectfully, so that your 'I' overlaps the physical space occupied by others. When we tried this before, some while ago, you watched for a feeling of 'unsafety', as they came too close to your boundary for comfort: this time—remembering from that previous example that you *can* 'disconnect' from them whenever you need—reach out to bring yourself 'into sympathy' with them. Notice how your feelings change as you link with the threads of 'We'—the *relationship* between your own 'I' and that of the other person. Focus your attention on one person at a time: anyone will do, but if they become aware of your 'connecting' to them — as they may well do, given the nature of the wyrd — it's best to withdraw back into 'I', and try again with someone else. In what ways do your feelings change as you expand into 'We'? In what ways do these feelings differ as you move into a felt sense of 'We' — a sympathy, and an empathy — with different people?

On some occasions, or with some people, all you'll get from 'We' is a sense of 'nothingness', or perhaps even a definite 'No!' If that's the case, you've hit a boundary: it's best to back off, and quietly 'disconnect' from that person — move yourself 'out of sympathy' with them. In other cases you might feel swamped, as you reach out to connect with some person: again, back off, and reconnect with your *own* sense of 'I'. Try again later with the same person: what difference — if any — do you feel? Watching what had previously seemed to be your own feelings change as you move into and out of sympathy with others — connect with and disconnect from that sense of 'We' between you — which feelings *do* only belong to 'I'?

Sympathy and empathy only exist in *relationship*: which means that, to make it work, we have to be fully aware of two people — both 'I' *and* the Other — *at the same time*. This takes some practice... it's all too easy, for example, to try to be sympathetic with others — or particularly to reach out in empathy to others — and become so focussed on trying to connect with the other person that we lose track of 'I'. Reaching out to others in sympathy or empathy shows us how we relate — interweave — with others: but unless we remember to retain a full awareness of 'I' as we do so, there's nothing left 'back there' to anchor that relating *to*...

For much the same reason, we can also fall into another trap — that destructive 'pseudo-sympathy' that we saw earlier — if our motives for reaching out to others are unclear. True sympathy and empathy only become possible when we're solidly anchored in 'I': and that can only happen when we're *asserting* 'I', not running away from it!

One of the hardest issues I've had to face has been a near-lifelong habit of trying to 'buy' being liked—in order to avoid responsibility for my *own* well-being. I'm the *nice* one: I'm very sympathetic, I'll listen to your troubles, I'll lend you—*give* you—anything you want; oh, but please, won't you be nice to me in return? Say you'll like me... I'll do *anything* to make you like me... please?

Not clever... *not* wise... and while the 'sympathy' was genuine, after a fashion — and often did seem to help those others, if rarely me — yet in a way it was also manipulative and dishonest — and hence abusive, both of others and, especially, of myself. About which I complained loudly, of course — "Why is everyone so *unfair* to me?"—and carefully avoided asking why... And *not* comfortable when I finally understood what I was doing...

In what ways do *you* pretend sympathy with others, in order to maintain relationships with them? In what ways do you suppress what you feel—suppress 'I'—'for the sake of the friendship'? For example, do you indulge in self-deprecation, or what Kate Fillion calls 'one-downmanship', putting yourself down in order to prop the other up, and maintain a semblance of intimacy and closeness? This may seem to work in the short-term, but when it becomes a habit, repeated over and over again over months and years, what does this pseudo-sympathy do to your own sense of 'I'? What does it do to the relationship? And when it finally falls apart—as it always does—who gets the blame?

True sympathy and empathy arise from a deliberate and aware choice of a *subject*-centred perspective: which means we also have to be aware of the dangers and drawbacks of that perspective, as we saw earlier. The object-centred perspective depends on a clear sense of separation, of boundaries; the subject-centred one on a sense of connection, of interwovenness, in which the other—whatever or whoever it may be—is seen as an extension of self, as a *part* of 'I' rather than something apart. In sympathy and empathy, this has to be taken a stage further: the Other is not merely part of 'I', but 'I' and the Other are one and the same. Both sentiments are subject-centred, and the difference between them is mainly one of emphasis and focus: in sympathy, we explore others' feelings as if they were *our* feelings, in *our* context; in empathy we in effect move our sense of 'I' into the *other's* context, and from there, as the old native-American image puts it, we 'walk a mile in their moccasins'.

> Empathy is often harder than sympathy, because we have to make a deliberate effort to let go of our own prejudices and assumptions: it can be very hard, for example, for someone from a materialistic Western background to fully grasp Mother Teresa's Eastern-influenced comment that "Loneliness and the feeling of being unwanted is the most terrible poverty"...
>
> It's always easiest to 'walk a mile in the moccasins' of someone who's similar to you: so make a specific effort to do so with those who aren't. For example, reach out in empathy with a prostitute, or a politician; with a mother in the last moments of childbirth, or a soldier in the chaos and terror of battle; explore life as an ant, or a cat — and at the same moment, as a sparrow cornered by the same cat. Reach out to grasp their challenges, their choices, from *their* perspective rather than your own. Being aware of both their life, and yours, in the same moment, notice how those same threads, those same choices, appear in your own life, in different forms, and in different intensities. What do you learn? How hard is it for you to avoid dropping back to a pseudo-'sympathy', aware of what is happening in their life, yet judging them from the preconceptions of your own?

Both sympathy and empathy are concerned with relationship: so it's important to remember that our first relationship is *always* with ourself—and hence we need our *own* sympathy and empathy at times. 'Self-sympathy' could almost be a synonym for self-awareness, or, for that matter, for assertiveness: it's about extending those threads of relationship and connectedness all the way back to oneself, acknowledging that we *do* 'have a right to be here, no less than the trees and stars'—yet also no more than the trees and stars, too. But in self-empathy, we acknowledge who we are, in our own context, *as if relating to a total stranger*—in other words, trying to see ourselves as others would, to understand our choices and our challenges 'from the outside'. (In a peculiar sense, it's so subject-centred that it ends up being almost object-centred: it's the nearest that we'll ever get to being 'objective' about our own actions!) It's particularly important to use self-empathy when looking at our own past: otherwise it's all too easy to wander off into delusions of self-importance or—more likely—to spiral down into a morass of self-pity and self-blame.

> To understand self-empathy, choose a moment that you don't like about your past — something deeply embarrassing, perhaps, or an act that now seems cowardly or cruel. That kind of judgement comes up easily, even when we try to be sympathetic, because we're looking at those incidents from our current context, with all the benefit of hindsight.
>
> So shift instead into empathy, viewing yourself-of-then as if a total stranger, in another context, another world. First look back into the past 'objectively', to help you rebuild an awareness and an understanding of your context — who, what, when, where and why — at *that* time, with all that 'benefit of hindsight'; then reach out not just to remember but to *feel* again the exact circumstances of that moment; and merge those two very different perspectives into one, viewing the actions of yourself-of-then within the *overall* context of the time.
>
> What were the choices and the challenges that yourself-of-then *believed* you faced, that led you to the actions that you then took? In what ways do your current judgements of yourself-of-then change? Seen from the wider perspective, in what ways *now* do those choices perhaps seem 'mis-taken' — or perhaps seem more understandable, given the full context of the time? Given

that hindsight, how hard is it for you to accept, simply that that *is* what you did — for reasons that, at the time, were simply the reasons that you chose?

Those were the choices, there, then; the results, here, now, are the twists... And yes, with the benefit of hindsight, perhaps you *could* have done things differently; perhaps you *should* have done things differently; but those 'magic' words — so commonly a cue for self-deprecation — don't actually help in resolving anything from the past, and usually only make things worse. The past is the past: we can see it, but we can never change it, and any attempt to do so, or to make others do so, only ends up abusing someone—usually ourselves.

Instead, use self-empathy's strangely dispassionate yet compassionate gaze to *accept* the choices of yourself-of-then: accepting that that is what you did, in what ways does it make it easier to be 'response-able' about it now?

In what ways does your 'response-ability' change — empowering you to do whatever needs to be done *now* to resolve the unpleasantness of that moment in the past?

Sympathy and empathy demand a lot from us: honesty and self-honesty, in particular. And in turn they help us to be more honest, with ourselves, and with others. But we can't do it all ourselves: and we don't need to, because those same threads of connectedness—if we allow them to do so—will show us allies at every turn. These allies are more than 'friends': they're in sympathy with us, yes, but they're not necessarily 'sympathetic' in the usual sense! True allies are able to be honest with us, and in turn we're able to be honest with them: which is why we need them so much when — as now — we begin to put our weird 'toolkit' into practical use.

13

ALLIES IN WYRDNESS

The wyrd passes through everything, everyone, everywhere, everywhen; so anyone and anything can be an ally in helping us find our own power and our own choices. *If* we let them be so, that is, and *if* we can understand and accept what they show us—which is not always as easy as it sounds!

"You get what you choose," says Reality Department: and it certainly *would* be wise if we could learn to make full use of the allies we have all round us—our allies in wyrdness. But the habit of hiding from our own choices in fear, or in the 'senses taker' of habit itself, is so pervasive that sometimes we *do* need a serious jolt before we'll stop and *look* at those choices, and look at where we are and where we're going...

Discovering allies

"It's well past midnight—why on earth do those meetings have to go on so long? It's cold, and it's wet, and I just want to get home... Wet. Cold. Turn here... one more street and I'm home. Wet. Fed up with this... I need a break... Tram tracks... get across the tram tracks... wet... slippery—No! No! Arrgh!!" The back wheel slides forwards as I turn, spinning the bike at right-angles to the road, pitching me sideways onto the ground. Everything happens in a kind of slow-motion, but it seems there's nothing I can do: I feel my elbow hit the ground hard, and then the much-hated mandatory helmet hits the road with a crack, leaving me momentarily dazed. For a brief moment, time stops—a kind of breathlessness—and reverts to a different kind of slowness... a painful slowness...

I can't quite see straight—my head's taken quite a knock, but nothing's bleeding. Okay. Let's get this straightened up, then. So I try to get up: but my arm's folded all wrong, and is obviously broken; and I can feel at least two ribs moving around in ways that they shouldn't. It's only now that I realise this wasn't a simple fall: I'm in trouble—*big* trouble... I can stand, but that's all: I'm stranded in the middle of the road, in the middle of the night, with my bike sprawled across the tram tracks, and there's nothing I can do about it. And everything *hurts*...

"Help me! Won't somebody help me!"

I've hardly said this, when a car comes past. And stops. Two young men jump out—and nearly get hit by another car that *isn't* going to stop. Dodging that, they come over, quickly understand what's wrong; almost without a word, one lifts the bike off to the side of the road and locks it, while the other helps me into the back of their car. Ten agonising minutes later, with every bump and turn finding a new source of pain somewhere in my body, they deliver me to the emergency room, and vanish from my life as quickly and as quietly as they came.

> One of the more noticeably weird aspects of life is that when we really *do* need help, it does tend to appear: and often as if 'from nowhere', with no questions asked or thanks expected—a human response, in sympathy with a human need. What's your experience of this? Go back through some examples of your own — both of times where you needed help, and of where you helped others 'with no questions asked or thanks expected'. What are the *feelings* you associate with this?
>
> There've been other times—rather too many of them — when I demanded 'help', but in which it'd be more accurate to say that what I really wanted someone else to take responsibility for my own mistakes... and in those

times there's often been a strong hint from the wyrd on the lines of "You got yourself into this mess: now you find your own way out of it!" Yet, for you, what was the difference in *feeling* between those times when you really needed help, and those when you were simply evading your own 'response-ability'? Looking back with the benefit of hindsight — and without the dubious 'benefit' of blame — what weird challenges did Reality Department require you to face in those times when help was *not* 'provided'?

Meanwhile, I'm meeting up with the weird world of hospital. I'm on my back, on a trolley. Faces appear and disappear, quiet urgency, questions, instructions, needles, someone easing off my jacket and shoes, scissoring through my favourite sweater, fitting a collar brace so that I can barely move. Sometimes it's crowded in this tiny curtained space, sometimes—for many long minutes, it seems — there's no one here but me, surrounded by the background chaos in the unseen, unknown world I can hear out there beyond the curtains. More faces appear, more voices: "Compound," someone says, as my arm is exposed; "May have internal injuries, need a scan"; "Lift up here if you can, need to get this plate underneath you." A tube is pushed gently down my nose and throat into my stomach: the weird sensation of drinking several pints of liquid through my nose. Being wheeled through corridors. A huge machine of some kind: "breathe in," says an electronic voice, "Hold... breathe normally... breathe in... hold," as I'm moved around inside this machine... all seems bewildering, a different, alien, painful world. More corridors, more faces, explanations—"Must operate immediately, need your signature to permit this"; more corridors, more bright lights, more pieces of plumbing pushed into me, more explanations, more instructions, more needles... and then nothing...

We live in an immensely complex world: as even a brief scan through the Yellow Pages would indicate, there are far too many threads of possibility for any one person to explore them all! So we specialise, exploring our chosen threads as far as we can take them, and leaving the rest to others. When we're outside our own areas of expertise —whatever they may be—we have to depend on others; and they, in turn, depend on us. In that most practical of senses, we act as allies for each other, within the total weavings of the wyrd.

Like any alliance, if it's going to work, it means that we have to *trust* those others: trust that they *do* know what they're doing, trust that they *do* have our best interests—as well as their own—in both heart and mind. How easy—or not—is it for you to find that trust? How do you reach a balance between over-trusting—abandoning your own 'response-ability'—and under-trusting, trying to 'control' those others even though you don't know what's involved? What do you *feel* when you know —as in the hospital—that you have no choice but to trust?

Go through some examples of everyday 'alliances' in which you have to trust others' judgement and ability and honesty: from the mundane, such as at the supermarket; to the technical, such as a computer store, a garage or a financial adviser; and on to those where your health—or even your life—is at stake, such as the doctor, the dentist or the emergency room at the hospital. Each in their own fields, those others each have their own concerns and priorities; and we have ours. Yet where is the boundary between those needs? What awareness, both of yourself and of others, do you need in order to achieve a balance at that boundary?

I wake slowly, painfully, to a different reality. It's daylight; that's about all I can see through half-awake eyes. My arm feels like it's weighed down with concrete—which is not far wrong, as it's wrapped in a heavy mass of plaster. There's a line of metal staples down my front; some kind of mask over my face; a rigid collar round my neck; tubes everywhere. A dull confusion: where am I? what's happened? what's going on? why can't I think straight? why does my chest hurt so much when I try to move? Then slowly, slowly, memory returns, showing the links between the past and the present—and perhaps a very different future to the one I'd planned... Through the haze, indefinite shapes resolve into definite faces, definite people: white uniforms, quiet voices, and a little light-hearted banter between people I can't yet see. A nurse close by sees I'm awakening; he stops to sit with me awhile, gently holding my arm, as I come to terms with the strangeness of it all. As he speaks, his words seem also to appear in writing on the wall, just like living in a cartoon-strip—a weird side-effect of the painkillers, they tell me later. Weird, all right...

Weird... and wyrd, I suppose... that wretched line about "There's always a choice, there's always a twist"... If this—stuck on my back in a hospital bed—is the twist, what on earth were the choices? If what I'm experiencing right now is in part the result of my own choices, what *did* I choose? All right, so I've been telling myself for weeks that I needed a break, but didn't do anything about it: and now Reality Department's given me that break—several of them, in fact! Work's going to have to go on without me for a while, I guess... don't know what'll happen about that, or anything, but I'll just have to wait and see: nothing I can do about that right now, is there? And I've lived on my own for years, keeping myself to myself, not really trusting much in anyone after so many weird disasters: but it looks like I have no choice now but to rely on others to help me—and trust that they *will* give me the help I need. Oh well, it's one way of finding out who my real allies are, I guess!

> "I've been telling myself for weeks that I needed a break: so now I have one—several of them!" I can see, quite clearly, the weird feedback from Reality Department about my own choices: and this time I can see it because I *know* I can't blame others—there was no one else involved. But there've been plenty of other incidents in the past when I've tried to hide from that 'response-ability', by blaming others for the results of what had in fact been my own choices... And looking back, I can see that much — if not most — of what I'd thought of as

intentional abuse by others would more accurately be described as feedback from the wyrd: which means that those 'abusive' others were more accurately my unintended allies, reminding me of my choices — if in a somewhat twisted sense! *Not* a comfortable realisation... though I slowly realise that it *is* a true one...

Explore some of your own examples of this. It's easier to first look at your own 'mis-takes', to see the choices you made that are hidden behind them; but then expand that outward to explore some of your more disastrous interactions with others.

Even if you *know* that their intentions were unhelpful, put the blame aside for a moment, and re-view them as your 'allies', whose weird task — regardless of what either you or they might have thought—was to show you your own choices and your power of 'response-ability' within that incident.

What do you learn, about your power and your choices—and the weird way in which we *do* bring to us all manner of 'allies'? Reframing each incident in that way, what happens to how you *feel* about the incident— and about yourself?

Soon after I wake up in the ward, I have my first visitor: it isn't either Mary or Kaye, as I'd expected, but a man named Martin, who works in our other office—he'd been talking with Mary when the call first came through from the hospital, and had decided, without being asked, that he wanted to help. I don't know him that well—he's a rather gruff and diffident character, an odd contrast to his garrulous partner Tina—but even before he's arrived at the hospital this morning he's already picked up my bike from the roadside, taken it home, and brought me a change of clothing: and for the next few days, whenever I need something, he's simply *there*. It's a good thing for me that he is, though, because my two closest colleagues are hardly able to help here at all: Mary's too busy handling my clients as well as her own, and Kaye's lost in sympathy—she comes several times to visit, but her only 'help' is to say, over and over again, "Does it hurt?"...

Kaye's been one of my closest companions over the past few years, so I'd expected her to help me the most: and was surprisingly angry—though at least managed to keep it to myself — when she didn't. Stuck in my own expectations, I hadn't noticed that it wasn't that she chose not to help, but that she *couldn't* help—being lost in over-sympathy, she simply couldn't cope with anything else. So it took me some time to realise that Martin had in fact done everything already: weird though it seemed, there was actually no need for Kaye to do anything other than what she was (or wasn't) doing. And that's when I finally remembered Inverse Murphy: that things *can* go right, if we let them — and that if we only let them 'go right' in the ways we expect, we're limiting our chances! The same applies with our allies: when we really *need* help, it often arrives from the most unexpected sources —and it's wise to notice this...

When you've been in trouble, from what weird directions has help arrived? In what ways was it different from what you expected? If it wasn't what you expected, what difficulties did you have in recognising that this *was* the help that you needed?

When others have been in trouble, you—like Martin — might well have found yourself prompted to lend a hand. Where does that 'prompt' arrive from?—the wyrd, perhaps? Sometimes the people you decide to help will be close friends, but at other times they may only be acquaintances, or even total strangers: for what weird reasons do you choose to help some people, and not others? — or to help at some times, and not others? What is the difference in *feeling* to which you respond— show your 'response-ability' — in these subtly different circumstances?

Out of hospital at last, and starting back at work: I've been warned that I won't be able to throw myself into it in my usual way, but it's still a surprise just how hard it is to come back to... all those things which seemed so important, so urgent, just don't seem so important any more... Yet even here there are more weird interactions with my 'allies': sometimes Kaye and the others recognise that I simply don't as yet have the ability to cope with everything that work throws at me, but at other times they get distinctly peeved. Which is fair enough, because although there's no visible difference, those are the times that I'm using—or rather *ab*using—their willingness to help, evading work that is not only my responsibility, but for which I *do* have 'response-ability'... When work seems difficult, it's hard to tell whether it's because it is difficult for me at present, or whether it's the result of my new habit of laziness: but by watching how others respond to my pleas for 'help', I can soon learn the difference!

> Like most of us, perhaps, I've learnt the hard way that nothing much happens when I'm wallowing in self-pity: and nor do I get any real help from others — though I may well get some of that useless pseudo-'sympathy'... Yet when I make a *choice*, and stop feeling sorry for myself, this state of mind ends up bringing me the help I need.
>
> Yet sometimes we'll need help from our allies even to reach *that* level of 'response-ability'... There's an old Native American tactic for this evasion of responsibility that I've seen used particularly well in women's support-groups: "You are welcome to come to the circle, and tell us your troubles, and we will advise you; you may tell us once more of the same troubles, and we will remind you of our advice; but if you come a third time, we will not comment, we will not criticise, but we will simply stand up, walk away, and re-form the circle without you."
>
> Others may be responsible *about* our needs, but cannot be responsible *for* us: they'll help where they can; but if we refuse to take responsibility for our own choices and our own actions, eventually they'll have no choice but to remind us, gently but firmly, that we *do* have the power to resolve our problems by ourselves, and that it *is* our 'response-ability' to do so... It's not exactly a comforting kind of support, but it's an honest one — and an honest ally is always the best kind to have!

> We all get 'needy' at times, demanding 'help' from others when all we're really after is attention — "that special attention which is the prerogative of the miserable".
>
> Look back at some of your own examples of this: what happened? At what point did your allies — your friends, workmates, support-group or whatever — "stand up, walk away, and re-form the circle without you"? You were probably more than a little angry about that at the time — it would have seemed like a betrayal rather than an act of 'power-with' — yet looking back now with the different eyes of the Inner Adult, what responsibility were you avoiding, and trying to export to them instead?
>
> In what ways did the challenge from your allies' weird withdrawal remind you — forcibly, perhaps — that the power and the 'response-ability' to change the situation ultimately lay with you, and you alone?

Looking round, and looking back on the accident, I can see that *everyone* is an ally: we all interweave in some weird way, whether we know it or not. But I can only use that awareness to help me—and to help me help others too—by accepting that it *is* weird: that we're allies *because* of the nature of the wyrd itself. We're not just weird allies, but allies in wyrdness: and to understand just what that means in practice, we need to review some of that wyrd 'toolkit' that we've gathered on our travels!

The wyrdness of allies

Everyone and everything can be an ally—*if* we let them be so, and *if* we can let them be who and what they are, rather than trying to force them to fit our expectations of them. Often we don't have much choice about who we meet: but we *do* have choice about *how* we meet them — and there can be plenty of twists in that...

> "Excuse me, lady!" calls the old tramp: she looks at his grimy clothes, snorts in disgust, and wafts away with an arrogant stride. At which point the university professor,

who admittedly *does* look a bit of a tramp in his old gardening gear, shakes his head sadly, and gives up in his attempt to warn the young woman that she's left the lights on in her car, and will have a flat battery when she returns...

Each of us has different parts of this weird puzzle we call 'life': I have an image sometimes that we're like explorers who occasionally meet to exchange notes on what we've discovered—here an uncharted valley, there an area of dangerous crevasses and loose boulders — and if we're going to make best use of what others have to show us, then it matters how we meet them! In what ways do you *allow* others to be your allies—or prevent them from being so? In what ways do you allow yourself to be *used* as an ally — without allowing yourself to be abused in the process?

Look back at some of your many brief encounters with others, especially strangers, and review them not as isolated incidents, but as interweavings of the wyrd you share with your fellow-explorers. Use that weird 'toolkit' of different perspectives on that interweaving — subject and object, blame and responsibility, use and abuse, assertiveness and self-responsibility, sympathy and empathy—to help you in this: what do you learn about how you've responded to those unexpected and unacknowledged allies? Understanding more of the nature of wyrd, in what ways can you use that toolkit to improve the quality of those encounters — and thus access more of the help you *are* offered through the weavings of the wyrd?

In the context of the wyrd, each person we meet is part of our geis, our 'fate with twists'. They help to move us — sometimes visibly, though often not—along a path which we may not *consciously* appear to choose, but with 'retrocognition' it often looks suspiciously like it! As the old Scottish expression puts it, we each 'dree our own wyrd', we each suffer — or otherwise — our own geis: and others, interweaving on *their* paths, often become our allies within the wyrd—whether they will it or no. And the same applies to us: by the nature of the wyrd, we'll often find our lives bending and twisting in sympathy with others' geasa.

Those are the twists: and though we don't have much choice about the *fact* of those twists, we *do* have choice about how we respond to them. So it's worthwhile aiming towards a fundamental shift in our general perspective towards others: a move away from the common notions of 'friends' and 'enemies', and towards regarding *everyone* in the same way, as 'allies'.

> Who do you regard as your friends? Why is this? What makes them *friends*, rather than acquaintances, or colleagues, or associates—or enemies?
>
> Who do you regard as your enemies — if any? Who do you think is likely to regard *you* as their enemy? Why is this so? What changes someone from an acquaintance—or even a friend—into an enemy? Perhaps more important, what changes an enemy into a safer acquaintance, or even into a friend?
>
> Now experiment with that shift in perspective: there *are* no 'friends', there *are* no 'enemies' — instead, all of them are 'allies' of different kinds, helping you along the path of your own chosen wyrd in their own different, and often unintended, ways. What happens to your concept of 'friends' if you do this? What happens to the way in which you view those previous 'enemies'? Perhaps more important, what changes do others — both 'friends' and 'enemies'—begin to see in *you*?

It's sometimes hard to see some people as anything other than 'enemies': yet looking back over the years, either they or their actions often turn out to be central to our personal growth, and our discovery of our own power. That's certainly true for me: without all those years of childhood abuse at the hands of big sister Anne, for example, it's unlikely that I'd understand how people interweave as well as I do — or be able to help others recover from similar abuse, as I so often find I'm 'asked' in some weird way to do. It still doesn't make it any less abuse, and certainly doesn't *excuse* the abuse: but it *does* mean that we can choose to turn it round, and use those understandings for *our* empowerment now—regardless of their intentions then.

The fact of others' existence is not in my choice, and neither, often, is their presence: but how I choose to perceive them *is* up to me — and it *does* make a difference. Yet I can't control how others perceive *me*: I can't *make* someone like me, for example — although I can easily provide conditions under which they may not like me at all... No matter how much I might hope otherwise, the ways in which others happen to interpret my various attempts at communication is *not* in my control: my 'communication' *is* what others make of it, which is not necessarily what I intended!

Allies are like mirrors: through the weirdnesses of our interactions, they reflect back to us the effective meaning of our own choices. So it's wise to pay heed to how others interpret our communications and our actions, because they're often more in sympathy with our wyrd than we are! Being allies with each other is a relationship of mutual 'use': and it's only if one or other of us fails to understand the nature of that relationship that it can fall into abuse. And allies are people with whom we can mutually explore issues—that image of 'explorers of uncharted worlds'—and take constructive risks: and with a little awareness on our part, and a fair amount of trust in the nature of the wyrd and its 'feedback', we can learn to do this with *anyone*—everyone whose paths we happen to cross in the interweavings of the wyrd.

Allies with *everyone*: does that sound impossible—or at least impossibly hard to achieve? Perhaps: but look back at what you've learnt about the nature of the wyrd, and you'll find it's not as hard as it sounds. Our lives weave and interweave through the wyrd, constantly moving in and out of sympathy with each other: and *everyone* we meet has something to show us, about their own wyrd and ours. All we have to do is *notice* this—and learn to listen out for that strange sense of 'impending wyrd' that warns us when action is needed...

Try it: using the various techniques in that weird 'toolkit' we've recently explored, experiment with the idea

—the *experience*, rather—that everyone you meet can be your ally. *If* you let them, that is—that part *is* up to you... How much do you need the 'sympathy' of your peers — friends with whom you already share similar feelings—before you can listen to what is said to you? What have they to show you? What have you to share? What is the 'We' that is created in the weird space between you?

With whom do you find this easy? With whom do you find it hard? What does creating that 'ally' relationship with others ask of *you*? Use the results of this experiment to show you more about your own prejudices and assumptions—and how they get in the way of your own empowerment within the wyrd, and your sharing of that power-from-within with the many others whom you meet...

In some ways it *is* easiest to practise this with our existing friends: but even here we need to be wary, because a 'fair-weather yes-friend' is useless to us for this... Our relationships with allies depend on *honesty*: so an ally is not simply a friend, but someone with whom the relationship will survive a level of honesty that can sometimes seem brutal. And that may not be true with many of our apparent 'friends': I've certainly been involved in many supposed friendships which, in reality, were little more than a codependent kind of 'double-entry life-keeping'—"I'll do this for you if you'll do this for me," with a rigid kind of 'account-keeping', and constant complaints about 'unfairness'... it can be quite a shock when the wyrd shows us what's *really* going on in some of our 'friendships'! It's essential to understand that, by its nature, the wyrd *is* 'unfair': there *is* a kind of feedback, and everything *does* balance, but the ways in which this happens can be very weird indeed...

And it's also essential to understand that often the *hardest*—and not, as we might expect, the easiest—person to achieve this kind of relationship with will be a close personal partner: the reason is simply that the emotional stakes can be—or at least *feel*—much too high to take that kind of risk. In the longer term, it's likely that our personal partner — if we have one — will indeed be our strongest ally: but unless we *do* take the risk to allow them—and they, in turn, allow us—to each find their *own* understanding of their wyrd, the relationship is all too likely to collapse into a mutually abusive chaos. For the relationship to grow, yes, it's wise to develop that understanding together; but in its initial stages, at least, it's wisest if that understanding develops *in parallel* with each other, rather than in a smothering and ultimately shallow 'togetherness'.

Perhaps the greatest single danger here is what I call the 'soul-mate/sole-mate' delusion: placing all our expectations on one person — and then getting upset when they are, inevitably, unable to 'deliver'. And a variant of the same problem is a kind of 'us against the world' mindset: basing our 'We' so firmly on the two (or more) of us that we try to exclude the rest of reality —a mistake which usually ends up in suitably weird results... So that's another issue we need to explore before we move on much further!

14

SOUL-MATES AND CELL-MATES

The idea that everyone can be our ally may seem weird enough, but it's going to get weirder still... in fact many aspects of relationship only begin to make sense when we start to interpret them in terms of the wyrd and its interweavings. One of the best illustrations of this is that weird sense of a 'soul-connection' with someone else—or the even weirder sense of a 'soul-mate' relationship with someone, where your lives feel as though they weave and interweave throughout space and time. It can seem very strange, and very special—which can be a problem, especially if we fail to realise that in some ways it's just a minor side-effect of the wyrd, and nothing 'special' at all. But once we grasp that that's what it is, it opens a whole new realm of possibilities in relationship, a whole new realm of choices—and, of course, some interesting twists...

Heart and soul

That sense of a soul-connection or soul-mate has two quite distinct aspects: a particular feeling, and a particular type of sympathy — a sympathy in *action*. We become so closely in sympathy with the other person that we'll find ourselves doing, quite unconsciously, what they most desire — or, with some people, what they most fear instead. (In a weird sense, there's no real difference: the state of being 'in sympathy' with another's emotions is exactly the same—all that's different is the emotions involved!) Once we become aware of this, it *feels* weird; yet it actually *is* wyrd.

> With whom have you had this kind of 'soul-connection'—finding yourself, quite unconsciously, doing either what they most desired or most feared? What was *their* response to you? If you realised what was going on—a weird kind of connection in which you'd made no *conscious* choice—what did you *feel*? And in what ways did you use this knowledge? In what ways—if any—did you try to use it to 'control' the interaction between you?

By the very nature of the wyrd, we'll move into and out of a resonant 'sympathy' with others all of the time. The same threads pass through everyone, everywhere, everywhen: and if we don't know this, or don't accept it, we're going to have problems... When we actually meet up with that reality — as in that sympathetic soul-connection — we'll either experience it as an overwhelming feeling of 'one-ness', or an equally overwhelming feeling of sheer terror, as we discover that others seem to know more about us than we do ourselves. And all manner of delusions can arise from a confused response to those feelings: from New-Age fantasies about 'soul-mates' or 'special powers' at one end, to full-blown paranoia at the other. Sure, there's a sense of 'something special' in that connection: but it happens to everyone, and *with* everyone, if only we'd let ourselves realise that it's there all the time anyway. And sure, there *is* something terrifying about the way that that connection can weave its way past even our most elaborate defences: but that connection *does* exist, whether we like it or not — and if we're afraid of it, the wyrd, helpful as ever, will tend to provide us with 'lessons' to remind us of that fact... It may not *feel* like it, but in fact it's entirely ordinary. Just weird, that's all... just wyrd.

In another sense, that soul-connection is a kind of direct communication with others through the wyrd — along the threads of the wyrd, if you like. And it also maps to a kind of *spiritual* desire — 'spiritual' in that sense of 'a sense of meaning and purpose, a sense of self and of that which is greater than self'. Through the wyrd we have access to everyone, everywhere, everywhen — hence that feeling of "our lives interweaving through space and time", because in effect that's exactly what it is. But it also means that, in the same way, we have direct access to whatever we think of as 'meaning and purpose' — or lack of it, from a more paranoid perspective. We get a sense of self, and yet at the same time a *loss* of the sense of self, because that connection shows us that the boundaries to our 'I' are entirely arbitrary; and in the same way we also get a direct *experience* of 'that which is greater than self' — whether we want it or not!

> If that soul-connection is 'communicating with others through the wyrd', with whom would you want that kind of communication? With whom would you *not* want that kind of communication?
>
> The twist here is that by the nature of the wyrd, we don't actually have much of a choice about this, and certainly not much in the way of control over it: the wyrd passes through everyone, everywhere, everywhen, hence that kind of communication is always possible, with anyone, anywhen — even when we least expect it. Which may explain a lot... Remind yourself of some examples of your own weird interactions with others — some that you'd very much wanted, others that you most definitely didn't. Reviewing them in these terms — of an entirely ordinary, if often strange, communication with 'the Other' directly through the wyrd — what happens to the way you now perceive those incidents? Do they still seem so special, or so 'suspicious'?

There's another serious source for confusion that can weave its way in at this point, namely that old childish need to be 'the centre of the universe'. In the paranoid form of this, the existence of any 'Other' *shows* us that we're not all there is in the universe: so we're likely to interpret any kind of communication from them — especially via the strangeness of the wyrd — not merely as a problem, but as a threat to our very existence. Which can lead to all kinds of 'pre-emptive' actions against that perceived threat—as may perhaps be all too familiar... And it can also lead to the old 'all or nothing' syndrome: if my notion of 'We' is so subject-centred that I think of you only as an extension of myself, the moment you do something I don't expect, I'll probably think there's no 'We' at all, and withdraw completely into my own 'I'... which will guarantee that there's no 'We' left!

Another side of the same problem gives rise to the 'soul-mate/sole-mate' mistake. When we resonate with each other through the wyrd in this way, there *is* a sense of being 'soul-mates': and that's no delusion. Yet if that awareness becomes entangled with childish needs for certainty and centrality, the results can not only be delusory, but even deadly. One form this takes is that this sense of connection becomes twisted into a statement of *ownership*, of exclusivity — "*my* soul-mate, my *only* soul-mate" — which leads straight into the dependent or codependent chaos around which so many 'love songs' revolve: "I can't live without you", "You're the only one for me", "You're mine, all mine" and so on. But it can get *really* tangled if we assume that this overwhelming sense of 'total connection' must extend to everything else: sex is one obvious problem-zone, but there are all too many others as well... And particularly if we've learnt to depend on others, or focus ourselves always on others — as women used to be so strongly socialised to do—there can be a sense that there's no way of connecting to our own soul *except* through 'the Other': which creates problems not only in personal relationships, but at other levels too — for example, at least one major religion has this dangerous dependency as a corner-stone of its creed...

All right, let's do our usual 'them and us' exploring here!
Who do you know who's fallen for that kind of trap:
mistaken that entirely ordinary soul-connection of the

wyrd for 'something special' — "You're the only one for me!" — and abandoned themselves to a bewildered 'Other'. What happened? At what point was the wyrd kind enough—or, from their perspective, *un*kind enough —to let them know that it was only a fantasy, a delusion built on childish hopes and fears? What kind of confusions arose when the bubble finally burst?

And, yes, let's ask when and with whom you've done the same... What happened for *you* in this? In particular, what were the *feelings* that you went through? Looking back a little more carefully, where was there a hint of 'impending wyrd' that was trying to warn you where the fantasy was going wrong?

Given the chaos, it's easy to be cynical, and say that it's *all* a fantasy — or a bad dream, more likely... No wonder that some people regard 'falling in love' as a short-term illness with rather worse side-effects than a dose of 'flu, and would rather give the whole affair a miss! And yet that would miss the whole point, because that soul-connection *is* 'love', and it *is* 'special': all we need is a strong dose of a rather rarer trait—namely 'maturity'— to bring it out into Reality Department in a rather more practical way...

So it's useful to invoke the Inner Adult for a while, to reframe this concept of the 'soul-mate'. The *feeling* is the result of a connection through the wyrd — sometimes momentary, sometimes longer—such that we *know* that there is no boundary between 'I' and 'the Other', between 'I' and 'not-I'. That felt sense of a soul-connection itself arises not from 'something special' between the two of us as such, but between *everyone* — the 'something special' being the wyrd itself. So a soul-mate relationship is not necessarily exclusive—the '*sole*-mate' delusion —and certainly not necessarily sexual—the 'soul-*mate*' delusion —but is simply a relationship of any kind with 'someone with whom we can converse from the soul'.

We know about 'body language', we'd understand 'a meeting of minds', or the subtle sympathy of 'a heart-to-heart talk': but what is communication at the level of the soul? In what ways does it differ from that of body, or heart, or mind?

The concept of a 'soul-connection' suggests communication at what I've earlier called a spiritual level: in other words it'd be a sharing of 'a sense of meaning and purpose, a sense of self and that which is greater than self'. In particular, the spiritual component — the 'soul-connection' component — would be the simultaneous experience both of a sense of self and of 'that which is greater than self'. What's your experience of this? With whom have you been able to share this — without movement, without words, without emotions, but just in a sharing of togetherness, of *being*?

There are times—many, perhaps—when words are not enough: but sometimes they suffice to hint at a meaning and an experience. When mind and body, heart and soul, all combine, and communicate, would that perhaps be what we mean by 'love'?

A soul-mate relationship is one in which we can share everything, 'good' or 'bad' — including an argument. "It's a bit like being in love," says Kim, "but a lot more like loving them for what they are, not what you think they are—or 'should be'..." And the wyrd weaves its way through everywhere and everywhen as well as everyone: hence, as Kim puts it, "It doesn't matter how far away they go — you always know they're with you. I call them 'forever friends', and they're as different from those soppy and soul-less teddy bears as you could get!" It *is* a form of love, but definitely a weird one...

In effect, a soul-mate is a learning-partner—an ally—with whom we can touch the full depth and breadth of the wyrd. There are no limits: and yet, strangely enough, there *are* boundaries. But before we can resolve that particular paradox, we need to look at another twist in the soul-mate saga: its weird sense of inevitability, that makes that soul-connection seem so much like an act of fate.

The chosen ones

Call it fate; call it destiny; more likely we'd call it geis if we're talking in terms of wyrd, but call it what you will: there are some people we're *stuck* with, whether we choose them or not! As Woody Allen once commented, in his usual wry fashion, "You can't divorce your mother..."; and even those from whom we *can* 'divorce' in one sense or another — a friend-turned-enemy, a much-hated boss—still tend to recur in our lives in one way or another, no matter how much we may try to avoid them. And at the same time there are also those who'll stick with us, and support us, through thick and thin—no matter what we do. Not so much soul-mates as cell-mates, perhaps...

Scan through your own 'cell-mates' for a while...

Who are you 'stuck with'? Who is inescapably part of your wyrd? Family, perhaps? Work-colleagues? Friends of friends? Or, looking a bit wider, those whose politics or attitudes you dislike, but seem unable to escape?

What is it about them — or what they do — that you dislike, that leaves you feeling that you're stuck with them? Remembering the weavings of the wyrd—and the way that every thread, every characteristic, passes through *everyone*—where do these same threads pass through *you*?

And who do you think — or even know — feels that they're stuck with *you*? Why? For what reasons?

Turning this around, which of your cell-mates are you glad to be stuck with? Which do you think are glad to be stuck with you? Which threads of the wyrd do they resonate with in you?

There's *always* a choice, says the wyrd: so it's arguable that we do actually *choose* our cell-mates — our family, our work-colleagues and so on—even though it's obvious that we don't do so consciously. A number of Eastern traditions — Indian in particular — base their philosophies on exactly this point, suggesting that in each incarnation we choose a family in which to be born, in order to best assist our growth towards 'nirvana' or, literally, release. (Release from the prisons of life, they say — and it sometimes does feel like that!) The idea has been much misused in recent times — for example, the all-too-common 'New Age' put-down of "You *chose* to be born into that environment, so any problems you may have are entirely your fault" — but even so it does have some validity. Whether we believe it or not, for example, it *is* useful to proceed *as if* it's true: because it puts the power to choose—and the responsibility to work with the situation—back onto us. We know, all too well, about the twists in our past relationships with our cell-mates: but once we remember that we *do* have choice, we also *do* have 'response-ability' in each moment, right here, and right now.

> Imagine that you chose your family; that you chose your work-colleagues, your clients, and all the other people you interact with every day: all the ones you like, and all the ones you don't. They're your chosen allies: your 'chosen ones'. Seeing them from this perspective, what difference would it make if this were true? What difference would it make to how you perceive what they show you?—and especially of what they show you of *you*?
>
> Friends are cell-mates we're more conscious about choosing, but the wyrd plays a strong part even in this! Look back through some of your friendships: how much did you make a *conscious* choice to create and maintain that friendship? There'll be some with whom there's a sense that you were 'fated' to meet, and yet it *was* your choice — and theirs — to make something more than a momentary 'meeting of explorers' out of that literal 'co-incidence'. But take this a step further, as with your other cell-mates, and imagine that your choices went further back: that you both *chose* to meet each other, in order to explore that soul-connection further. What difference does this make to how you perceive that friendship — and *your* power of choice within it?

The real complications arise when we *know*—or think we

know, or want to believe — that there's a soul-connection between us and someone else: but they don't share the same belief. And the opposite is true, of course: I look back at all too many occasions when someone thought they'd found a 'soul-mate' in me — which may have been true, but they somehow forgot to recognise that I'm also a perfectly ordinary human being... There may well *be* a connection through the wyrd to the other's 'core-I' — their super-ego, in classic psychology terms — but it doesn't happen to match their beliefs as to where they are or want to be: and in those circumstances the ego usually wins!

The ego, in classic psychology, is responsible for maintaining our boundaries: a mismatch of expectations in a supposed 'soul-connection' is an equally classic example of a boundary-problem, and we've already seen the chaos that can arise from that... An object-centred approach tries to *make* the other share the same belief; a subject-centred approach tells the other that they *ought to* want to share the same belief, and gets resentful when they don't; both of these approaches—lost in the child*ish*-ness of the Inner Child—somehow manage to forget that the other person *is* 'Other', and *is* entitled to their own choices, no matter what we might think!

There may also be another problem here — one of our own making. In one of the old Sufi tales, the mad priest Nasruddin is sitting slumped in a dark corner of the tea-house, the very picture of dejection. "What's wrong?" asks the host. "I've been searching — *searching* — all of my life for the perfect woman," sighs Nasruddin, "and today I found her..." "But... shouldn't you be happy?" asks the other man. "She told me that *she's* searching for the perfect man," comes the sad reply, "and she's... she's... still looking..."

Are you still waiting for the perfect partner? On a more cynical note, would you 'trade in' your present partner — if any — the moment you find that 'perfect partner', or even a 'better' one? What are you looking for?

The wyrd passes through everyone, everywhere,

> everywhen: so in principle, the same threads that you're looking for in that 'perfect partner' can be found in *anyone*—though sometimes they may be hard to find... The choice is up to us: what do *you* choose? And notice the twists that follow from each choice...!

The crucial point here is to be aware not only of the feedback that we're getting—or not getting—from the other person, but also from the wyrd. I want to believe that there's a 'We', a soul-connection, with Nicky, for example, but given that we keep managing to miss each other, no matter what I try to arrange to happen, maybe the wyrd's trying to tell me something...

Perhaps the only way to resolve this is to keep aware of our choices—and not abandon our choice of 'I'—yet at the same time accept that the feedback we get from the wyrd *is* the feedback that we get. That's the hardest part, of course... But it's also useful to notice that the feedback that we get from the wyrd about our supposedly 'failed' relationships is also our soul-connection with each person: it may not be the threads that we want, but the connection *is* there. It isn't easy — "When we hugged again, it still hurt really deeply," said Jen, about a relationship that hadn't gone the way she'd wanted. "When I don't see Davey, it *is* okay ... mostly..." she says, getting teary...— but it's almost certainly the wisest way to go: and it's the only way in which we retain our power, and our response-ability, to create something new.

The love connection

The wyrd passes through everywhere, and contains everything within—and through—itself. There are no limits—and that's what we experience in that moment of soul-connection. We *know* that there is something 'greater than self' — and in that moment we're part of it, and *are* it. That's *magic*, in a very literal sense of the word.

Another word for this would be 'love'—but in both a more

specific sense of 'love' than the usual one, and also in a much wider sense. It's love in that somewhat mistranslated Christian sense of 'Faith, Hope and Love' — mistranslated in that it's described more closely in the older phrasing of 'Faith, Hope and Charity', with 'charity' in its original deeper sense of *caring*. In this sense of love, there's an interweaving both of sympathy and empathy, and an awareness both of sameness and of difference —a weird dance of 'I' and 'not-I', of 'I' and 'We' and 'I'.

> Familial love; 'brotherly love' and 'sisterly love' in both their biological and wider sense; the love shared with a teacher, or a respected elder; that deep respect of a colleague or a friend which we'd have to call love: what's your experience of these? In what ways are they differ-ent from each other, and from the more usual romantic meaning of 'love'? In what ways do you experience them as being the same? And in what sense is it true that there are no limits in these relationships—and yet there are clear, definite boundaries?

If that's love, what's hate? It's often thought of as the opposite to love, but in many ways it's exactly the same energy twisted into a different form: there's still the same intensity, and still the same sense of inevitability — though perhaps more in the sense of a cell-mate we'd like to banish from our lives, but can't, because we're stuck in the same cell... So the real opposite of both love and hate is *indifference*—the negation of that weird soul-connection. An *absence* of either sympathy or empathy — just a sense of nothingness, or often no sense of anything at all.

One of the cruellest forms of this is when someone — vaguely aware of both the strength and significance of that soul-connection—deliberately blocks it, or uses the promise of it, as a means to control the other: "How can you possibly say you love me when you don't give me flowers for my birthday?" or "I'll love you if you do this for me... and then this... oh, and this too..." It's a form of abuse, and an extremely common one—so common that many songs, at least, seem to suggest that's all that 'love' is... 'Conditional love' is no joke; and in the sense that that deeper sense of love *depends* on maintaining that soul-connection, it's probably no real love at all.

> That may have stirred up some unhappy memories, but if so it's probably a good idea to explore them a little, to lay them to rest...
>
> What's your experience of 'conditional love'? What is the *feeling* when someone arbitrarily places conditions on what you'd thought — or felt — was the soul-connection of love? Who did this to you — family, friends, colleagues, partners? And — rather more difficult to face — who have you done this to? What conditions do you place on the love — the self-acceptance — that you offer to *yourself*?

Unconditional love is quite different: and given the realities of being human, it's almost impossible to achieve! It's perhaps best understood simply as *acceptance*: that this is who they are, this is who we are, and we acknowledge and celebrate our samenesses, our differences, and the threads that weave between us. But it's much more than that: in one weird sense, for example, 'unconditional love' is actually highly conditional — because there's a *commitment* to that soul-connection of 'We'. It's also an acceptance that is both non-attachment and non-*de*tachment—a soul-connection that exists because there is no 'need' for it to exist. And because of that soul-connection, there's a *shared* sense of meaning and purpose, and a shared sense of 'I' and 'We' and 'I', which can link back through the wyrd to perhaps the weirdest emotion of all: *joy*.

> Back to the café for some more people-watching: but although you'll be watching others, the key person to watch is yourself... And although this one's about 'unconditional love', there's no need to panic — because there's nothing that you'll need to do, or to say, to anyone. Unless you want to, of course!
>
> Choose your usual quiet place in the café, and go to that usual quiet place inside yourself. Right now, these

people around you in the café are your cell-mates: who are they? You know them—or some of them—on what we might describe as a surface level: but who are they at the level of the soul? What are their hopes, their fears? Move sideways in the quiet space within, so to speak, so that you can now see yourself as just one of those people in the café: what are *your* hopes, *your* fears, at the level of the soul?

Watch, and gently reach out, along the threads of the wyrd that stretch between you, to all of these people —including that person out there that you call 'I'. Like the wyrd — and as an aspect of the wyrd — love is everywhere, is everyone; like the wyrd itself, love simply *is*. 'Doing no-thing', explore that soul-connection with each one: dispassionately, yet with all the passion of your heart and soul; attached, yet not attached; detached, yet not detached; involved, yet without involvement; without conditions, without limits, yet with clear and certain boundaries; somehow *beyond* empathy, beyond sympathy, the glimpse of soul-connection with each person there simply *is*.

For example, over there in the far corner are Geoff and Julie, trading horror-stories of past relationships — and it's clear what's going to happen next! And, knowing them, the explosions that are all too likely to follow in the next few weeks... But just watch, quietly: an acceptance that they are who they are, and that this is what they choose—no matter how much they may protest otherwise! In this moment, they're your cell-mates, and your soul-mates; and despite their internal — eternal? — chaos, they are, in this moment, soul-mates for each other. Watching yourself, watching you, watching them, involved, yet not involved, attached, yet not attached, what do you *feel*?

Would it make sense to describe that feeling as a quiet kind of joy? Would it make sense to describe it as love?

Unlike the schmaltz and self-delusions of so much 'romantic love', there's no abandonment of 'I', so there are still boundaries: and yet there are no limits — there's no need for them, because the boundaries of 'I' and 'We' and 'I' are clear. *Anything* is possible: but precisely because it *is* possible, there's no need to try to make it so. Instead, what happens between you is what you *choose*—tempered by an awareness, through that soul-connection, of the twists that weave through every choice...

And there's one choice, one possibility—perhaps too often associated inappropriately with 'love' — that you've probably noticed I've carefully 'forgotten' to mention here. That's because sex — that weirdest of all human activities — really needs a chapter of its own: so that's what we'll turn to next!

15

WYRD SEX

First page you turned to, after reading the contents? If so, it would illustrate one point: the weird fascination that sex has for so many of us! So why is it that a relatively minor human activity — certainly in terms of time — should occupy such a central place in so many people's thoughts, and so often portend such a weird choice of conduct? Time to look at this weirdness a little more closely...

The weirdness of sex

In one sense, sex is entirely ordinary: it's simply part of the mechanism by which the human species propagates itself. Nor is it even an unusual one: in varying forms, it's common to most so-called 'higher' species, from earthworms and insects to mammals and many plants. Sex itself, and hence the two distinct human sexes, provides an essential 'randomising' function which allows faster species-response to a changing environment: so although, as some of the more extreme feminists have argued, males are technically "biological parasites on the parental care of females", without them we would all be riddled with disease! And in most species, sex—or even *interest* in sex, especially from females — is something relatively unusual: just once a year, in most longer-lived animals, and sometimes less than that. So it's interesting to stop for a moment, and realise just how weird human sex really is.

> Probably worth while to stop here for a moment, and have a look at your own experience of 'human sex'... Any comments? Any 'weird experiences' that stand out? Or is the *ordinariness* starting to sound a little weird—or the weirdness ordinary?

In principle, as with any animal, sex is part of procreation. Much of it is built-in, so to speak, with many of our responses— for all we may want to believe otherwise — 'hard-wired' within us, in much the same way that baby animals seem cute — to ensure they're cared for by their parents—while adolescent ones suddenly aren't—and are often kicked out with unseemly haste! In most animals, procreation is effectively the only purpose of sex, and it's tightly timed by the seasons, to match the availability of resources that young animals need. But humans? Anytime, anywhere, and almost, it seems, anyone... and procreation is often —usually?—the one thing humans are trying to *avoid* in sex!

Males are necessarily the sexual 'show-offs' in many species, perhaps most; yet in humans it's equally true of females. Much though the fact may be unwelcome to some, even the anatomical build of women — by comparison with most other female animals—is little short of permanent sexual advertising: the hip-waggle that is a direct result of the different shape of the pelvis in women compared to men, for example, or the breasts— permanently filled-out, unlike almost any other mammal — which dance like the sexual equivalent of a fishing lure for the whole of an adult woman's life. Weird... almost as though there's something extra in human sex... wyrd, perhaps?

Whatever it is, and for whatever reason, it's a weirdness that 'civilised society' — especially in nominally Judeo-Christian cultures — often tries to sweep under the carpet, to make it 'disappear'. It doesn't work: the threads of the wyrd will always come out *somewhere*: and if we try to deny a thread as major as sex, and shove it out of the back door of our lives—"Not *now*, it's not *nice*!"—it'll simply drift back in through the side-door of the unconscious again, with even weirder results...

> What are your own attitudes to sex? How easy, or hard, is it for you to accept that—physiologically speaking, if nothing else — you *are* a sexual animal? Whether it's easy or hard for you, notice that for others it's not: what do you *feel* about that difference? Without an empathy for that difference, what kind of complications do you think are likely to arise, and in what kinds of relationship?

Sex is weird: like all other aspects of the wyrd, it's never truly under our control—and it has its own weird versions of Murphy's Law!. "I used to think that sex was something you did with your spouse, and *only* with your spouse," said a friend; "I'm damn glad, now, that I wasn't a virgin when I married. And I also thought that you didn't find anyone else attractive when you were firmly committed into a marriage—but it doesn't happen that way... and it certainly makes life complicated!" Whether we like it or not, sex has its own imperatives: which means that we need to find a way to work *with* them—because fighting against them simply won't work.

Lust—the natural desire for sex—has an energy all of its own: the word 'lust' is closely related to 'lustre', which means 'to shine'. But plain, ordinary, old-fashioned, uncomplicated lust gets dressed up in romantic guise, to make it more socially acceptable, or to pretend—either to others, or to ourselves, or more often both — that it's something that it's not: and *that's* when all the complications start to happen... Lust is a *feeling*: and it's important to remember that we don't have any control over feelings as such —they simply *are*, and it's best to let them be that way. But we *do* have choice about how we respond to those feelings: we do have that 'response-ability', and it's up to us to use it wisely. Given the downright dishonesty and denial that underpins almost all of our society's attitudes to sex—and the real dangers, for both sexes, if anyone makes any kind of a mistake—this isn't exactly easy...

> This isn't easy at an individual level, either. I'm at a social evening at the offices of one of our clients: I'm chatting away with Pat about business, when I become aware of an undercurrent that's suddenly in our conversation, and a strong sense of arousal — too strong to ignore, or to pretend that it isn't there. The old sexual chemistry again... and *totally* inappropriate here, especially with a client! I'm not going to say anything *at all*: and as my face starts to blush with embarrassment— which I'm sure *must* be visible to everyone — I make a strangled excuse to Pat, and flee!
>
> What are some of your own examples of where you feel you've had to stifle your natural sexual response to others? Why was this? What effect did this denial have on your own self-image — or on how you perceived the other person?

It's from that stifling of feelings that all the prurience and prudery starts—often building to a chaotic crescendo of blame and counter-blame: "It's *their* fault that I was aroused! *she* led me on! *he* did it *to* me! they *made* me drunk, it wasn't *my* fault!" and so on... But we've seen all this before, when we explored the problem of blame in a more general sense: and as we saw then— as with that small boy who wanted to blame his hand rather than face his *own* responsibility for breaking a plate — trying to 'export' responsibility to others actually hurts *us*, because in doing so we throw away our power of 'response-ability', and hence lose our power of choice. So it's useful to step back, and look a little more closely at the *feelings* that arise from the interweavings of our mutual sexuality: and recognise that we *do* have choice in how we respond to them. If we're not going to abuse ourselves or others, we do need to *manage* our sexuality, and direct it towards our choices: but that's not the same thing at all as trying to 'control' it — which, as we've seen in other contexts, rarely works well at all...

The wyrd, being weird, has no boundaries: it contains everything within itself, and weaves through everything, everywhere, everywhen, everyone. When it meets up with the arbitrary boundaries of social custom — the literal meaning of 'morals' — there can be some interesting confusions: especially around sexuality. For example, it's not uncommon for someone to take a moral stance about homosexuality, describing it as immoral, evil, unnatural, *wrong*: and yet the morals of pre-Christian Greece, from whence so much 'Christian' philosophy arose, were highly homosexual. Heterosexuality was regarded by many as pointless and loveless, fit only for procreation and nothing else: and while Socrates and his compatriots sang the praises of their beautiful young boys, Sappho and her followers on the island of Lesbos—hence 'lesbians'—wrote some of the most powerful and erotic poetry ever known. Many people might have difficulty with such attitudes in our present society: yet like everything else, the way we express our sexuality *is* a choice—which means there's also, as always, a twist.

Another Sunday, another café — this time close to the beach, a favourite haunt of the city's arts crowd. Over there, at the far table, are two young women, fingers clasped across the table in a lover's embrace. They reach over, and kiss each other. As they do so, I hear a sharp intake of breath beside me: at the next table, two teenage girls start sniggering and making pointed comments, while their mother glares at the lovers in frosty disgust, and orders her daughters to look away. In a world of their own, the lovers don't seem to notice this: they'll have seen it often enough, anyway. But I just look on in sadness, at the way our arbitrary, subject-centred 'morals' can so easily intrude on others' private lives and private loves...

I'm prudish and shy, and probably moralistic too, trying to hide from a sense of shame about my own rather restricted sexuality. Watching others who are freer in this sense — particularly those whose sexuality is different from my own — can be quite a challenge: if nothing else, it's an interesting exercise in empathy! So try it for yourself, perhaps?

If you're a woman, try looking at other women as if

214

through a man's eyes; if you're a man, try looking at other men through a woman's eyes. Reach inside yourself, to find those threads of the wyrd, and then reach outward, to find those 'different eyes'. In what ways do your morals intrude, trying to force the picture to fit a certain way? Working your way past that filter as best you can, what do you discover about how *you* respond to your own sex?

Still reaching out in empathy, turn those others' eyes — a woman's eyes, a man's eyes — towards you. What do you feel of the beauty and the lustre that they see in you? What do you feel of your power in this? And in what ways do you fear it?

Human sex is a great deal more complex than simple procreation: seeing people describe a car, or even a computer program, as 'sexy', it's obvious that, like the wyrd itself, sex pervades pretty much everything—especially if we choose it to do so. Given the confusions, it's all too easy to make 'mis-takes': "If we feel a sexual response with each other, it must be love," I say, but in fact it's probably nothing more than mutual lust... And yet sexuality is as much a *spiritual* quest as anything else: a way of understanding and exploring both self and 'that which is greater than self'. To make it work, we need a rigorous honesty and self-honesty about what we *feel*; and while for much of it we do *need* the involvement of others, it's up to *us* to take the responsibility to ensure that it's a relationship—a sharing—of mutual *use*, not mutual abuse... It's up to *us*, in other words, to bring our sexuality into a joyous, and fulfilling, dance with the whole of the wyrd —or, as the Greeks would have put it, a dance with Pan.

The dance of Pan

Like the wyrd—and as an aspect of the wyrd—Pan is *everywhere*: that's literally what the name means. (If you're familiar with Greek mythology, one of the simplest ways to understand the concept of wyrd is to merge the imagery of the three sisters of Fate with that of the Greek notion of Pan, or his later embodiment as Dionysus.) Pan has been much-maligned in Christian times, partly because of long-forgotten religious politics — although in fact several key elements of Christian imagery (such as "This is my body; this is my blood") are clearly Dionysian. But more than anything else, the depiction of Pan as 'the Devil' is a classic example of denial and projection: any symbol that includes *everything* within itself is obviously going to cause problems for a philosophy that has fixed ideas about 'good' and 'evil'... That concept of 'the Devil' has little to do with Pan, and for the most part is an *invention* of the early Church, without which their 'survivalist'-style 'good versus evil' worldview could never make sense. In effect, 'the Devil' is a dumping-ground for all the aspects of their own humanity which the 'founding fathers' of the Church — writers such as Saul of Tarsus and Augustine of Hippo — could not face within *themselves* or in anyone else: and that particularly included sex.

> Like Saul of Tarsus — 'Saint Paul' — Augustine was no saint in his youth: until his sudden 'conversion' in later years, he's reputed to have been a particularly abusive playboy — which suggests that his diatribes against the sins of sexuality — women's sexuality in particular — might possibly have had more to do with envy and blame than with anything 'spiritual' as such...
>
> In what ways do you blame others for *your* desires — especially when those desires aren't satisfied? If you're on your own and lonely, and you see others enjoying each other, how much do you want to suppress *them* so as not to face the hurt within yourself? Then look around, and see how much the same thing happens in society at large... could this sad envy and other-blame perhaps be the *real* source for many of our apparent social problems?

There was *some* validity in their concerns, as we'll see shortly, but there's perhaps a more useful way to view this: that our sexuality is one of the most direct ways in which we can *experience* the unity of the wyrd. Within sex, not only do the separate boundaries of 'I' and 'I' tangibly dissolve into a shared 'We', but in that weird moment of orgasm both 'I' and 'We' release themselves into the wyrd — a literal 'union with everything'. Exactly the same happens in what one friend euphemistically described as 'one-sided sex', other than that there's no immediate sharing: "The closest experience I know," she said, "was in a 'past-life regression', where you focus on a tiny spot within, which is your sanctuary, and the place you return to after the regression; but in this, everything centred on that growing spot of ecstasy, until the rest of the world just shrank away..." But it's not just that 'the world shrinks away': in that brief, timeless moment, there is *only* 'I', *and* everything, all in the same space. That's weird... that's wyrd.

What we might call the 'mechanics' of sex play their part in this, obviously, but that alone is not enough: it's the *context* that seems to matter most—especially if we're to reach that moment of union with each other and with the wyrd. "Orgasm?" asks Lisa, with her usual wry grin, "'S kinda like a tiny little shy, furry critter what needs coaxin' an' teasin' out of its hole—*if* yer know what I mean!"—she winks, and grins again—"Weird, but it's like that: an' it don't take much to make it scamper right back where it came from—which is annoyin'. *And* upsettin'. More than just a *little* bit, I can tell yer...!'" Much like that notion of 'doing nothing': a great deal may have to be done in order to reach that state, but trying too hard can be very trying! It's a dance with Pan: a dance with plenty of energy, perhaps, but still a delicate one...

The same applies to all those adolescent images of 'weird sex': strange postures and positions *do* make a difference, but only in a context which few adolescents would have the patience to achieve! Those complex contortions of the *Kama Sutra* and tantric yoga have exactly the same purpose as classical yoga, or the transpersonal postures for ecstatic trance researched in recent years by people like Felicitas Goodman and Belinda Berkowitz: they *might* just work as 'sex games', but they're essentially meditations in a spiritual sense — they take the form of shared meditations in a sexual context, but the overall aim is the same. They need to be approached with practice and discipline if they're ever to work in the way that they're intended: but far too many people take a shallow 'gosh-wow' attitude to tantra and the like — which is precisely why it so often seems pointless. Those postures seem weird, but in practice are rarely wyrd enough: as with ecstatic trance, the intertwined positions are very precise, and need to be held, without moving, for fifteen minutes or more... and in a sexual context that's *not* easy!

And in any case, for most purposes, they're entirely unnecessary. Being aware of the wyrd, everything and anything can be experienced as sexual, or with that same sexual intensity — *if* we let it be so. In some ways it's our old friend Inverse Murphy again: things *can* work, if we let them—and if we only let them work in expected ways, we're limiting our chances... One friend commented that what most turned her on was watching her husband wash up—and she wasn't joking, because it was the fact that the sex had a context of *caring* that made it meaningful.

> Yes, they're right, this singer-guitarist is *good*, and she also reminds me a lot of Lisa: big and burly, with bawdy backchat and lots of laughter — "Everybody's lookin' for the... Big O," she sings. She invites a couple of other musicians to join her. I've seen them before: offstage, they're a pair of dissolute drunks, but here, in this context, *magic* happens. The atmosphere is suddenly electric — and highly sexual. It's the lead guitarist I'm watching: he's drunk, of course, but his fingers dance over the fretboard in a joyous interweaving with the singer's guitar — does he need the alcohol to let go enough to play this well, or is it the drink that's playing *through* him? Weird... But it's the body-language, and the glances that flash between them, that are so fascinating: she's centre-stage, secure in herself and her laughter, and able to *share* that with everyone; he's like a kaleidoscope of sexual archetypes, at one moment a small child with a wicked grin, the next a leering lepre-

chaun; and through it all, the music, weaving its dance for Pan between them. And yet they're both sitting firmly in their seats, on opposite sides of the stage: it's so sexual *because* there is no contact — and it's clear that this 'shy furry little critter' of musical magic would vanish if either of them made a move to make it so. That's wyrd...

Partly because of those domineering demands of lust within us, it's easy to assume that sex *must* always be physical, or else it isn't sex: but as in that example on the stage, there are many times when the *intensity* of the experience — its truly weird component — only exists when physical sex *isn't* an option. What are some of your own examples of this: a hug with high sexual energy with a workmate, perhaps? And when you *can* contain that intensity of energy within you, where does it go?

Flirting is the obvious example of this: and yet flirting is also, in its own way, a sexual equivalent of play-fighting — 'a weird cross between competition and co-operation'. It *is* a 'power-game': but it works as long as the emphasis is on 'game' rather than 'power' — and especially so, as long as it remains focussed on power-with rather than power-over or power-under. It's a kind of sexual wrestling: when it's done well, with 'response-ability' and a rigorous self-honesty, it helps everyone explore and extend the limits of their sexual power; but when it's done badly, with denial and blame, all hell can break loose...

Jody, one of the engineers at the research establishment, was an absolute master of flirting, playing that edge of sexual tension to the hilt, yet playing it so perfectly that no one ever misunderstood what was going on. She was also brilliant at parodying all manner of sexist stereotypes — pretending to be the secretary of the other engineers in her office, for example — but in a way that made that office *fun*, for everyone. Perhaps it worked so well because she was good at her job, and everyone knew it: she had no need to play 'power-games' to cover up her own faults. But Kara, by contrast, was a disaster-area when she worked here: she had an horrendous habit of chasing after our male clients in a blatantly sexual manner, and then making wild accusations of 'sexual harassment' whenever she couldn't make a sale—so it was a huge relief for everyone when we were finally able to 'let her go'... Yet we're still stuck with our 'office creep' Andrew, who's just plain dishonest in this: and he still purports not to notice why Kaye carefully keeps her distance whenever he's around...

Flirting is a sexual version of play-fighting: so in what ways do *you* 'play-fight' by flirting with others? What do you *feel* when you play that edge between co-operation and competition, between sharing and selfishness in a sexual sense?

The game collapses as soon as anyone takes it too seriously—stops seeing flirting as a *game*—and tries to 'take control', or to force the game to go a particular way — either to physical sex, or to a prudish nothingness. What do you *feel* when the game collapses in that way? What do *you* feel towards the 'giggle-wrecker'—the one who took the game too seriously, and spoiled it for everyone? When you've been the one who made that 'mis-take', what do you feel towards yourself? And how much do you try to cover up those feelings by blaming others instead...?

This dance with Pan is a dance of power: and as we saw earlier on, about use and abuse in a more general sense, the crucial distinctions lie between power-from-within and power-with on one side, and power-over and power-under on the other —not in what is actually done. Despite what our morals might have to say about pornography, or about sado-masochism and the like, there is no such thing as 'abusive sexual behaviour': but there certainly can be—and all too often is—such a thing as abusive sex... And despite the shrill moralism of those who would play the subject-centred, and ultimately abusive, game of 'God's Police', it's up to us, and no one else, to develop our 'response-ability' in sex. In reality, the God's Police mindset is grounded in fear, not power: it lives in terror of the dance of Pan. It may believe it's helping when it tries to 'protect' us with its rigid rules and regulations on 'correct' behaviour, but, in practice it actively *hinders* us, not least because it has no grasp of the weird twists of Inverse Murphy — or that, by the nature of the wyrd, the only valid 'law' is *'anything goes'*. Once we understand this, we at last gain the power to choose what *we* want from our own sexuality: and gain access to our own power, and responsibility, in sex.

The power of sex

Sex can be mutual use, or mutual abuse: it's up to us. And it's up to us *as individuals*—not the State, or some other self-appointed group playing at 'God's Police'. It seems obvious, stated like that: but for many people it can be a concept that seems strangely hard to grasp... One of the tragic ironies of current cuckoo-feminism is the degree it tries to censor and suppress women's sexuality, when an earlier generation of feminists fought so hard to free it. Sex can be power-with, or power-over, just like any other form of power: and it's becoming clear that the standard gender-stereotypes about sexual abuse are as inadequate as we saw they were about most other forms of abuse. And although it's rarely acknowledged in our sexist society, in reality males are as much victims of sexual abuse as females are; and lesbian relationships turn out to be the most common site of sexual abuse — rather than the least, as the usual gender-stereotypes would suggest. So the bleak reality is that the power of sex can be used, or abused, just like every other thread of the wyrd. Yet it knows no boundaries: especially not simplistic boundaries of sex or sexual preference... and to try to conceal that perhaps unpalatable fact beneath a morass of 'politically correct' delusions is just another form of abuse...

That's the twist, says the wyrd: but there *is* always a choice —and the choice is ours. And the choice is a simple one: to be honest, or not. If we're not, we're going to abuse *someone*: either ourselves, or others, or both. So if we're to avoid abusing anyone —through sex, or any other interaction—we actually *don't* have a choice: we have no choice but to be honest—rigorously honest —with others, but especially with ourselves.

> The first requirement for being honest with ourselves and others in a sexual sense is that we need to be clear about what we *feel*: it's hard to be 'response-able' about our sexuality if we don't even know what our responses *are*... But all those subject-centred expectations of us— about what we 'should' and 'shouldn't' feel—or internal-ised self-blame and self-shame are bound to get in the way: how easy—or not—is it for you to work your way past these? How easy—or not—is it for you to express your *own* feelings and choices about your sexuality? If it's not easy, what 'response-ability' do *you* have to change *your* involvement in the situation, so that you *and* others can feel safe expressing their own sexuality?

Our sexuality gives us a direct experience of union with each other and the wyrd: 'making love' is perhaps a weird euphemism for this, but it'll have to do! But even in this we have choices: as my friend Lynn puts it, we can make love *to* the other, make love *with* the other, or 'make love' *at* them — the latter being, at best, a misuse of others in a sexual sense.

Making love *to*, says Lynn, is 'body first, person afterwards': "One takes a fancy to a body, a face, and starts to build fantasies about how they'd be in bed" — in other words following the dictates of lust. The risk is that someone may have the wrong idea... but as long as it *is* clear that it's mutual, it's use, not abuse: and it depends strongly on being able to *receive* pleasure as well as to give it, and to allow ourselves to be given pleasure in our own right. Often that weird sense of union comes not in the physical sex itself, but in what Lynn describes as the 'afterglow'—a quiet sense of sharing and contentment after the urgent demands of lust have been placated.

Making love *with* is the other way round: 'person first, body afterwards'. The physical sex arises out of, and as an expression of, an already-existing context of *sharing*. "Friends end up making love," says Lynn, at a point where the boundaries on sexuality—usually softer with a partner than with other friends—happen to fade away. The risk here is that one person may be indulging the other, or agreeing to — or even setting up — a sexual involvement 'for the sake of the friendship'. As Lynn puts it, "There is the risk of need coming in: not just the real human need of this sexual experience, of sharing and touching—which is no risk, really—but of sex as a cure for a problem." But when it *does* work, the sexuality provides an immensely powerful support to 'I' and 'We' and 'I'.

Making love *at* is where it goes wrong: 'the Other' becomes just an object or a subject for our own confusions and desires. This is the valid part of the Christian 'founding fathers' fears about sexuality, except that their own self-dishonesties have helped to make it the chaotic confusion that it now so often is... One of the problems is that, just as it's easy to become addicted to adrenalin to provide an illusion of 'meaning and purpose' in an otherwise empty-seeming life, it's also easy to get addicted to sex—or to the internal hormones that drive it and result from it. And responding always with sex when the real need is for *sharing*, or simply for physical contact—that *need* to be 'in touch' with others—can eventually lead to some *very* crossed wires... There's a danger, too, that sex may be perceived as the *only* way to achieve that sense of union with the wyrd; and there are all the old traps about dependency on another to 'get high' — which leads us straight back into those 'soul-mate'/'sole-mate' delusions again. We've probably all had more than enough experience of those particular lessons: yet they can be surprisingly hard to get to 'lessen'—especially if we don't pay enough attention to what we actually feel...

> Making love *to*, *with* and *at*: I have my own experiences of all of these, but what are yours? Looking at those examples where that crucial sense of connection just wasn't there—and where, all too often, you were stuck with the feeling of having to just wait it out, thinking of

anything else so as to get away from the emotional discomfort of the situation — what were the *feelings* — that sense of 'impending wyrd', perhaps — that warned you that this was not going to work out the way that you'd hoped? And looking instead at those situations where it *did* work out, in what ways can the feelings that you remember from those situations help you to regain and retain your 'response-ability' if 'making love at' happens to you again — or if you find *yourself* doing it again?

Trust is crucial in this: facing our fears, as Lynn puts it, about "whether one's wobbly bits will be laughed at, or if one's left hip will dislocate while trying out that new position!" These fears will always be worse if you've had too much experience of being 'made love at'... but how easy — or not — is it for you to trust the other person *or* yourself in sex?

Sometimes the confusions and miscommunications seem so bad that it's just not worth the trouble: "I think I'll just give up and go to a monastery somewhere," I say to myself, in one of my bleaker moments; "or perhaps just give up entirely..." But in fact we don't have all that much choice about this: as the sad stories of some of the ascetics would indicate, Pan won't let us get away *that* easily! We *are* sexual animals: and when we're faced with something that fundamental to our being, it's generally wisest to try to work *with* it rather than fight against the imagined 'unfairness' of our fate...

A pagan view of sexuality provides an interesting contrast to that of civilised suburbia — often a weird contrast, since it aims always to work *with* the energies of Pan. One of the more common pagan concepts is the notion that sexuality is not so much a choice as a kind of 'possession' by the Goddess and the God — particularly at the May Day revels which the Puritans struggled to suppress. In mediaeval England it was even considered that any children resulting from such 'plesant pastimes amidst the woods, groves, hils and mountains' were the progeny not of their physical parents, but of Robin Hood and his merry band of followers — hence several common English surnames, such as Robinson, Johnson, Tuck and Merryweather. It was a way of acknowledging sexuality within society which we'd rarely understand now...

Or would we? Has sex, for you, sometimes felt like a 'possession by the Goddess and the God' — a feeling of being *used* by 'that which is greater than self'? What difference did it make to your own sexual experience, and that of your partner? Acknowledging that the 'possession' was taking place — and that it was not in your control as such — what choices did you still retain? Being 'used' in this way, how did you ensure that you were not *ab*used by this weird energy that seems so much 'greater than self'? And if you tried to ignore that energy, or to suppress it in you or in others, what happened?

We *are* sexual animals: one result of that is that almost everything we do to 'feel good', especially with others, is likely to be hard-wired within us either as 'sexual advertising' or a sexual response. Dressing up may make us feel good, but will almost inevitably draw attention to us; lipstick simulates the slight reddening of the lips in sexual arousal, and most other make-up has much the same effect; and perfumes smell 'good' precisely because they simulate human pheromones — men's perfumes in particular are often based on musk for exactly that reason. Whether we know it or not, much of what we do is sexual advertising: hence it's actually abusive of *us* if we attack others for responding to that 'advertisement'. If we're not clear who we're trying to 'attract', and send out a generalised 'come here' message in a sexual sense, we really can't complain if the 'wrong' person responds...

Given the impact that it's had on society in the past few decades, it's unfortunate that so much feminist theory shows such a lack of realism on this issue. "We have an absolute right to go where we want, and dress as we please," says the 'Take Back The Night' slogan, and it's true: but if we do so, we also have absolute responsibility in what happens — which is exactly what the slogan tries to deny, demanding that others must be responsible for us instead... We're never responsible *for* others, but it's actually an act of abuse if we refuse to take responsibility *about* others: and attacking others for responding to our blatant sexual advertising would certainly come under that category. But at the same time it *is* disempowering to feel that we constantly have to 'dress down', to hide ourselves, or to suppress our own sexuality for fear of triggering the wrong person's response. It *is* a real dilemma: but it's one that won't go away simply by playing 'God's Police' with it...

We'll be coming back to this problem later, but how do *you* resolve this dilemma — if at all? If you have difficulty with it — which most of us do — notice how easy it is to project the blame entirely onto others, rather than face the power — and 'response-ability' — that we *do* have in each situation... in what ways can you work with what you know, and what you *feel*, about your own sexuality, to help create a 'win-win' for *everyone* in this dilemma?

Sex can be a problem, or not: ultimately, it's up to us. It's our sexuality, and our 'response-ability': there's always a choice, says the wyrd, but remember that there's always a twist...!

But sex is also one aspect of the wider issue of gender: the physical, social and other differences and problems that are specific to the type of body into which we were born. "Is it a girl or a boy?": there are some weird assumptions—and possibilities – that can arise from the answer to that question, so that's where we next need to turn our attention!

16

GIRLS AND BOYS

Fairly early in pregnancy, a single chromosome in the growing embryo triggers a minute change in the amount of a hormone in the mother's bloodstream: and that's what determines those major shifts in body-structure that we see as the two different sexes. It's weird that a tiny difference in an otherwise unremarkable body-chemical can lead to a huge divergence in life-experience: but just how much of these differences between the sexes are due to nature, or to nurture? How much of the problems, and the advantages, that we have in our lives *really* derive from our sex — and how much from plain old sexist stereotypes, about what we 'ought' to be? Whichever they may be, a wyrd perspective will probably help...

Nature...

The two sexes *are* different: our experiences of sexuality — to continue our previous theme — are distinctly different, for a start.

> Another 'exercise in empathy': how well do you under-
> stand how sexual experiences *feel* for the other sex? If
> you don't know — which most of us don't — then *ask*...
> which may bring up some weird responses! Notice the

> difficulties which arise for you in doing this — or even in response to the *suggestion* to do this... why should this simple question seem so difficult?

Some of the differences are not so obvious, and could certainly be described as 'weird'. In their work on the trance-effects of postures, based on religious sculptures from around the word, Felicitas Goodman and her colleagues found that exactly the same posture can create entirely different experiences for men and for women, and that different postures are sometimes needed if both sexes are to experience the same effect — and that these sex-differences have been recorded in different traditions throughout history. Goodman's 'Chiltan Spirits' posture from Uzbekistan, for example, requires the women to sit cross-legged, and the men to stand, in order to experience the same trance-image — usually of a circle of women seated round a fire, in this case. Another matched pair of postures, from Cernavoda in Romania, appears to be used for a healing trance: the woman sits in a rather awkward position with one leg straight and the other bent, while the man sits in a kind of pensive or sorrowful position: the men in this posture hardly experience anything at all — other than exhaustion — but their presence means that "the women report having access to powerful reservoirs of energy to do their healing work". Weird... the threads of wyrd do pass through us all, yet it does seem as though our sex can make it harder for us to access some threads, but much easier to access others...

Another subtle difference is simply the different experience of *change*: adult women are changing all the time, weaving their way through many different cycles of the body, whereas men — although they do have their own cycles — tend to experience change as something less internal, and more 'out there'.

> There's a beautiful African tale that illustrates this point. Imagine an old woman sitting in front of her hut in the heat and the dust of an eastern evening, with a gaggle of girls squatting in a semicircle in front of her. "A long time ago," she says, "I was a girl, just like you. And then my

body changed, and I became a maiden. And through each month, and through each month, my body changed, and I knew myself as woman. And I met my husband: and through each month, and through each month, my body changed — but he was always the same. Then by him I became pregnant: and through each month, and through each month, as my baby grew within me, my body changed — yet my husband was always the same. Then I bore my child, and I fed my child: and through each month, and through each month, my body changed — but my husband stayed the same. Then I bore my second child, and my third: and with each child, and with each child, my body changed — but my husband, he was always the same. Now I am an old woman," she says, "and my body has changed: I can bear children no more. But my husband, he's still much the same as he ever was. How boring!"

Whether you're a woman or a man, in what ways are you aware of the rhythms and cycles of your own body? In what ways are you aware — if at all — of those of others? Without awareness, there can be no empathy; and without empathy, relationship can become more than a little problematic...

We're never responsible *for* others, but it's useful — to *everyone* — to be responsible *about* others and their constantly changing needs. Reaching out in empathy with others along the threads of wyrd, sensing within you the ways that *they* change, and change in response to you, what can you learn about your *own* cycles, your own changes?

It's if we're *not* aware of our cycles that the problems can arise — because we're then likely to project the changes in our behaviour onto others instead, blaming *them*, in a subject-centred way, for changing, when the changes are actually in *us*. Unhappy memories, for example, of trying to co-exist with Kara in that office, because, to her, everything was *always* our fault: "You should have *known* it's 'raging hormones' season," she'd yell, "I'm not responsible for my damn hormones, am I?" For the existence of the hormones themselves, no: but even under their

influence—especially if aware of it, which she obviously was—
she surely had *some* 'response-ability' to manage how she related
to others? But then I can hardly talk, I suppose: "*Why* are *you*
angry?" I snarl, when it's clear that it's just one of *my* mood-
swings that's going on...

Pregnancy is perhaps the extreme example of this — so
much so that some women describe it as like being taken over by
a kind of parasite: symbiotic, perhaps, but not always benign—
especially in terms of what *we* may choose. "I'll tell you what was
wrong," says Ursula Le Guin's character Takver, in her novel *The
Dispossessed*; "I was pregnant. Pregnant women have no ethics—
only the most primitive kind of sacrifice impulse. To hell with
the book, and the partnership, and the truth, if they threaten the
precious foetus! It's a racial preservation drive, but it can work
right against community; it's biological, not social. A man can be
grateful he never gets into the grip of it. But he'd better realise
that a woman can, and watch out for it." She may be right on the
last point: but looking around in our society, particularly at many
fathers' *felt* response to the complex issues of abortion, I'm not
so sure about that...

> Mark, one of our grumpier technicians, is obviously
> having trouble at home: "Don't ever let your ol' woman
> get pregnant," he says, while we're sitting in the tea-
> room; "her brain'll go to pudding, and then you've *really*
> had it..." A few of us start muttering: "Hey, that sounds a
> bit sexist, Mark..." But then a quiet voice cuts in,
> unusually excited: it's Mai, one of the senior program-
> mers. "It's *true!*" she says. "All the time I was pregnant
> with Anna, I had to struggle to keep my mind working,
> and I still don't think I've got it all back yet." Mai's done
> both her master's degree and doctorate *and* had her first
> child since moving here from overseas seven years ago:
> she's no sluggard, and no fool. For all his surly sexism,
> perhaps Mark might have a point...
>
> Pregnancy affects everyone differently — including
> the fathers who so often get forgotten, and who *can* help
> a great deal when they're allowed to be involved! It can

> be a time of wild changes for everyone: so once again, it
> calls for mutual respect — and for empathy, not sym-
> pathy. In what ways can *you* help in creating this?
> Whether you're a woman or man, what 'response-ability'
> do you have?

The one obvious difference between women and men is that women can bear children, and men cannot: and that in itself has some weird results. Women have a kind of literal immortality built into them — an immortality which men can only access through women. If she so desires, a woman needs no *direct* contact with a man in order to become a mother; but to be an active father, a man is entirely dependent on a woman's presence — a dependency which can easily lead to all kinds of abuses, in both directions. Some societies try to resolve the problem by building a philosophy of *personal* immortality — either by 'redemption', as in Christian theology, or through reincarnation, as in eastern religions or early Celtic concepts. But where the only available 'immortality' is through children and grandchildren — such as in Judaism — it tends to lead to 'ownership' of children (and arguably of women too): hence, for example, all those endless 'the son of... the son of... the son of...' lists of patrilineality in the Bible...

> It's useful to explore this dependency through empathy,
> by the age-old trick of inverting the options — and explor-
> ing the reality of that inversion.
>
> If you're a woman, imagine that you have no way of
> bearing children on your own: if you want to be a parent,
> you have no choice but to involve a man, to bear the
> child for you. Explore how you'd *feel* in that scenario:
> would you succumb to a sense of emptiness and pur-
> poselessness if no man would have you, perhaps — or
> even try to trap a man into depending on *you*, to hide
> your dependency on him?
>
> If you're a man, imagine that you have 'immortality
> built into you', in the ability to bear children: but the
> responsibility — and the risks — are yours alone, and
> women have no way to reach that sense of immortality

> except through you. How does it *feel* to be depended on in that way—and to have that responsibility for others as well as for yourself?
>
> Both these scenarios are inverted from physiological fact: but how much are they true in other senses? Explore those twists in reality for a while...

Many of the old stereotyped gender-roles arose from real physical differences: many of them quite small, but crucial in terms of survival for a society always on the edge — as most were until well into this century. A surprising number of sex-differences can be categorised under the old 'gatherer/hunter' split: male anatomy focusses the strength in the upper body, and is geared for high-power but lower-endurance tasks typical of a hunter, while female anatomy focusses the strength more in the lower body, and is geared for lower-power but higher endurance tasks typical of a gatherer — hence the comment, from the Vietnam War days on the Ho Chi Minh Trail: "Women can carry only four-fifths of a man's load, but can carry it half as far again." Even in city-based societies, the same stereotypes still have their validity: women tend to be better than men at 'multi-tasking', and in working with repetitive detail, but tend to have more difficulty than men at some kinds of problem-solving, and with spatial tasks such as reading a map 'upside-down' or judging the exact distance between their car and the next. It's these weird differences that emphasise that it's useful for *everyone* if we *can* be allies for each other.

> Given the omnipresent 'incentives' to complain—such as that "special attention which is the prerogative of the miserable"—it's all too easy to see the disadvantages of our life, or the advantages that others seem to have: but what are the *advantages* of being the sex that *you* are? What do you *not* have to face because of the type of body that your 'I' wears?
>
> And how true for you are those stereotypes about the 'typical' man or woman? How much is the *opposite* of that stereotype true for you?

Quite minor physiological differences can have significant effects on our emotional behaviour, too. Most men will remember all too well the childhood admonition that 'big boys don't cry': but it would have been more accurate to say that big boys *can't* cry (whereas small ones certainly can...), because a specific 'female' hormone, tightly linked with the ability to cry, shuts down in males during puberty. It's the reason why many women — often to their intense frustration — find themselves crying when in reality they're angry; and the inability to express emotion in tears, as they were able to do in childhood, often leads men to express sadness as anger — especially in times of grief. Weird... but that's the way our bodies work — and it's important to learn to work *with* it.

There *are* differences between the sexes — and important ones at that. Yet in many ways the differences between the sexes, in practice, are far less than the differences between individuals — each one of us — regardless of their sex: the *intra*-gender differences, technically speaking, are far greater than the *inter*-gender differences. But often it won't seem that way: not because of our nature, but because of our nurture — the expectations that were thrust upon us by others in the society and family into which we were born. Often we don't have much choice about what we've been handed by nature (though a little persistence can often pay dividends!); but we *do* have choices about our nurture — especially once we start to unravel some of the weird twists that can *seem* so 'natural', 'just the way things are'...

...or nurture?

Feminist theory draws a useful distinction between sex — the facts of physiology — and *gender*, which is more of a stereotyped role imposed on us by society's subject-centred expectations of what boys and girls 'ought to be' — constructing, from infancy onwards, a picture of 'proper' behaviour for women and men. For example, there's that pervasively nasty little nursery-rhyme:

What are little girls made of?
   Sugar and spice and all things nice
—that's what little girls are made of.

What are little boys made of?
   Snips and snails and puppydogs' tails
—that's what little boys are made of.

"Oh no, not *that* nursery-rhyme!" said Fred, who's now in his sixties. "My mother thought it was wonderful: she put a framed copy of it above my bed, and she used to recite it to my sister and me every night—she had no idea how much I *hated* it. It made me feel like I was being blamed for everything, and that my sister was always perfect, whatever she did—and that's certainly how it seemed, because I was always getting into trouble on her behalf. I hated it so much that in the end I *did* start to act like I *was* made of 'snips and snails and puppy-dogs' tails': and Mother didn't like that *at all*—even though that's what she'd told me, night after night, that I was supposed to be..." "Fair enough," says his partner Sylvia, "but how would *you* like to be told, endlessly, that you have to be *nice* to everyone? 'Sugar and spice' indeed!—we always had to look so damn 'nice' that we were never allowed to play out in the street, like you could, in case we got our clothes dirty!" They both laugh: a healing laughter...

Innocent nursery-tales — or a serious source of sexist stereotypes? What do you *feel* in response to what that rhyme says about *you*, about what you're 'made of'? Explore some other songs and stories of your early childhood: looking back through the *feelings* of that time with a more adult empathy, how much have the gendered 'morals' of those tales pervaded your life—and your choices now?

Nature and nurture are so closely interwoven that it's often hard to tell the difference: though they're both part of our wyrd, that much is for certain! One solution to the problem is to take the stereotypes *as if* they're true, and then twist them around a bit... This is what Jungian psychology does: it starts with basic stereotypes of 'the feminine' and 'the masculine', and weaves outward through the complex threads that are described as 'archetypes', until it arrives at a richer, deeper, wider fabric that approximates to a description of the wyrd itself.

It's a useful tool: but like all such tools, there's a real danger in taking it too literally. I've seen quite a few 'women's spiritual-ity' texts, for example, that insist, almost in a kind of Jungian parody, that the moon—or whatever—is *always* 'feminine', and likewise that intuition, nurturing, sharing, peace-loving and so on are human attributes that only women have, while only men are violent, competitive, controlling... Not only are such 'essentialist' ideas little more than an embellished version of those childish sugar-and-spice/snips-and-snails stereotypes, but they're also exactly what earlier feminists fought *against*—because they knew how much they stultified women's choices. As Jung's concept of the 'animus' and 'anima'—'the man within the woman' and 'the woman within the man'—make clear, *every* thread passes through *every* one of us: everyone, everywhere, everywhen. As we saw earlier with those issues of use and abuse, perhaps the only real 'gender-difference' here is in which threads tend to show more easily on the surface...

It's worthwhile looking at some of the standard gender-stereotypes — 'masculine' strength and courage, 'feminine' beauty and nurturing — and exploring their opposites *within yourself*. So, for example, what is *feminine* strength, *feminine* courage? What is *masculine* beauty, *masculine* nurturing? What form do they each take within *you*? What form do they take in others — particularly those of the 'wrong' sex, according to those stereotypes?

Take a look around you — at how you interact with others, at how others interact with you, at images in the media and elsewhere. How much do those standard gender-stereotypes dictate how you, and others, relate with each other? Make a point of looking for those 'opposite' threads — such as feminine courage, or

> masculine nurturing — in everyone you meet: what
> difference does it make to how you perceive them, and
> relate with them?

Another important 'nurture' issue arises from the dominant role of the mother in most children's upbringing: even where the father is permitted to be present at all—which he's not for a surprisingly high proportion of families—he's far more likely than the mother to be away from the home, at work or elsewhere, in the times when younger children are awake. The result is that girls and boys tend to have quite different problems in what Jung described as 'individuation'—the *spiritual* process of identifying 'I', and defining boundaries between 'I' and 'not-I', which comes to a head in adolescence.

The problem for girls is to *separate* from the mother, to identify herself as an individual in her own right. From birth onwards, she's known herself as 'same as' her most prominent— perhaps only—active parent: so it's easy for her to regard herself as an *extension* of the mother — and courtesy of the usual subject-centred confusions, many mothers do treat their daughters in that way, even to the extent of sharing each other's clothes. So the late teen years, when the *need* for individuation usually becomes too strong to suppress or ignore, can be a suddenly explosive time—and particularly hard for the mother, who may well feel she's been betrayed, or at least unfairly attacked. But it's actually a kind of wrestling, in which the daughter is trying to find *her* own strength and power—and *needs* someone to push against, someone who will push back hard, but will still let her 'win'. As one wise friend — a grandmother — commented to me the other day, "Of course it's 'unfair'—but the main task of the mother of a teenage daughter is to be in the wrong!"

The boys' problem is somewhat different: they've known from birth that they're *not* 'same as' their mother, but that's about it. Right to the end of primary school, they've lived in a world populated either mostly, or entirely, by women: hence many, perhaps most, boys have no idea of who they are, or what they're 'for' at all—and almost the only images they have about what it is to be male come from the media's mangled stereotypes, or from women's often disparaging remarks. Sometimes the only kind of 'self-definition' that boys have is a fear-driven *negation* — that they're not-female, not-homosexual, not-weak, not-cowardly and so on; and since, by its nature, the wyrd keeps reminding them that they *are* all of these things, in one sense or another, they may well try to export those fears to others, through 'gay-bashing' or similar kinds of scapegoat-abuse.

The systematic, if not obsessive, 'pro-feminist' denigration of masculinity and maleness in the past few decades has certainly made the problems worse — there can be no doubt about that. But throughout history, boys have always been easy 'marks' for any group or cult that seems to offer them *any* sense of meaning and purpose: and the spiritual *need* for 'a sense of meaning and purpose, a sense of self and of that which is greater than self' is so strong that it almost doesn't matter what the group is or does, as long as it *does* seem to offer that spiritual security. The fanaticism of many sports-fans may seem pointless to most of us, but it's actually one solution to this problem: and at least it's a relatively benign one, because many cults and cliques are not. Where most girls seem simply to need someone to wrestle with—in one sense or another—most boys do seem to *need* this sense of group-membership to provide them with a stepping-stone to personal identity: and if our society doesn't seem to care what form this takes, it can hardly complain at the results! Inaction and indifference are *choices*, even at a societal level: "There's always a choice," says the wyrd, "but there's always a twist..."

Look back — or within — your teenage years, at that crucial period of individuation: that time of becoming *yourself*, as an independent—and sexual—being. Was it a time of turmoil for you, as it was—and is—for so many others? Understanding a bit more about the nature of abuse, and being aware that blame for the past — whether of others, or yourself—helps no one, look a little closer: what did you do to others, and to yourself? In what ways did you try to export those confusions to others — or try to 'buy being liked' by 'importing' others' inner chaos? How much do those choices then still affect your life now—especially in the ways in which you relate with others?

What was happening to your peers then — how did *they* cope? In what ways did you allow *their* choices influence how *you* relate with others — both then and now?

By the time we get to adulthood, the basic gender-stereo-types can be summarised in two simple matched pairs of statements. The first of these 'summaries of sexism' is the ubiquitous assumption that 'men *do*; women *are*'. Men are defined in terms of what they *do*—"What are you? Oh, a used-car salesman... How nice... See you!" — or in terms of some arbitrary, external definition of success—"February's 'Salesman of the Month': sounds *good*"; but they often struggle to be acknowledged for who they *are*, as human *beings* rather than 'human doings'. By contrast, women are acknowledged for who they are (or rather, who they *appear* to be — hence a huge and highly profitable cosmetics trade...), but often have to struggle to receive any acknowledgement of the vast amount of work that they *do*—"Well, isn't that what women are *supposed* to do? what's so special about that?" These stereotypes permeate through every aspect of our society: every Mother's Day the cards are about 'motherly love', and the advertisements are for flowers, for fashions, for perfumes, or (the nearest to acknowledgement that mothers *do* indeed work!) for household utensils; every Father's Day they're for tools, for car parts, for paints and glues — and ghastly socks and ties!—and the cards talk more about 'fatherly *duties*'. But these are stereotypes which are surprisingly hard to challenge—even within ourselves. It all seems so much a 'fact of life': and yet the weird twist is that it is, in reality, nothing more than a *choice*—though one that greatly affects how we relate with each other.

The other matched-pair makes stereotyped assumptions about our inner worlds: "Women don't think, *can't* think," it says; "men don't feel — *can't* feel." Although some male politicians, and some feminist theorists, seem determined to prove the stereotypes true in their own case, they *are* no more than assumptions. Perhaps because they'd gone against those stereotypes, most of the women engineers at the research establishment were above the average of their male counterparts; the same seemed to be true of the male nurses at the hospital. But breaking free from those stereotypes can be surprisingly hard work...

To illustrate this point, let's do another of those inversions, and assume a stereotype of 'men *are*, women *do*'. It's just another choice: but it may seem a weird one...

Imagine, as a woman, that you will only get acknowledgement for what you *do* — or appear to do. People aren't interested in *you* at all, and especially not in what you feel: they're only interested in the size of your purse. Everything hinges on status: without that, you're *nothing*, especially to the other sex — so status, and a sizeable purse, are your only hope for a family, or even for friendship, of a kind. If that's the stereotype, how would you relate with others of your own sex? If the other sex seems interested only in your status and your ability to act as their 'provider', how would you relate with them? If status is everything, how safe would you be in expressing what you *feel*? And how much would you rely on outward 'symbols of success' to shield yourself from inner uncertainty? Since no one takes any notice of how you feel, how easy — or not — would it be for you to care about your *own* appearance and health — or would you expect to have to sacrifice it in the desperate search for that elusive 'status'?

And imagine, as a man, that you will only get acknowledgement for what you are — or *appear* to be, rather — and even that 'acceptable appearance' is set within tightly defined limits which change wildly according to the whims of fashion. Although people will pay lip-service to what you say you feel, no one seems to have the slightest interest in what you think, or even in what you do—everything you do is either unnoticed, or taken for granted. Everything hinges on how you look: without that, you're *nothing*, to anyone—especially as you get older, and are less 'desirable'. If that's the stereotype, how would you relate with others of your own sex? If the other sex seems interested only in your appearance, and in your ability to prop up *their* all-important status, how would you relate with them? If appearances are every-thing, how safe would you be in expressing what you *really* feel? And how much would you rely on artificial aids to prop up your appearance, in order to shield yourself from inner uncertainty? Since no one seems to notice what you do, how easy—or not—would it be for you to care about your work?

Again, these do have their counterparts in the so-called 'real' world: but how much do those 'natural' stereotypes—"Men do, women are; women don't think, men don't feel"—still dominate in our society? Those are the choices that our society 'chooses' for us: yet what are the twists that arise from them?

Sometimes breaking free of the stereotypes can seem more trouble than it's worth. The weird fuss over 'the first woman to...' — doing something that seems quite ordinary to the woman concerned—leaves many a woman feeling more like a perform-ing monkey than the professional that she is. And 'nice guys' often pay a painful penalty for being open and empathic, because many women want to "practise having a male friend without causing emotional damage"—as one friend put it—but fail to notice the damage they cause while they're 'practising'... So it's often essential to be well aware of what we're doing before we breach the stereotypes — and to be clear about the boundaries of 'I'.

Yet the wyrd passes through everyone—every one of its threads. And each of us — and the choices we make — are expressions of the wyrd and its weavings. These gender-stereo-types place artificial boundaries on those interweavings, and greatly limit the range of possibilities available to us — for no real benefit to anyone. In the name of equality, if nothing else, it's wise to challenge them—especially within ourselves.

But George Orwell's famous warning applies here as much as it does in politics: if we don't take care in creating our 'equality', "All are equal" can easily mutate into "Some are more equal than others" — and that's exactly what's happened with those gender-stereotypes. Over the past few decades 'Western' societies have done a great deal to tackle the women's side of those matched-pairs: much has been done to acknowledge what women *do*—and have always done—and no one can reasonably doubt that women *do* think, and have as much right as men to say what they think. But the other side of the equation — acknowledging who men are, and what they feel — hasn't yet happened: if anything, the stereotype has become even more entrenched, and few people—feminists especially—seem willing to face it. That's been our society's choice, if only by default: but there's always a twist, says the wyrd, and the twist seems to be that unless we tackle the *whole* of the problem of sexism, we'll end up right back where we started—which would *not* be a good idea... If we want genuine equality of the sexes, nurturing the full expression of the wyrd within each and every one of us would seem to be the only way to go.

Nurturing the wyrd

Equality is a difficult concept, and gender-equality especially so: as we saw a while ago, in all sorts of issues such as the public provision of toilet space, identical treatment is often far from 'equal'! But the wyrd passes through us all: with very few exceptions, most of which *can* be attributed to nature rather than nurture, almost all so-called 'gender-issues' are essentially *human* ones. And it is disturbing to see just how one-sided most ideas of 'gender equality' have become: most governments now have an 'Office for the Status of Women', or some such department, for example, but few — if any — have anything resembling an

'Office for the *Safety* of Men', which — given the social stereotypes of gender — would be the effective equivalent for men's
concerns.

> The front page of the newspaper today consists of a
> story about a TV anchorwoman who'd 'collapsed' at the
> newsdesk, and all the worries about her health; the back
> page, of course, is full of sport. Women's safety; men's
> status... priority news, it seems. Yet side by side, tucked
> away in a forgotten corner near the middle of the paper,
> are two tiny items apparently almost too trivial to men-
> tion: about a leading woman novelist winning a major
> international award; and a man crushed to death in
> another building-site accident. Women's status, men's
> safety — or lack of it — as invisible as ever...
>
> We can't do much individually about major social
> stereotypes like these, but it's certainly worthwhile
> exploring how they affect the way we think — and the
> way we interweave with others in the wyrd. If true
> equality would mean that "the needs, concerns, feelings
> and fears of women and of men are of exactly equal
> value and importance", how much do the images in the
> media and in our society in general support this? How
> much do those images influence your *own* attitudes to
> men and to women? And once you start to see those
> influences, what can *you* do to counter them — both in
> yourself, and in your relationships with others?

Equality goes far deeper than merely that between men and
women, or girls and boys: it's about understanding that *everyone* is
"equally deserving of respect" — simply for being who they are,
as an expression of the wyrd. There's always a choice, there's
always a twist: given the nature of the wyrd, choosing to nurture
a genuine equality for everyone will bring us face to face with
some very twisted attitudes — especially within ourselves...

There's always a choice: so what do *we* choose? If power is
'the ability to do work, as an expression of choice', what is *our*
power? That's up to you, says the wyrd...

> Germaine Greer once commented that feminism was about "exploring all the possibilities of what it is to be fully human, in a woman's body, and from a woman's perspective": a committed exploration of the wyrd, yet understanding, and accepting, that there *is* such a thing as sex, there *is* such a thing as gender — and there *is* such a thing as our own, peculiar, particular body. The same could be said for men too, in their own way, of course—otherwise it wouldn't be equality!
>
> In what ways do you commit yourself to "exploring all the possibilities of what it is to be fully human", in your *own* body, and from your *own* perspective? In what ways can you support others in doing so? In what ways can you support *everyone* in doing so?

Each of us is an expression of the wyrd, a clustering of its threads; a series and sequence of *choices* — each with its own inevitable twist, and its own ending. Our power arises from awareness—awareness of ourselves, of others, and of the wyrd itself—and from choice, for ourselves, and *with* others. So what *do* we choose? Answer: it *is* always up to us. But nurturing choice in the infinite 'We' that we share with others—treating everyone, including ourselves, as "equally deserving of respect" — eventually weaves its weird way back to us: it's a wiser way to go.

The catch is that what it asks for from us is *trust*: trust in the wyrd, trust in ourselves, trust in others — boys, girls, everyone. And it also asks us for commitment: to be ourselves, to be *here*, to be *now*, and accept the wyrd for what it is — the interweaving of everyone, everywhere, everywhen. Yet there are times when trust and commitment can be very hard to find... and that's when trusting just a little — enough to trust our *knowing* in the wyrd—can make all the difference in our relationships with others, and with ourselves.

17

TRUST AND COMMITMENT

Whenever we're in difficulty with others, or with the world in general, it often *seems* easiest to say 'No', regardless of what's going on: and worry about the consequences—or lack of them—later. "Defend the boundaries!" I cry; "Repel all boarders!" And it works! But eventually I start to notice that there's no one around any more, and no one seems to want to know me... "Lower the drawbridge! Tear down the walls," I cry, in lonely desperation: and fail to notice, until rather too late, just who and what it is I'm 'inviting' into my life. Up go the boundaries again—quick!—and the cycle starts all over again. Up and down, up and down: "round and round the garden..."

There *is* a way out of this loop: but it involves commitment, and trust. Commitment is about saying 'Yes'—and being clear about what it is that we're saying 'Yes' to! And trust is about working *with* the wyrd, working *with* the weird twists of Inverse Murphy — so that whatever we choose to commit ourselves to, we *can* allow it to happen. This is perhaps the place where our allies can help us most: but only if we let them help us!

Commitment

Power is the ability to do what *we* choose: so commitment consists simply of saying 'Yes' to what we choose—and sticking to it. But it's not always quite as simple as it sounds... and it's only once we grasp our 'response-ability' here that we can begin to move forward.

For a start, we'll often find ourselves in a tangle over our own choices, because commitment usually requires doing things we'd prefer—'choose'—not to do. I prefer to live in reasonably tidy surroundings: I commit *myself* to that choice. But since I live on my own—and at the moment choose to have it be that way—then the only person who can keep the place tidy is *me*: and tidying-up is often exactly what I *don't* want to do! If I try to force myself into doing it, or mock myself—"Useless, aren't you, Chris—can't even remember to wash up, can you?"—to try to shame myself into doing it, I'll only make things worse. Yet if I don't do anything, the place descends into chaos very quickly indeed... The weird solution is to 'do no-thing': keep quietly reminding myself of the commitment—in this case, keeping the place tidy—and don't allow myself to get in my own way when I find that I'm doing it!

> I don't *like* coming home to a sinkful of dirty dishes: but no matter how much I usually hate washing-up, no one else is going to do it, are they? Yet 'discipline' just doesn't work: I find myself saying "Shan't!" in a very childish manner. So I've become what I suppose I'd call "being disciplined about indiscipline": it's like a weird dance, leaving a corner of my awareness open for exactly the right moment to act. I don't 'try' at all, I just wait until the right thread of the wyrd arises to the surface —which it always does, and usually sooner rather than later. The 'right thread' in this case is one of *wanting* to wash up—and up comes an odd feeling: "Hey, it's really *satisfying*! You know, I have to work with some clients for days or weeks or months to get any reponse: but here, I

get a tangible result — clean dishes! — in a matter of minutes! Amazing!" A weird approach to commitments, perhaps... but it works!

In what ways do you try to force yourself to do things that you don't want to do? How well — if at all — does force or self-bullying work, in terms of giving you a sense of satisfaction in those tasks?

If it doesn't give you a sense of self-empowerment— which for most of us it doesn't—then try 'doing no-thing' about it: be disciplined about the indiscipline, and use Inverse Murphy to *allow* yourself to keep those commitments to yourself. If you do this, what happens? What are the twists by which you find yourself holding to your choices?

Projecting the responsibility for this kind of internal conflict onto others, and blaming them for what are actually our choices—"I don't *want* to do this, but I *have* to: they *made* me do it"—can be a *really* quick way of wrecking relationships: and one that we do need to be careful about. But with awareness, we can use—rather than abuse—our allies to trick ourselves past this block, using them as mirrors, in either a passive or active sense, to reflect our own choices back to us, and remind us of our commitments to *ourselves*.

"Damn! I forgot — Jean and Peter are coming over tomorrow night: and unless I sort out that pile of papers on the table, and all the other stuff that's lying around, Jean'll be full of all her usual nasty put-downs about my 'untidiness'... I don't want to have to tidy up *at all*—it's all *her* fault!" But just as I start to throw things into a semblance of order, grumbling away as I do so, up comes another of those little 'messages' on the winds of the wyrd: "*You* invited them here, Chris, didn't you? — was it perhaps to remind you of *your* commitment to keep this place tidy?" Oh... not directly, of course, but I suppose it *is* a hidden part of the reason, yes... in which case I'm tidying-up for *me*, aren't I? Better get on with it, I say to myself, with a wry grin!

Sometimes the mirroring can be a lot more active—

such as asking a friend to keep reminding you of your intention to hold back on the chocolate for this month at least — but in what ways do *you* use others to reflect back to you your commitments to yourself? Knowing how easy it is to project onto others the blame for the parts of those commitments that, like any child, we don't *want* to do, how do you protect yourself — and them — from this? When you *have* done so — which all of us do, at some time or other — what kind of courage do you need in order to acknowledge this, and take 'response-ability' for making amends?

The same applies to our choices with and about others — our commitments to 'We'—and also others' commitments to us. But it's essential to remember that a commitment is a statement of *intent*—and nothing more. There's always a choice, says the wyrd, but there's always a twist: if our 'commitment' to and from others becomes a rigid expectation, then it's no longer a choice, but a kind of enslavement or self-enslavement—and the results can be very twisted indeed... And there are some things we simply can't commit to: not won't, but *can't*. Feelings are one example: we can't commit to maintaining a feeling for someone, because feelings are simply not in our control — they're either there, or they're not. So, as Alanis Morrissette sings about a now-departed lover, "You told me you'd hold me till you died: *but you're still alive*", it's understandable enough as a *feeling*, but it's unrealistic—if not dangerously subject-centred—as an attitude to hold about relationship with others...

Oh, the joys of 'love-songs', most of which are about nothing of the kind! Dependency, projection, blame, self-centred and subject-centred fantasies therein aplenty: but quiet, self-honest empathy — the core of a genuine love of and for others — is a bit like good news — it doesn't *sell*, and is mostly conspicuous by its absence!

Yet take a look at your own 'failed' commitments, both to and from others: you may well feel a fair amount of anger about them — but what is that anger hiding?

> What was *your* 'response-ability' in the 'failure'? Were
> you expecting 'commitment' about things which are
> outside of the others' control, such as their feelings? In
> what ways did you abandon your commitment to
> *yourself*?

We *can't* commit to feelings; in many cases we can't even
commit to actions. I was upset for a while because Kaye — my
best friend at work — gave me no help at all while I was in
hospital: it took me some time to realise that she was so lost in
her own feelings about what had happened that she could hardly
help herself, let alone anyone else... the commitment was still
there, but she wasn't *able* to follow it through. So that weird
statement that "there's *always* a choice" eventually comes down
to a simple question: "We have a commitment: what is *negotiable*,
right now, within this commitment?"

Whatever the difficulty, there *is* always a choice available
which maintains a relationship — whether that relationship is
professional, personal or whatever. And there's also always a
choice to move *out* of a relationship: but we then have to face
and accept full responsibility for that choice too... Because of
that weird 'mirroring', where each person reflects our own issues
back to us — whether by intent or not — relationship *always*
brings challenges: some of those issues need to be faced at a
deeper level than others, but we always have *some* 'response-
ability' in this—if only in our commitments to our own 'I'.

And it does help if we have some clarity about that
commitment to 'I': some kind of 'purpose in life'. The black
philosopher Howard Thurman once commented that there are
two questions we need to ask ourselves: "Where am I going?"
and "Who will go with me?" But if we ever get those questions
the wrong way round, he said, we're in *deep* trouble; and we also
need to accept that sometimes—perhaps often—the only valid
answer to the second question is 'no one'...

> I can't count the number of times I've made those two
> mistakes: assuming that there *must* be someone who

> will choose to 'go with me', wherever I go; and trying to base "Where am I going?" on what I thought *they* wanted, on the rare occasions when I *did* find someone who seemed to want to go with me! *Not* wise... especially since what I know of my own 'purpose in life' means that it is, by its nature, often a lonely one — whether I like it or not.
>
> Do *you* have a sense of your own 'purpose', the geis of your wyrd—an overall direction or theme for your life? If you do, how often have you found yourself asking "Who will go with me?" without regard for what you *know* about your own purpose? Abandoning 'I' in favour of an inevitably illusory 'We' in this way is an easy mistake to make, but a costly one...

In effect, our 'purpose' in life' is a commitment not just to ourselves, but to the wyrd: it's the way we work *with* our wyrd, rather than endlessly wasting energy trying to fight against it. And it's also an acceptance of our geasa — our bond with life itself. But first we need to recognise that it *is* our own commitment: and central to that is the need for *trust*—trust in ourselves, trust in others, and trust in the wyrd itself.

Trusting 'I'

A counterpart to 'trust' is *courage*—literally 'coeur-rage', 'heart-madness'. It's both a kind of 'heart-knowing'—or of the gut, or soul, rather than the head — and *action* on that knowledge, trusting, as the Desiderata puts it, that "Whether or not it is clear to you, no doubt the universe is unfolding as it should." And it does take a lot of courage to reach that level of trust in the universe — or even in ourselves. Given our society's constant pressures towards self-blame, even to say "I am who I am" — that "I have a right to be here, no less than the trees and stars"— can be hard work: and for most of us, Edith Piaf's famous phrase "Je ne regrette rien"—'no regrets', I regret nothing—will seem an impossible ideal—or impossibly *wrong*...

What do *you* regret—about relationships, or your own or others' actions or inactions, or anything? How easy—or not — is it for you to shift to Edith Piaf's position of "regrette rien", 'no regrets'? How much are those old regrets tied up with resentment, 'a demand that the Other feel guilty' — where 'the Other' can also be *yourself*?

In particular, what would it ask of you to move away from regret, and towards a position where all that matters is the commitment, and the 'response-ability' to reclaim your *own* commitment — whatever form it may take—whenever an action you'd regret *does* take place?

Trust is also an attribute of the Inner Child: but here again we need to remember that distinction between child*ish* and child*like*. "You've *betrayed* me—I trusted you totally!" is not trust at all: it's a childish export of responsibility to 'the Other', and hence is — as we saw earlier — actually an act of abuse. Trust relies on the Inner Child's fragile innocence, it's true: but innocence is not a synonym for self-righteous subject-centred stupidity! A child*like* trust is innocent, yes, but it's also open and *aware*: like the Inner Adult, it understands that trust is not an abandonment of 'I', but a process of constant renegotiation. By the nature of the wyrd, *nothing* is fixed, and every thread has its twist and its ending: no matter how much we may want things to be predictable and certain, so that we can place 'absolute trust' in them, Reality Department will eventually provide conditions in which that 'absolute commitment' *must* be broken. It's wise to accept that this sometimes bleak reality *is* fact, and learn to work *with* it...

It's important to remember, too, that feelings are often far from rational: we first need to accept that they *are* what we feel, and *then* assess our 'response-ability'. A sad example of this: back at college, one of my friends was waiting for her father to collect her, to take her home for the holidays. After two hours' wait, she rang home: he'd left on time, her mother said — probably just taken a detour, as he sometimes did. Half an hour later, though, her mother rang back, distraught: the police had just visited her, to tell her that, on his way to collect her, a truck had crashed into his car—and he'd been killed. My friend was horrified to find that her own first inner response — fortunately unspoken — was "How *dare* he die on me like this! How on earth does he think I'm going to be able to get home without him?" Weird... and yet it was an entirely natural response, because to the ever-dependent childish side of the Inner Child, death *will* seem like a betrayal... And the hard part is that we do need to accept that this *is* what we feel: because only then will that inner childishness allow room for a more adult response.

Trust is a process of constant renegotiation: so how do *you* negotiate a sense of inner trust, between the different aspects and layers of yourself — especially in times of stress? In what ways can you accept that there are weird aspects of yourself which *are* 'selfish', almost to extremes—and which will not allow you to reach inner peace unless they *are* at least allowed to have their say?

A commitment is about saying 'Yes' to something; if we don't trust, there'll be no viable commitment. Yet the opposite of 'Yes' is not 'No', but more like 'let's negotiate': the *intention* behind the commitment to our choice of 'I' remains the same, but the way in which we get there is always open for negotiation! "Okay, I'm committed to keeping this place tidy, Chris," I say to myself, "and I don't want to wash up right now: so what's negotiable in this commitment? What else can I do, right now, to keep to that commitment?" It sounds weird, perhaps, but it *does* work: and if we can't even negotiate a kind of peace within ourselves, we're unlikely to be able to negotiate clearly with others...

What's called 'personal development' is simply the process of creating this weird 'negotiation with I'. Exploring our own power and 'response-ability', exploring our boundaries, developing our understandings of subject and object, of the problem and prevalence of blame, of use and abuse, of assertiveness, and of sympathy and empathy, we move towards a state of *self*-trust in which, as the Taoists would put it, "The tiger can find in me no place to rest its claws": we become safe with others by trusting *ourselves*.

> It's late at night, and Lynn is walking home down one of the grubbier back-streets in the night-club district of the city. Up ahead, in the dimly lit street, two burly young men are walking towards her, down the middle of the road. A moment's apprehensiveness... then she reasserts her choice of 'I', her personal *commitment* to 'I': "I am who I am, they are who they are; I'm going about my business, and they're going about theirs, and it's nothing to do with me." Without a pause, but with a clear sense of inner certainty, she walks on. They pass; a moment's brief glance of acknowledgement, and that is all. But as they continue on, Lynn hears the quiet comment from one man to the other: "I do wish Margaret would learn to power-walk like that... it'd help her a lot, wouldn't it?"
>
> Fear isn't pleasant; yet we *can* always find a way to face it, even if sometimes we can only do so, as one friend put it, by 'collapsing in a puddle' once we're safely round the corner... Given the omnipresent fear of abuse — and our society's incessant exaggeration of the facts behind that fear — it's not easy to find the trust that "the tiger can find in me no place to rest its claws": so how do *you* find that trust? And how much do you notice of what *doesn't* happen—the fears that do *not* come to fruition?

Trusting ourself, it becomes easier to trust others, because we know that even if others — for whatever reason — may 'fail' us, *we* won't let ourselves down. Not being a 'victim' to ourselves, we're no victim to anyone. Trust is a kind of 'feedback loop': and it's usually up to us as to whether it spirals upward, into greater empowerment for everyone, or becomes a downward spiral into despair. But because it's a loop, we can use trust to help us create trust: and sometimes the only way in which we can learn to trust ourselves is by trusting others.

Trusting 'We'

Trust *should* be easy: but it isn't, simply because of that dominant belief in our society that "where there's fear, there's power" — and hence, almost everywhere we look, we'll find fears being exaggerated, inflated, invented, to give someone a short-lived illusion of power, for a short-lived personal gain. Fear is the absolute antithesis of trust: more to the point, it *destroys* trust. Before we can fully let go into trusting others — our 'We' with others—we need to be aware of our own confusions about fear and power: we need to trust that what we're creating with others is power-with for everyone, rather than power-over or power-under for a self-selected few.

> It's probably worth taking a moment here to review the work you did earlier on power and fear: in particular, the *practical* distinctions between power-with and power-from-within on the one hand, and power-over and power-under on the other. And since trust in action is mutual *use*, it'll probably also be worthwhile reviewing the work you did on the practical distinctions between use and abuse, and on the *practice* of self-assertiveness. It's been some time since we first looked at those themes: what's changed in your understanding of them?

Once again, the childish side of the Inner Child may cause us some problems here. Among its other attributes, trust is a *feeling*: we can provide conditions which will foster its growth, or hinder its growth, but ultimately it's either there, or not—and it's not under our control. But it's easy to get lost in a kind of emotional investment in 'trust', as though it's something that others *should* or *ought to* give us: "Why don't you trust me?" I wail. "I've done everything I can to help you, haven't I?" Yet those 'magic' words 'should' and 'ought' give the clue as to what's really going on: I may have thought that my intentions were 'pure' enough, but it's more likely I've been caught up in a subject-centred attitude, hoping to prop up my own ego by trying to make them like me, or support me—which isn't so much trust as a minor act of abuse, and certainly not suitable for trust!

Since trust is a feeling, there are no excuses — and no excuses needed—for either trusting or not trusting: trust either *is*, or *isn't*, and there's not that much we can do about it. A friend is someone we probably overload with trust; an enemy is someone we probably don't trust enough; whereas allies are those we trust to be *themselves*—we trust them simply to be who they are, and nothing else.

> A few quick questions to play with!
> Who do you trust? Why? And who do you *not* trust? Why not?
> How much do you over-trust your friends—or expect too much trust from them? How much do you under-trust your 'enemies'? And who are your allies — the people you trust simply to be themselves?

There are reasons for trusting or not trusting, of course— and again, there are no excuses, or excuses needed. If I promise to help you, and let you down once: well, fair enough, that's an ordinary happenstance in Reality Department. I do the same thing again: that's coincidence, and that's part of Reality Department too. But three times, or more? Perhaps not 'enemy action' — especially if it's obvious that I'm trying to be helpful— but certainly not a good reason to trust that I'll be able to deliver what I promise, no matter what my excuses may be.

> So how *do* we redevelop trust when trust 'fails' — especially when it fails with others? "With difficulty" is the real answer, sometimes... But the key is to go back to the commitment, and renegotiate: the *form* that the commitment takes often doesn't matter that much, but the commitment itself does.
> For example, I'd arranged with Kaye to have a quiet wander downtown together this afternoon: nothing special, just a bit of shopping and some coffee and cake

in one of our favourite cafés. But she's late — as usual — and I'm feeling frustrated, and angry: "She *said* she'd be here by one, and it's nearly two o'clock — why on earth can't she turn up on time?" Yet I've already given myself the clue on that one: she *is* usually late, so expecting her to come when she says would be treating her as if she's my 'subject' — and not trusting her to be *herself*. So let go... accept that she is who she is... a wry grin crosses my face... and a moment later, the doorbell rings — Kaye, of course! Weird, that, isn't it?

Where does trust repeatedly 'fail' between you and some of your closer friends? Whatever form the 'failure' takes, just accept that they are who they are, and that you are who you are; keep clear on the commitment between you, but allow the *form* of the commitment to shift in whatever way it needs. What happens when you do this?

The wyrd being what it is, there are no 'absolute rules' that can always tell us what to do. It's here that a distinction between ethics and morals can become painfully clear: morals — 'rules for living' which arise from the assumptions of a given society — may be useful as general guidelines, but there's always some point at which they simply cease to work, or cause more problems than they solve. Eventually, we have to rely on our ethics: which usually comes down to trusting ourselves, and others, and the wyrd.

It isn't easy. An old friend, visiting from another city, comments to me about the inner turmoil of an extra-marital affair: "I don't like not being one hundred percent open with my partner; yet I don't like not being able to get a very basic need met because there's a lack of trust on both sides. All I can do is follow my nose as far as behaviour is concerned: picking out a narrow trail of what feels right *for me*. Morals — at least the old rigid ones — mean less to me than ever I thought: it was hard to grasp that, and to follow it through." My friend pauses; looks at me again. "Sometimes a thought that I'm just being selfish comes through, and certainly a feeling of being alone. There aren't many who'd understand this, Chris—I'm glad that you do. I just have to accept that the most important person in my life has to be me: I have to get what I need from *me*, as far as possible. Only with that understanding of myself can I actually relate properly with anyone else..."

> Ethics arise mostly from an understanding — an *experience* — of empathy: "Do as you would be done by", and so on. What are *your* ethics? In what ways do they differ from — or define — your morals, or the morals you've learnt from the society and family in which you've lived?

Trusting our allies to be who they are, and nothing else, creates the weird space for something else to come through— something wider, more open, more inclusive. For example, as my visiting friend explains: "I didn't ask to be listened to when I was debating where I was going with Mo: but Kim did listen, and intuitively created enough atmosphere of trust for me to be able to unload. At that stage I really needed someone to talk to—and not someone who would think it was all romantic and lovey-dovey. Someone practical, who pointed out the practicalities, even though I'm sure I've looked at the practicalities — or impracticalities — and risks myself. It also helped to have a second viewpoint, and to look at what I was planning, through someone else's eyes. It helps to reiterate that a choice feels right: it's no longer 'immoral', it's just *me*."

Morals are a kind of pre-packaged 'lazy man's ethics': if we follow the simplistic rules of our society's morals, we usually don't need to give a second glance to the far greater complexities of individual ethics. If we *do* have the discipline to understand those ethics, we can live without morals—or *beyond* morals—if need be: but without ethics, we're nothing. Aleister Crowley's infamous expression, "'Do what thou wilt' shall be the whole of the Law!" may sound weird, but it's probably not wyrd enough: in reality, it's usually twisted by Reality Department into something more like "Do what you will—but be *very* sure that you will it..."

> "Do what you will — but be *very* sure that you will it..." Look back at some of the moral tangles and ethical dilemmas into which you've found yourself projected in the past — your own version of the story of Diarmid and Grainne, perhaps. What were the choices that led you there? What were the twists? The way out of these twists usually involves an uncomfortable lesson in ethics, and in the deeper meaning of *trust*: what was it in each case, for you?

Trust is a feeling; trust is empathy; trust is, in its own way, a form of ethics; above all, trust is weird. So trusting ourselves, and trusting others, often depends on trusting the wyrd itself: a choice which, of course, always has its own twists!

Trusting the wyrd

Just as we need to trust ourselves to be who we are, and trust others to be who *they* are, we need to accept — and trust — that the wyrd is what it is. Perhaps the hardest part is accepting that not only is there always a twist in every thread of the wyrd, but there's also always an ending — often with a weird twist of its own, as a geis. So there's *always* a risk, in anything that we do, or even in what we *don't* do; yet we'll always find that we have to trust *something*, and however carefully we may plan, and prepare — we think — for every eventuality, there's always a chance that whatever we've placed our trust in will break down. That fact *hurts* — hurts our pride, hurts our need for certainty — but it *is* a fact: so it's best to work with it — trust it for what it is — rather than try to fight against it.

Nothing is certain, *nothing* is 'fail-safe': which is why the best engineers, acutely aware that the only real 'law of nature' is Murphy's, spend so much effort trying to design their systems to 'fail gracefully' whenever they meet up with that aspect of the wyrd. 'Mis-takes' are how we learn: some of the wyrd's 'lessons' are so expensive — in many different senses — that we never want them to happen again: but 'mis-takes' are how we learn, and sometimes it *does* take many repetitions before we finally get a 'lesson' to lessen...

> This is true on every scale, of course: some 'mis-takes' are so huge that we never have a chance to try again, and recovery—if any—happens at a societal rather than personal level. Much of the history of engineering has consisted of finding ways to reduce the human cost of large-scale 'mis-takes': but the same will have happened, on a smaller scale, in your 'engineering' of your own life.
>
> Each time we 'fail'—meet up once more with one of our weird 'lessons'—it takes a bit more courage to start again, and trust that what we've learnt in each iteration means that the lesson will indeed 'lessen' next time we face it.
>
> What does it take for you to trust the wyrd in this way? From where within you do you find that courage?

Each thread has its ending: so there's always a risk that what we've trusted will fail us — not someone else, somewhere else, somewhen else, but *me, here, now*. Exactly the same is true of everyone else: being human, we're fallible — and we're *all* struggling with our geis, our very own 'lessons' from the wyrd. So true trust is not a wild abandonment of faith — a child*ish* 'trust'—but an *acceptance* that we are who we are, others are who they are, and the wyrd is what it is. We trust ourselves, and others to be *human*, and nothing more—yet also nothing less.

There's also an old magical expression, echoed in the Taoist tradition, that "Those who do not trust enough will not be trusted." Trust is a feedback loop, but with all the usual weird twists: if we allow our courage to fail us, and succumb to fear, we're actually *increasing* the risk of that which we fear coming about; but if we *can* find the courage to face the fear, and trust in ourselves, in others, in the weavings of the wyrd, our own feeling of fear reduces — and that which we fear withdraws further from our life. Like fear itself, the risk never vanishes completely; but it *does* get smaller, once we accept that it *is* a risk —and, being fully aware of the risk, do it anyway.

> This feedback loop between fear and risk is a bit like 'non-attachment': ignoring the risks is dangerous, but worrying too much about them can sometimes be even more dangerous! So we trust enough to 'do no-thing' about it: we're not attached to the risks—worrying about them — nor are we detached from the risks — ignoring them—but accept that they *are* risks, and learn to trust ourselves, and others, and the wyrd to warn us when we *do* need to pay attention to them!
>
> Driving a car is a good example of this—especially when we're learning. The risks are real: and if we ignore them, we'll put ourselves—and others—in danger. But being over-cautious is sometimes even more dangerous: we make the wrong decision, too early, or too late, or pay attention to only one aspect of the problem, missing the much larger one that's coming at us from another direction... And we *do* have to accept that the risk is always there — whether we like it or not, every thread *does* have its ending—and understand that, for the most part, the 'response-ability' for everyone concerned lies with *us*, *here*, *now*.
>
> Go back to your memories of learning to drive: how did you work your way past the fear — fear of the machine, fear of your own lack of skill, fear of other drivers—and find acceptance and trust in yourself, and in others? When you're driving now, how do you achieve that balance of fear and trust?

By trusting the wyrd, and its connection within us, we trust our connection with others. Trust is the way by which we contact each other through the wyrd: in trust, we reach a natural sympathy with others—or at least an awareness of others—and hence, being aware of the echoes of the choices within *us*, the risks reduce for everyone. We trust in ourselves—acknowledge that we are 'response-able' for ourselves — and hence allow others to be responsible for themselves in turn. We have our choices, they have theirs; we're responsible *about* others' choices, but we're never responsible *for* them—nor they for ours. There's always a risk that there may be disagreements at the edges, at the boundaries where those choices meet: but instead of fighting, or reacting in fear, we simply say "Let's negotiate..."

Life, we could say, is a process of constant renegotiation with the wyrd, watching and responding to its feedback on where our choices are taking us. Since the wyrd weaves its way through everywhere, everywhen, everyone, the weird answer to that question "Who will go with me?" becomes more evident the more we explore and accept our own wyrd; but the choice of how to answer that first question—"Where am I going?"—is *always* up to us. Yet we do have a weird world of allies out there: and it's up to us to reach out, with trust and commitment, to make use of the help they offer us.

18

A WYRD WORLD
OF ALLIES

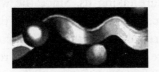

The wyrd weaves through everywhere, everywhen, everyone: so anyone and everyone can be our ally—if we let them! Wherever we go, whatever we choose, there's a world of allies for us out there—allies whose own wyrd interweaves with ours. There's a whole world of power to share, and a whole world of choices for each of us; but before we can reach them there is, as we've seen, a whole world of confusions to work through... So it'd probably be useful to summarise where we've been together on this weird journey of ours, before moving out on our separate ways once more.

A world of confusions

There *is* such a thing as fate: we each have our own wyrd to face, each with its own weird twists. So as we extend what we've learnt in our personal explorations out into the wider world, everyone we meet not only has *their* own wyrd to face, but will usually act as an unwitting—and often unwilling—agent in ours. And the same will be true of us: interweaving with them by choice or by chance, we too are likely to find ourselves becoming part of their wyrd, or acting out the sometimes cruel twists of their geasa. There's plenty of room for confusion in this... for *everyone*...

But we do have a choice: to carry on as before, going 'round and round the garden', learning nothing; or accept our responsibility — our 'response-ability' — and face the fears that are always hidden within these weird loops of interaction. Nothing changes overnight, perhaps — though sometimes change can be quicker even than that — but nothing changes unless *we* change, and face what those changes truly mean for us. The weird part is that as we change, others change too...

> Even while reading this book — if you've put these ideas into practice, as shown in these 'boxes' — you're likely to have found some changes happening already: what are they? With whom and in what kind of situations have you seen most changes: with co-workers, perhaps, or family — or with 'ordinary' people in the shops and on the street?
>
> You'll probably see these changes most in minor conflicts with others: the disagreements and 'boundary disputes' are still there, of course, but in what ways do the weird lessons within each start to lessen as you explore your 'response-ability'? And as you explore and accept your *own* 'response-ability', what happens to others' acceptance of theirs?

Everyone has their own wyrd; *everyone* makes 'mis-takes', as they face — or refuse to face — the twists in their own wyrd, and what it shows them of themselves. As we've seen, unpleasant though it may be, abuse — the harshest face of the wyrd — is an entirely human mistake: it arises when we, or others, are too afraid to face what the wyrd shows us, and hence try to export that fear, or that confusion, to others. *Everyone* abuses others: perhaps most those who pretend that they don't... When faced with abuse — ours or anyone else's — it's up to *us* to choose differently, and find the 'response-ability' to change it into mutual *use* of each other, for everyone. That's often hard — very hard — but it's the only way to go!

What makes it harder still is the 'blame-game' that's endemic in our society's paediarchy: "Round and round in the usual old game, I take the credit and you take the blame—*so it's all your fault!*" As we start to take responsibility for ourselves, and about others, we'll find that this gets *worse*—for a while. That can make it hard to keep going... or even to trust that we *are* progressing at all...

Part of the problem is that, by the nature of the blame-game, anyone who *is* willing to take responsibility for anything is likely to be blamed for *everything*: which doesn't help, of course, but that's the way the blame-game works. But perhaps a more serious side of the problem, from our own perspective, is that as soon as we *do* start to face our 'response-ability'—especially in relationships, of any kind—things will often seem to get visibly *worse* rather than better: and we may decide to stop, quickly! But the reason this happens is that, by breaking free of the 'senses-taker' of habit—and often our own habitual involvement in the blame-game—the habits and patterns become visible: and for a while, until we go a bit further in developing our *response*-ability —our ability to respond differently—it'll seem like there's little or nothing we can do about it... So it's at this point that we need to remember to *trust* — trust in ourselves and our own inner knowing — and hold to our commitment to ourselves and to what we choose to share with others. It may well seem hard— especially if we're facing the reality of past abuse by ourselves or others—but it's best, as the old expression puts it, just to "keep going, keep going, one step at a time".

> A simple question, but perhaps not an easy one: what help can you find from your allies — in effect, everyone you meet — to help you face *your* part in the blame-game? In what ways can you use them to reflect back to you, through the wyrd, the twists of your own choices — especially in relationship with others?
>
> It may be useful to go back through some of the examples in this book—particularly in the 'toolkit' section —to help you in this...

Another aspect of the same problem arises whenever we or others take too much of an object-centred or subject-centred approach to relationship — especially the latter, as it's often harder to recognise, and because it links so strongly into the blame-game. It's useful to be wary of that trap—and not drift back into the chaos of the blame-game ourselves, by blaming others for doing it!

Although there's all too many options for confusion, ultimately *everything* is relationship. Whether we like it or not, *everyone* is our 'soul-mate', with their fate interwoven with ours on the threads of the wyrd. And whether we like it or not, we'll find ourselves moving into and out of sympathy with others — and even with ourselves—all of the time, as our boundaries — however well-defined, however well-defended — rise and fall with the weird currents of our geasa. So it *does* help to commit ourselves to developing our empathy with others, even though it may take a deliberate effort at times to do so: because it's not only how we can find hidden sides to our own power, but also find ways to *share* it with others—with all of our weird allies.

A world of power

"Where there's power, there's fear; where there's fear, there's power": once we start to face our own fears, and work our way through the tangled confusions about power—both our own, and in our society as a whole—we find that we *do* have power— and plenty to share. Power is the ability to do work, as an expression of choice: and it's not just what *I* choose that matters, but what *We* choose, sharing the work—the common goal—as power *with* each other. If we allow our fears, or the confusions of our society's paediarchy, to take over, all we'll be left with is either power-over, or power-under: and that'll help *no one*—especially ourselves. So here too we'll need to remind ourselves constantly of our 'response-abilities' in this: and keep a careful, constant check not just on what we choose as our 'I', but also on what we choose as our part of any 'I and We and I'.

264

We *do* have that power to choose: but at times it's all too easy to forget this...

> Using your own power-from-within to change power-over and power-under into power-with: how easy—or not—is this for you to put into practice now? If you *have* started to put the examples in this book into practice, how much has this expression of your 'response-ability'—and your own power—changed both in your own life, and in the world you see reflected 'out there' in the weavings of the wyrd?

The wyrd weaves its way through everyone, everywhere: what seems to be the inside—our own private world—is also the outside, and vice versa; and any boundaries between 'I' and 'not-I' are always somewhat blurred. Our allies are separate from us, and not separate, at the same time: so that weird state of empathy—aware of both 'I' and 'not-I', in the same moment, and experiencing the world from both perspectives—is always available to us, as one of the most powerful and empowering tools in our 'toolkit'. Through the weird awareness of empathy, we learn to trust our allies to *be themselves*—nothing more, and nothing less; and in the process come to trust that we too need only be *ourselves* —we need be nothing more, and nothing less, than that.

> Empathy is a strange state to be in: needing to be aware of two people—both 'I' and 'not-I'—and in effect experience two lives in two places in the one moment, it can place some interesting strains on our sanity! How easy—or not—do you find it to maintain your boundaries, your own sense of 'I', while exploring another's life-experience in this way? How easy—or not—is it for you to accept that 'Other' for who they are, in *their* terms, from *their* perspective, without judging them from your own? If you still find this hard—which most people do—what kind of 'no-thing' would you need to do in order to change this? 'Trying harder' rarely works well, in this or anything like it: so look within, perhaps, for your *own* weird answer?

We each have our own answers; and we each have a spiritual need to share those answers with others, in order to be part of 'that which is greater than self'. As we become more aware of our own solutions to the impossible ethical dilemmas that face each of us, it's easy to try to impose them on others, as moral precepts that *should* apply to everyone: but the 'should' in that statement would warn us that we're probably being a bit too subject-centred in our approach to 'not-I' if we do so... trying to enforce our 'response-ability' over others' lives while probably not facing our responsibility for our own...

If we take that attitude too far, we'll end up with an ideology, trying to impose our fixed ideas about 'right' and 'wrong' onto the tortuous complexities of Reality Department. But it doesn't work: and it's also a quick way of making enemies out of our allies! I've heard plenty of people say that feminism, or 'the patriarchy', or whatever, is 'the enemy': but I'd argue that the only real enemies we have are cowardice and complacency—especially in ourselves... What we may choose to believe is up to us: no '-ism' is an enemy of anyone, in itself. But there can be no doubt that ideologies of almost any kind can easily act as the agents of those twin enemies within us: the chaotic conceits of cuckoo-feminism, for example, actively incite emotional coward-ice and intellectual complacency — because according to its blame-based worldview, everything 'bad' that happens to us must always be the fault of someone else. Such a belief helps no one, especially us: the only real 'response-ability' for our lives lies with us, and us alone.

> This may still be a hard one, because belief-systems such as feminism so much inform our lives and filter our perceptions, especially about how people 'ought to' or 'should' interact: but how easy—or not—is it for you to break free from ideology altogether, and accept each person, here, now, for *who they are*? And if it is still hard for you, notice that this is also true for almost everyone: understanding that this is so—that we *all* may struggle with the twisted nature of our wyrd—in what ways can

> this help you find that compassion for others — and for
> yourself?

Ideologies and '-isms' of all kinds have their place, and may well help at times, by showing us a different perspective on the world: but weird though they sometimes may be, they're rarely wyrd enough. An ideology, almost by definition, provides only fixed answers, which can never cope with the full complexities of Reality Department; whereas a wyrd perspective accepts that all we have are questions—hence *quest*—and any 'answers' that we find exist only for us, and perhaps only in the moment. Ultimately, what we may choose is up to us: that's our power, and our responsibility. Yet wherever there's a choice, there's always that weird twist: and it's usually wise to remember this!

A world of choice

'I' is our choice, and yet not always entirely our choice, because our 'I' is also always changing in interaction with others: their wyrd weaves through ours as much as ours weaves through theirs. But 'I' is not that which changes, 'I' is that which *chooses*: so once again, it's wisest to 'do no-thing' about this—keep clear about our own choice of 'I', and work *with* these currents of change, rather than trying to fight against them. As long as we remain clear about our overall aim — what we might call our 'purpose in life', or the weird kind of quest that's inevitably woven into it — then the route by which we get there doesn't matter all that much: and if we allow those strange twists of Inverse Murphy to work in favour, the winds of the wyrd can show us much that's of interest!

> Inverse Murphy — "Things *can* go right — if you let them"
> — is rarely easy to accept: it takes a lot to trust that
> much! But if you've been putting these examples into
> practice, have you noticed any difference in your aware-
> ness of Inverse Murphy? If so, what form did it take? And

> what kind of courage did it ask of you, in order to let its
> weird twists work for you?

Every thread of the wyrd has its geis; every choice has its ending, its weird dénouement. And although we share the wyrd with everyone, its *expression* in our life is our choice alone: so it's up to us, and no one else, to know when we need to switch threads, to change our choices, in order to deal with the weird complexities of the world. Often what we need is a peculiar kind of perspective, almost an anarchic one in the real sense of the word: a wry acceptance that 'anything goes'—and that we need to 'do no-thing' about it. Given all those confusions of the blame-game on one side, and all the cultural imperatives to be seen to be *doing* something on the other, it's rarely easy to hold back and just 'do no-thing'—especially in relationships. But by keeping our inner awareness open to those strange messages of 'impending wyrd', we can *know* when to shift sideways — and share that safety with others. "Listen; wait; listen," says the wyrd; "listen; *act*; listen..."

> Listening for that strange sense of 'impending wyrd'
> often isn't easy — and neither is waiting! But look back
> for a while at what you've learnt in this weird journey of
> ours: what *has* become clearer to you—especially about
> your own choice, and power, within the wyrd?

Waiting — or rather impatience — can be a problem, especially when we desperately want something to change: but change happens when it happens to happen, and in its own weird time, not ours — yet it's up to us to set the course, our chosen direction for any change! That's the wyrd: it *is* our choice —but only if we let it be so...

The wyrd weaves its way through everywhere, everywhen, everyone. So we're always in relationship, with everyone — our allies in wyrdness. Those weird strands of sympathy and empathy, which weave our lives together, exist only in relation-ship — in some ways *are* relationship. Interwoven with each other, we reflect each other, and each other's issues: and while others do have their own choices, which interweave and intersect with ours, we always have exactly as much 'response-ability' as we choose.

Relationship is weird; relationship is wyrd. Ultimately, though, it *is* down to us: "Issues pass through me on the threads of wyrd, are unchanged by how much I am unchanged." We share the wyrd with everyone: yet weird as it may feel, for each of us the interpersonal world begins and ends with 'I'. And since our 'I' is perhaps the only true choice we have, would it not be wise to choose it?

FURTHER READING

You may find some of the following books helpful for further exploration of the ideas in this book. Some may be out of print, but will be available through libraries or used-book dealers.

Wyrd

Brian Branston
   The Lost Gods of England, Thames & Hudson, 1957
   Gods of the North, Thames & Hudson, 1955, 1980
Tom Graves
   Positively Wyrd, Gothic Image (Glastonbury, England), 1995

Self-exploration

W.I.B. Beveridge
   The Art of Scientific Investigation, Heinemann Education
      Paperbacks (London), 1961
John Bradshaw
   Homecoming, Bantam (New York), 1990
Felicitas Goodman
   *Where The Spirits Ride The Wind: trance journeys and other ecstatic
      experiences*, Indiana University Press, c1990

Susan Jeffers
> *Opening Our Hearts To Men*, Ballantine (New York), 1989

Hugh Mackay
> *Why Don't People Listen?*, Pan (Sydney), 1994

Gerald M. Weinberg
> *The Secrets of Consulting*, Dorset House (New York), 1985

Philosophical perspectives

Paul Feyerabend
> *Against Method: outline of an anarchistic theory of knowledge*, Verso (London, New York), 1978, 3rd ed. 1993

James Gleick
> *Chaos: making a new science*, Penguin (New York), 1987

Robert M. Pirsig
> *Zen And The Art Of Motorcycle Maintenance*, Bodley Head (London), 1974

Lao Tsu
> *Tao Te Ching*, tr. Gia Fu Feng and Jane English, Wildwood House (London), 1973

Fiction on wyrd and geis

Bryan Bates
> *The Way of Wyrd*, Beaver Books, 1986

Marion Campbell
> *The Dark Twin*, Turnstone Books (London), 1973

Alan Garner
> *The Owl Service*, Collins (Toronto), 1967

GOTHIC IMAGE PUBLICATIONS

Gothic Image Publications is a Glastonbury-based imprint dedicated to publishing books and pamphlets that offer a new and radical approach to our perception of ourselves and the world. These are some of our current publications:

The Avalonians
Patrick Benham

Conflict in the Caucasus
Svetlana Chervonnaya

Devas, Fairies and Angels
William Bloom

Dowsing the Crop Circles
edited by John Michell

Dragons: Their History and Symbolism
Janet Hoult

Glastonbury Abbey
James Carley

Glastonbury: Maker of Myths
Frances Howard-Gordon

The Glastonbury Tor Maze
Geoffrey Ashe

The Green Lady and the King of Shadows
Moyra Caldecott

Labyrinths: Ancient Myths and Modern Uses
Sig Lonegren

The Living World of Faery
R J Stewart

Meditation in a Changing World
William Bloom

Needles of Stone Revisited
Tom Graves

The New Ley Hunter's Guide
Paul Devereux

New Light on the Ancient Mystery of Glastonbury
John Michell

Positively Wyrd: Harnessing the Chaos in your Life
Tom Graves

Robin Hood: Green Lord of the Wildwood
John Matthews

Sacred England
John Michell

The Sacred Magician: A Ceremonial Diary
William Bloom

Saint or Satan? The Life and Times of Russia's New Rasputin, Anatoly Kashpirovsky
Galina Vinogradova

Spiritual Dowsing
Sig Lonegren

Symbolic Landscapes: The Dreamtime Earth and Avebury's Open Secret
Paul Devereux

Gothic Image Publications are available from all good bookshops or direct from

7 High Street • Glastonbury, Somerset • England • BA6 9DP
Telephone +44 1458 83 1453 • (Fax +44 1458 83 1666)